POEMS
OF THE
ELIZABETHAN
AGE

POEMS
OF THE
ELIZABETHAN
AGE

An Anthology by
Geoffrey G. Hiller

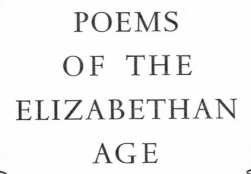

METHUEN & CO LTD
LONDON

to Diana

First published in 1977 by
Methuen & Co Ltd
11 *New Fetter Lane London* EC4P 4EE
© 1977 *Geoffrey G. Hiller*
Printed in Great Britain by
Richard Clay (The Chaucer Press) Ltd
Bungay, Suffolk

ISBN 0 416 83200 8 (*hardbound*)
ISBN 0 416 83210 5 (*paperback*)

CONTENTS

BARNES

DRAYTON

SHAKESPEARE

CONTENTS

ix

CONTENTS

SATIRES

CONTENTS

PASTORALS

CONTENTS

Preface

This anthology seeks to represent the poetry of the Elizabe-
than age by a selection of poems written in five of the literary
genres which were highly popular at the time: the sonnet,
lyric, satire, pastoral and Ovidian romance. An arrangement
of the poems by their genres rather than in simple chrono-
logical order has several advantages. It avoids the risk
of bewildering the reader with what is likely to appear an
amorphous and diverse poetic miscellany. More importantly,
it enables the conventions of style and subject matter appro-
priate to each genre to be the more readily appreciated;
accordingly, it encourages a fuller understanding of indivi-
dual poems because each one is placed in a significant literary
context. Indeed, it is the way the Elizabethans themselves,
who were so conscious of literary genres, would have wished
their poems to be read. Within each genre-section poems by
individual authors appear in chronological order so that a
general sense not only of the development of the genre but
also of an individual poet's skill in it is maintained.

Some few poems have been included chiefly for their his-
torical interest (the extract from Gascoigne's *The Steel Glass*

and from Turbervile's translation of Mantuan, the poems in quantitative measure by Sidney and Campion), but all others have been selected for their literary merit alone. This means that many works which might usefully have demonstrated the variety within each genre have been excluded on the grounds of inferiority. Rather than to offer a completely representative survey of each genre, the anthology is designed to enable the best poems of the Elizabethan period to be read in the best possible light.

The design of the anthology has necessarily involved some difficult decisions of classification, and it is hardly to be expected that the reader will always agree with the inclusion of a particular poem in a particular section. The Elizabethans themselves, while they classified poetry as fervently as they classified everything else in the cosmos, were also aware of overlapping. There was nothing to prevent a poem in one genre from employing elements of another. 'If severed they be good, the conjunction cannot be hurtful', as Sidney wrote of heroic and pastoral poetry. Many of the pastorals here are also lyrics; some have elements of satire; the Ovidian romance has a strong pastoral flavour. It must be emphasized that while this anthology is intended to draw attention to the Elizabethans' awareness of the 'kinds' of poetry, its categorization of poems is not inflexible and each section is not to be considered completely self-contained. Naturally the reader is free to disagree with the category in which a poem has been placed, since he may prefer to read it in a totally different context. But it is hoped that he may appreciate too the reasons why it appears where it does in this anthology.

The selection of poems is intended to represent the 'high period' of Elizabethan poetry, from the late 1570s, when Sidney was writing his *Arcadia* and when Spenser published his *Shepheardes Calender* (1579), to the end of Elizabeth's reign. However, a few poets who wrote earlier in the Queen's lifetime have been included: Wyatt and Surrey, both for their individual worth and because they were regarded as the 'two chief lanterns of light' illuminating the way for those who followed; Turbervile and Gascoigne, who were lesser poets but whose works are nevertheless of much interest, particularly in relation to the greater that were to come. The last year of Elizabeth's reign, 1603, is taken as marking the end of the Elizabethan period of literature, and the boundary has been overstepped on very few occasions and only for reasons which are fairly evident (the best sonnets of Drayton, for instance, were not published until 1619, but it would surely be improper to omit them). The lyrics of Jonson and Donne have not been fully represented, partly because their complete works are readily available, but chiefly because they are usually, and rightly, considered poets of a new age, even though their early works were written in Elizabeth's reign: their subjects, attitudes and techniques belong to the seventeenth not to the sixteenth century. Consequently only their early lyrics and those which are most 'Elizabethan' in style have been represented here.

Texts have been taken from early editions or manuscripts, as indicated after each poem or before each group of poems. Emendations of the copy texts have been made sparingly, and in every instance they have been recorded in footnotes. Only obvious misprints in the original texts have been corrected silently. In a few cases variants which are possibly superior, or are otherwise interesting for the interpretation of a poem, have also been recorded in footnotes. In these instances, if the work in which the variant occurs bears the same title as the copy text, it is designated simply by its date of publication, placed in parenthesis. In all cases an indication of the date of composition of a poem has been given in a footnote if it differs significantly from the publication date. Titles which have been given to extracts from longer poems are placed in square brackets, as they are the editor's own.

Since the orthography and punctuation of Elizabethan poems is so varied (and often not the poet's own in any case), spelling and punctuation of the text and of variant readings have been modernized for the sake of uniformity and clarity. However, the original spelling in Spenser's poems has not been altered. Just as Spenser's deliberate use of 'olde and obsolete wordes' (as E.K. wrote) brings 'great grace' and 'auctoritie' to the verse, so too does his spelling, and the archaic flavour of his poetry would be greatly reduced were it to be modernized. Spenser's original punctuation has also been retained, but in a few instances, when the meaning would otherwise be obscure, it has been silently emended. The use of *i, j, u, v* and *f* has been regularized, ampersands have been expanded, and (as elsewhere) diphthongs have been replaced by separate letters.

Except in Spenser's poems, the final suffix *-ed* has always been printed in full, with the *e* marked with an accent when it is intended that it should be sounded. If the *e* is sounded in normal pronunciation it is left unmarked. This policy has the virtues of simplicity and consistency, and should be helpful in reading the lines as their scansion requires them to be read.

ACKNOWLEDGEMENTS

I should like to acknowledge the help I have received from many of my friends and colleagues in the Department of English at Monash University. My thanks are due in particular to Professor David Bradley, Professor Arthur Brown, Dr Harold Love, and Mr Philip Martin for their valuable criticism and advice during various stages of the anthology's preparation. I am indebted also to Miss Elizabeth Cook of Homerton College of Education, Cambridge, for making useful suggestions on some detailed matters. My grateful thanks go also to Miss Gail Ward and Mrs Sheila Wilson for producing the final typescript.

I should like to thank the Bodleian Library, Oxford and the Folger Shakespeare Library, Washington for permission to reproduce illustrations used in the text.

Introduction

More love sonnets were written in the last two decades of Elizabeth's reign than in any other twenty-year period in England. It was a literary form attempted by most poets whether or not they were in love, and by most lovers whether or not they could write poetry. Matthew in Jonson's *Every Man in His Humour* was by no means alone in his ability to 'overflow you half a score or a dozen of sonnets at a sitting' when he indulged a melancholy mood, and, for better or worse, many such overflowings found their way into print.

The genre achieved this enormous popularity partly because the Petrarchan sonnet gave the Elizabethans a set of conventions, appealing in themselves, which formed a secure foundation on which an endless number of themes and variations could be constructed. The sonnets of the four-teenth-century Petrarch, expressing his humble love and devotion for the unattainable Laura – at once a human being and a symbol of divine virtue and beauty – provided a series of poetic attitudes, images and conceits which could readily be imitated by future poets. Furthermore, the sonnet's form of (usually) fourteen lines was considered the ideal length, being 'neither too long for the shortest project, nor too short for the longest', as Samuel Daniel wrote. Elizabethan poets were conscientious craftsmen, and the sonnet provided a challenge to a poet's artistic ingenuity. Daniel saw the sonnet as a well-furnished room:

... is it not most delightful to see much excellently ordered in a small room, or little gallantly disposed and made to fill up a space of like capacity, in such sort that the one would not appear so beautiful in a larger circuit, nor the other do well in a less, which often we find to be so, according to the powers of nature in the workman.

(*A Defence of Rhyme*, 1603)

The Elizabethan sonnet developed by testing and experiment, as poets tried out new furniture and new ways of constructing their small rooms.

The structure of a sonnet naturally influenced the treatment of its subject. The Petrarchan form, which normally rhymed *abba abba cde cde*, was never popular in England. Wyatt, who first brought the sonnet to England from Italy, was the first to introduce the couplet ending, which could be used to good effect for a pithy epigram or a climactic conclusion, and almost every later sonneteer followed suit. Sidney experimented with variations on the Petrarchan form in *Astrophil and Stella*, but most of his sonnets end with a couplet. Spenser used an ingenious spiralling rhyme scheme *abab bcbc cdcd ee*, which recalled the *Faerie Queene* stanza. Shakespeare and most other sonneteers used what came to be known as the 'English form', *abab cdcd efef gg*. This rhyme scheme, first used by Surrey, was relatively easy to manipulate for a great variety of ends, and its seven rhymes proved less constricting than the five of the Petrarchan form.

The sonnets of Petrarch and his imitators provided a vast storehouse of conceits and images for later sonneteers: the servitude of the lover, his sleeplessness, his desire to bestow immortality on his lady, the lover as huntsman, as a storm-tossed ship, love as ice and fire, pleasure and pain, honey and gall – all these recur with amazing frequency, and a cursory glance through any collection will reveal many more. It must not be believed, however, that a poem necessarily suffers because it employs a conventional theme or a common conceit. Shakespeare's greatest sonnets use images which have appeared countless times before. It is what the poet makes of the conventional material that matters; the freshness, and what Sidney called the 'forcibleness', which he brings to the old material is what makes the sonnet convincing as poetry.

The question of the sincerity of a sonneteer is one which is often raised. The fact is that it is not necessary to be in love to write poetry: it may even be a hindrance, since great poetry depends on the detachment of the writer as well as on his involvement. Donne himself said that he wrote best when he had least truth for his subjects. Whether or not a poet is in love is beside the point: what matters is that his poem should give the impression that he is, and it is this illusion which the sonneteers attempted to create. The fact that sonnets were written in the first person does not prevent them from being fiction, and it is primarily as fiction that we must read them. It is important that the reader should not assume that the 'I' of a sonnet is the direct voice of the poet writing the sonnet.

This is particularly so in the case of Sidney's *Astrophil and Stella*. Sidney shared many characteristics with his Astrophil (they were both courtiers, politicians, heroes of the tourney), but to identify the two completely is to misinterpret Sidney's aims. It is not Sidney who is having difficulties writing poetry in the first sonnet: it is Astrophil. And in Sonnet 74 it is Astrophil who boasts of the smoothness of his verse in a poem carefully contrived by Sidney to move anything but smoothly. Sidney often views Astrophil with a comic detachment, gently mocking his 'star-loving' hero – for his vanity as a

sonneteer (3, 74), as a jouster in the lists (53), and for his smug
conviction that as a lover he is unique among lovers (54).
Indeed, it is important to realize that there is humour as well
as pathos in Sidney's sonnets. The strain of humour did not
escape Thomas Nashe, who in his preface to the sequence
called it 'the tragicomedy of love . . . performed by starlight'.
Astrophil endeavours self-consciously to be the perfect
Petrarchan lover and sonneteer, to wear and to 'paint' the
blackest face of woe. But he discovers that the courtly code
is inadequate to account for his experiences: his love for
Stella is unexpectedly at odds with both reason and virtue.
He sees in Stella the image of true beauty and goodness, but
at the same time physical desire cries out irrepressibly for
food (71). No matter how hard he tries his lover's feelings
will not square with love's philosophy. Sidney puts the
Petrarchan convention in a new light by depicting with
grave humour a naive, introverted, slightly puzzled lover
who is constantly struggling to express his feelings, to analyse
them, and to make them conform to his conception of the
courtly code, while, all in vain, he tries to obtain his beloved's
grace.

Sidney's sonnets, which formed the first major sequence in
England, inspired a vast number of imitators. Between the
writing of *Astrophil and Stella* (1581–2) and the publication of
Shakespeare's *Sonnets* (1609) over twenty sequences appeared,
as well as hundreds of individual sonnets. The majority of
these are greatly inferior. They use conventions without
imagination, their poetry lacks the power of new insight into
the experience of love, and all too often, as Sidney himself
complained, their 'fiery speeches' are applied much too
coldly to be convincing. Some poets, however, were more
successful. Daniel and Drayton at their best at least make the
reader feel the validity of the commonplace, the reality behind
the convention, and find a pleasing freshness in an old sub-
ject. Daniel's sonnets are lyrical and elegant *statements* – of the
poet's power to immortalize his beloved, of his humility as a

4

lover, of the powerlessness of fragile beauty to withstand 'the dark and time's consuming rage'. Drayton's are more robust, more colloquial in tone; they contain an excitement and a liveliness absent in Daniel. They also show a welcome sense of humour. However, while the virtues of both poets are not to be underestimated, they as a rule do not reward us with new experiences of what it is like to be in love. Inferior sonneteers merely assert, while the better explore and question; the poorer poets write to define love, while the greater – Sidney, Spenser and Shakespeare – persuade us that love in the end is indefinable.

Spenser's *Amoretti* was published with his *Epithalamion* in 1595. To some extent the sonnet sequence and the marriage hymn form a unit which narrates the course of the poet's courtship and marriage. However, while autobiographical references exist, the relationship between the story of the poetry and actual events is by no means clear. What is significant, however, is that the poet's wooing is not to lead to an epilogue of despair, as Astrophil's did, but to reconciliation and marriage. In Spenser the lover's bark, which had been wandering tempest-tossed on benighted seas ever since Petrarch, at last descries the 'happy shore' where is 'eternall blisse' (63). The deer, which in Wyatt's sonnet fled the advances of the wearied huntsman-lover, in Spenser returns to the pursuer and 'with her owne goodwill' allows herself to be made captive (67). A new turn has been given to the Petrarchan sonneteering tradition when the lover finds that his wooing is not entirely in vain. Spenser's sonnets in general reflect not the despair of frustrated love but the hopeful anticipation of a worthy lover's reward.

In Sidney's sequence the lovers' relationship was never anything but a distant one, and Astrophil alone was at the centre of Sidney's vision. The *Amoretti* presents us with two well-characterized lovers and shows us the ever-deepening relationship between them. Like the Petrarchan mistress, the lady is beautiful and virtuous, *but* she is also accessible. She is witty and, one suspects, something of a tease. In the later sonnets in particular, there is a strong sense of understanding between the lovers, a rapport erstwhile unknown in the Petrarchan tradition. It is as if they are taking a mutual delight and satisfaction in watching each other play out the game of wooing and being wooed.

The quiet tone and easy flowing movement of the verse reflect a certain calmness of mind in Spenser. The conflict of reason and passion which tormented Astrophil is absent; the love of the body 'fayre' and the love of the 'mind adornd with vertues manifold' are perfectly reconciled. Moreover, in the great Easter sonnet (68) love is set triumphantly in a Christian context. While for Sidney earthly love leads but to dust ('Leave me, O love'), in Spenser it is seen as an inspiration for, and a lesson in, divine love, and is to be cherished by both man and woman accordingly.

Shakespeare is the outstanding sonneteer of the Elizabethans. He writes with the dramatic immediacy of Sidney and Drayton, the mellifluousness of Daniel, and the tenderness of Spenser, but with a compression, a density of thought and imagery like none before him. More than any other sonneteer's, his poetry is of the intellect as well as of the ear. In his sonnets there is no empty music: he makes one *think* as well as *listen*. Because of his intense awareness of the complexity of things, of the multi-faceted nature of truth, his statements are often paradoxes, his assertions in themselves suggest alternative points of view. His irony is often so multi-layered that it can never be fully fathomed. His sonnets, moreover, range over an extraordinarily wide area; they explore a variety of human relationships which are placed in the broader context of the problems and paradoxes of life itself.

Shakespeare is the most anti-Petrarchan of the sonneteers. The courtly code was clearly inadequate to deal with love for a youth who is found to be as unfaithful, self-centred and hypocritical as he is beautiful, and with love for a woman who lacks both beauty and morals. Yet in one way too Shakespeare

was indebted to the Petrarchan stock of images and com-
monplaces. One need not read many lines before encounter-
ing metaphors of the stage of life, of lawsuits, or accounting,
or warfare, or siege. But in Shakespeare's sonnets the
substance of the old images has been forged anew. His
images have a unique complexity and power; they bear
little relation to the commonplaces of the Petrarchan store-
house, the furniture of which had been borrowed or pillaged
mercilessly by many a lesser poet.

Shakespeare presents us (as Sidney did also) with a highly
sensitive and thoughtful lover, who is forced by the circum-
stances of a love which bewilders him to analyse and criticize
his feelings, and to question all things, including morality
itself. His self-examination is intense and painful. He loves
deeply, but his mind is actively at odds with his heart, reason
with passion. He constantly finds himself excusing the youth's
faults, while reason tells him that he is corrupting and de-
meaning himself as he does so. He despises himself as the
vassal of a woman who professes no constancy and to whom
not one of his physical senses is attracted (141), but he cannot
explain the fascination she holds for him. Human under-
standing between the lovers is discovered not in mutual love,
as it was in Spenser, but in mutual lust, deception, and con-
scious self-deception. But despite (or perhaps because of) the
lover's willing surrender to what neither reason nor con-
science can explain, he never loses his self-respect. Nor is
there any self-pity:

> I am that I am, and they that level
> At my abuses reckon up their own;
> I may be straight though they themselves be bevel; . . . (121)

Paradoxically, in yielding himself fully and consciously to
love he reaches self-discovery. His earlier advice to the young
man proves applicable later to the lover as well: 'To give away
yourself keeps yourself still'. Sidney's Astrophil loved and lost
and knew not why; he had no aptitude for self-discovery or

7

self-analysis. Shakespeare's lover, on the other hand, has; and in the process of his self-searching we come a good deal closer ourselves to realizing what love, and the self-sacrifice of love, are like.

If the last quarter of the sixteenth century was the great age of the sonnet it was also the age of the lyric, when the companion arts of poetry and music together reached a high peak in their development. It was the period of the great madrigal and air composers – Byrd, Dowland, Morley, Campion, Gibbons – whose musical achievement gave England an envied reputation throughout Europe. Music was played and heard in every rank of society. Part-singing and family concerts were popular in homes; men of most trades sang as they worked; folk-songs were sung in streets and taverns. In such a musical climate the lyric as a poetic form could emerge into prominence because both poets and composers could find support and encouragement in each other's work.

Poetry and music were closely associated in Renaissance thought. The poet, like the musician, found his prototype in Orpheus, the mythical Greek singer who tamed wild beasts and made trees and rocks move around him in a circle by the magical, civilizing power of his music. Spenser in the first stanza of his *Epithalamion* compares his role as poet and bridegroom with that of Orpheus, and the refrain of the poem which follows perhaps suggests the echoing harmony between man and nature which Orpheus's playing established:

> So Orpheus did for his owne bride,
> So I unto my selfe alone will sing,
> The woods shall to me answer and my Eccho ring.

Poetry was regarded as the re-creation on earth of the music made by the heavenly spheres as they circled in their orbits; it was, in Drayton's words,

> The language which the spheres and angels speak,
> In which their mind they to poor mortals break
> By God's great power, into rich souls infused, . . .
>
> *(The Moon-Calf, 1627)*

The poet and musician were alike in being privileged to hear the heavenly harmony and in being able to communicate it to mankind.

Of the lyrics collected here, some were written for existing musical settings, some were set to music afterwards, others were not set to music at all; but all have the kind of *verbal* music, the melodious diction and language, which is essential to lyric verse. From a purely literary point of view (which is our concern here) the musical settings are not of great importance. Without them the lyrics can still be appreciated as poems, just as many of them were when they appeared in sixteenth- and seventeenth-century anthologies. On the other hand, of course, the words alone cannot give us the full experience of the lyric when it is sung.

The Elizabethan lyrists wrote on a wide variety of subjects and used a great number of forms of versification. Like Feste in *Twelfth Night* they could turn their hands with ease to a 'love song or a song of good life'. They produced epithalamia, lullabies and epitaphs, gay light fancies on the joys of spring and the pastoral life, and more sage and serious meditations on religious subjects, on worldly transience, life and death. Some lyrics – the religious poems of Southwell, for instance – have a didactic purpose, and their language is consequently direct and plain. The poetic style of these lyrics does not call attention to itself, but remains subordinate to the matter in hand. In the majority of lyrical poems, however, the subject matter is either trivial or commonplace. The poet's concern is less with his content than with the 'garment of style' in which he dresses it: the poem is adorned with all the 'kindly clothes and colours' of Petrarchan decoration, or it is dressed with exquisite simplicity and grace. The beauty of most

9

lyrics exists above all else in the sheer artistry of the poetic expression.

The Elizabethan poet who wrote lyrics for singing was well aware of the effect which the extra dimension of music has on poetry. Since the capacity of the listener to absorb and comprehend is more restricted than that of the reader, the song is not a suitable medium for intellectual argument or for the expression of complex emotions. There is little opportunity for deep psychological insights, for subtle or involved use of wit, or for strange and unfamiliar imagery. Consequently in the sung lyric the poet usually portrays a mood rather than develops an elaborate argument. This was so not only in the madrigal, which was polyphonic and in which the complicated part-singing tended to make the words in any case subservient to the music, but also in the lute song or air, in which the musical accompaniment remained subordinate to the solo voice.

Lyrics intended for singing were written in clear and relatively uncomplicated language which would not hinder immediate understanding. Rhetorical figures were used with care that the sense of the poem was not lost or obscured; they were, for instance, directed usually towards elaboration or repetition rather than towards compression. At the end of the anonymous 'Weep you no more, sad fountains', for example, the mood of quiet restfulness – the 'rest that peace begets' – is beautifully sustained by the gently insistent repetition of certain words in a slow rhythmical movement:

> Rest you then, rest, sad eyes,
> Melt not in weeping,
> While she lies sleeping
> Softly, now softly lies
> Sleeping.

Poets often used formulaic patterns of words from stanza to stanza, as Sidney does in his first song in *Astrophil and Stella*, where he praises each of Stella's features in turn. Such a device not only contributed to the melodious quality of the verse but also helped the listener's understanding of the sense, since familiar phrases are repeated or varied as new subject matter is introduced. The refrain too was manipulated by the best lyrists in numerous artful ways. It afforded a musical close to a stanza which was all the more satisfying because of the listener's anticipation of its recurrence. It could be especially effective if it appeared in a different and unexpected context. In Wyatt's 'In eternum' the refrain gains an added poignancy at its final appearance when it refers not (as it had before) to the poet's vow of steadfast faith, but to his lasting memory of woman's fickleness:

> In eternum then from my heart I kest
> That I had first determined for the best;
> Now in the place another thought doth rest
> In eternum.

It is not surprising that the lyric, the most musical of all literary genres, should so often draw on music for its imagery. The airs of Campion are full of examples. Campion was a musician-poet who excelled as a lyrist, not only for his meticulous craftsmanship in coupling his 'words and notes lovingly together', but also in creating poems which, when read without their accompaniment, have a verbal music unsurpassed by most other lyric writers. Because he was a musician, Campion's mind turned naturally to instruments, notes, echoes and music for imagery and metaphor. In 'Follow your saint' the 'sad notes' of the singer take on an almost tangible form as they are bidden to pursue the mistress as the messengers of love. When Corinna sings to her lute Campion readily likens himself to the instrument:

> And as her lute doth live or die,
> Led by her passion, so must I;

and as Corinna's lute-strings break at the sound of a melancholy song, so too the poet's heart-strings break in sympathy.

The Elizabethan lyric seldom expressed private and personal emotion. The identity of the many lovers who sing of their joys and pains is unimportant; they are virtually anonymous. This does not mean that the lyrics are emotionally under-charged in consequence: only that the emotion is not par-ticularized. There are of course exceptions. In Spenser's *Epithalamion* the joys of the wedding day take on a personal significance since the poet who celebrates them as a detached 'observer' is at the same time the bridegroom who is experien-cing them. The poem is in one sense a public celebration, in another a private 'Song', a personal gift of the poet's to 'my beautifullest bride'. But in other lyrics – even those in plays – the singer is not characterized by his song to any significant extent. If he is in love, his emotions are neither intensely private nor presented as very different from those of any other lover in his audience.

At the end of the Elizabethan period, however, we find certain changes taking place in lyrical poetry, among them being the emergence of a personal voice. Donne's lyrics insist on the uniqueness of the individual's experience of love. His colloquial diction, the harsh rhythms, and (often) the direct abruptness of the tone strengthen our awareness of a dis-tinct personality:

> 'Tis true, 'tis day; what though it be?
> Oh, wilt thou therefore rise from me?
> Why should we rise because 'tis light?
> Did we lie down because 'twas night?

> (*Break of Day*)

Donne gives the impression of talking rather than of singing. His style is uncourtly; he rejects the 'soft melting phrases' of the Petrarchan lyrists and writes with masculine vigour and forthrightness. His debt to earlier poets both in his style and subject matter is not to be underestimated, but his wit and irony are sharper and more sustained, his imagery and comparisons more ingenious, his departure from convention more defiant than any other lyric writer before him. Donne is the poet of a new age, an age when a stronger personal consciousness was developing side by side with a growing disenchantment with the old Elizabethan order and its traditions.

SATIRES

In the Renaissance hierarchy of poetic kinds, satire was far removed from lyric poetry. The lyrist portrayed the beauties and joys of earth and heaven; his aim was to make the 'too much loved earth more lovely', from a brazen world to deliver a golden. The satirist's attention was fixed steadfastly on the brazen world itself. His style was 'lowly', 'pack-staff plain'; his muse was earthbound – if indeed he had a muse at all: Marston in his *Scourge of Villainy* invoked no deity or muse except 'grim Reproof' and 'Fair Detestation of foul odious sin' to guide him. He was inspired by his own misanthropic passion and needed no celestial aid.

The satirist insists that he is depicting the *actual* world, mankind as it really is, not as it ought to be. Gascoigne set out to show men to themselves, not in a crystal glass which would flatter them because it 'shows the thing much better than it is', but in a 'glass of trusty steel', which reflects nothing but the truth and shows men 'How foul or fair soever that they are'. The satirist refuses to be gulled by appearances. Like Wyatt, he prides himself in not judging by 'outward things ... Without regard what doth inward resort'. He sees that the saintly courtier is a hypocrite, that under the sumptuous clothes of the gallant is an 'incarnate devil', and that the 'outward fair' of the snow conceals a dunghill beneath. Many of the common topics for satirical attack were inherited direct from classical writers: flattery, religious hypocrisy, fraud, ambition, lust, drunkenness, fortune hunting; other satiric butts – such as fops, Puritans, tobacco smokers, travellers – were added to the list by the Elizabethans. But for the satirist by far the majority of men's faults were contained in the sin of deceit, or the foolishness of being deceived: 'Thus with the world the world dissembles still', wrote Lodge. The satirist's aim was to uncover the truth, to draw the veil from the world's villainy, and show mankind to mankind.

All Elizabethan writers agreed that the purpose of satire was to induce men to laugh at or to scorn folly and evil, but the satirists' methods varied according to their outlook and indeed depended to a great extent on their regard for their predecessors in the genre. While literary influences on sixteenth-century satire can be traced from France, Italy and (particularly in the case of Gascoigne) from medieval England, the Roman satirists Horace and Juvenal were by far the most influential. The work of each was very different. The satires of Horace (65–8 B.C.) dealt with the folly rather than with the wickedness of vice. They are goodnatured, without bitterness or aggressive vehemence. They often have a personal intimate tone and a quietly ironic wit which allows the urbane sensible personality of the satirist to emerge. They reflect the optimistic view that man might turn from his sins if he is brought pleasantly and tactfully to a knowledge of them. The satires of Juvenal (A.D. c. 60–c. 130), on the other hand, are characterized by direct and scathing invective and by the dramatic and vivid realism of his portrayal of corrupt society. They display (even flaunt) a detestation of mankind, a totally pessimistic outlook, and a belief that man's evil is inherent and therefore incurable. Juvenal's cynical melancholy and powerful rhetoric appealed to the taste of the Elizabethans and his work was the model for most of the satire of the late 1590s.

The influence of Horace appears most prominently in the satires of Wyatt and, to a lesser extent, in those of Donne and Lodge. The direct source of Wyatt's poem *Of the courtier's life, written to John Poyntz* is the tenth Satire of Alamanni (from whom he also derived the Italian metre, the *terza rima*), but his calm stoic outlook, his sophistication, and the informal intimate tone are all ultimately Horatian. In explaining why Wyatt has fled the 'press of courts' the poem tells us as much about the poet as it does about court life. The technique of the satire is to expose the corruption of high places by asserting the integrity of the man who delights to be remote from them. It is largely the sanity and self-control of the satirist which persuade the reader to his point of view, and the personal confiding air afforded by the epistolary style places him in the privileged position of Wyatt's friend Poyntz himself. Lodge's satirical epistle *To Master E. Dig[by]* proceeds in a somewhat similar way. In Horatian satire the reader may often find he has struck up a friendship with the satirist: in Juvenalian satire he knows he is despised along with the rest of the world.

Donne's satires have none of the calmness and urbanity of Wyatt's. The first and third (reprinted here) are personal meditations, but the thought is vigorous and forceful, the imagery arresting, the verse rugged and often irregular. The third Satire, in particular, does not quietly expound a philosophy already resolved upon but rather dramatizes the poet's attempts to formulate one, with an earnestness and urgency unknown in Horatian satire. It is as if Donne is working out his own salvation as he writes. There is Juvenalian *saeva indignatio* in the vividly presented encounters of the 'motley humorist' with the fools in the street (*Satire I*), and in the cynical characterization of men of various religious sects by their sexual partialities (*Satire III*). However, while there is anger in the satirist's heart, there is also compassion for the weaknesses of man. 'Kind pity' is there to choke his spleen. The 'motley humorist' is in the end a ludicrous figure, despised but not altogether rejected, and the 'railing' of the third Satire is tempered with reason and good sense.

This 'Kind pity' is not at all evident in the work of the later satirists, Hall, Marston and Guilpin. Hall, who was the first of the three to publish (his *Virgidemiarum* appeared in 1597), claimed, to the fury of Marston, that he was the first of the

English satirists. His justification presumably was that he was the first to imitate faithfully the style of Juvenal's satires. The works of these satirists embody no tolerance of man's weaknesses. Nor are they directed at persuading man to laugh at himself and to reform. Their aim is to rebuke and chastise. The satirist is the Scourger of Villainy; he carries a bundle of rods (*virgidemia*) with which to whip the guilty. He is appalled at the extent of man's corruption and claims (following Juvenal) that in such decadent times it is difficult *not* to write satire (*difficile est saturam non scribere*). His bitter invective issues without either restraint or discrimination:

> Who'll cool my rage? Who'll stay my itching fist?
> But I will plague and torture whom I list.

> (Marston, *The Scourge of Villainy* II)

To some extent, of course, the character of the satirist was an assumed one. The Elizabethans mistakenly thought that the word 'satire' was derived not from the Latin *satura* ('medley') but from the Greek *satyros* ('satyr'); they believed that the genre of satire had its origin in the ancient Greek satyr play, in which actors adopted the role of satyrs in order to inveigh against the vices of their fellow-citizens. The Elizabethan satirist often posed as the savage and rude creature of the woods, whose wild nature gave him licence to rail freely against mankind. The 'low' style of the formal satire, with its 'rough-hewed' harshness of language, its frequent tortured obscurity, and its ragged metres, was justified not only on the grounds that such was the style of Persius and Juvenal but also because this was the kind of speech befitting the lips of the coarse satyr.

The vision of life of the later Elizabethan satirists is grimly pessimistic. The satyr, wrote Marston, might sooner 'draw Nilus river dry, As cleanse the world from foul impiety'. Man has lost his reason and sunk to the level of the beasts. Animal imagery is abundant in these satires. Hall's lawyers are flies feeding fat on poisonous carrion. Marston's Diogenes in the seventh Satire searches the crowded streets looking in vain for a man; but the whole world appears 'brutish':

> ... for nought but shades I see;
> Resemblances of men inhabit thee (141–2)

and in the shape of men he finds swine, rats, eels, dogs and apes.

Marston is probably the most powerful of the later satirists. Hall is more restrained, Guilpin's bitterness is alleviated by a certain warmth of humour. *A Cynic Satire*, however, is a *tour de force* of passionate invective. Marston's view of mankind is warped and perverted. He transforms men into hideous caricatures and grotesques. His jaundiced eye is fixed on the most sordid and vile side of man's nature and he refuses to believe that any other exists. The Cynic Diogenes is hardly less bestial than the people he despises as beasts. But the satirist's lack of reason, his twisted cynicism, and his obsession with all that is repulsive serve to make his satirical invective all the more forceful. What Marston wrote of Hall in another context, he might equally well have applied to himself:

> Who would imagine that such squint-eyed sight
> Could strike the world's deformities so right!

> (*Certain Satires* [1598], II)

In 1599 the authorities prohibited the printing of satires and called in (among others) those of Hall, Marston and Guilpin. *The Scourge of Villainy* and *Skialetheia* were burnt. There may have been political and religious reasons for the censorship of satires; it may also have been due to the increasing salaciousness and grossness of their subject matter. The restrictions which were imposed, in any case, were sufficient to stay further significant development of the formal satire until the middle of the seventeenth century.

PASTORALS

The pastoral as an Elizabethan genre had a close affinity with satire. Both were written in the 'low' style which befitted the humble nature of the satyr and shepherd. Both in one way or another were critical of the evils and follies of the city and court. Some pastorals (like those of the Italian Mantuan [1448–1516]) were little more than satires in disguise; the poet intended, as George Puttenham wrote, 'under the veil of homely persons and in rude speeches to insinuate and glance at greater matters'. The shepherd was a popular pose for the satirist to adopt since he could calculate that the pastoral virtues of honesty and plainspokenness which he assumed in his persona would elicit a sympathetic response from the reader. In other pastorals (and they are by far the majority), while satire may not be the primary concern, the vices of the city are nevertheless criticized indirectly and by implication: the celebration of the simplicity, happiness and purity of the pastoral life becomes a tacit condemnation of the complexity, misery and corruption of city life. Often the pastoral world is praised not so much for its positive virtues but for its freedom from the very evils of civilization which the satirists so often attacked:

> Here nor treason is hid, veilèd in innocence,
> Nor envy's snaky eye finds any harbour here,
> Nor flatterers' venomous insinuations,
> Nor cunning humorists' puddled opinions,
> Nor courteous ruin of profferèd usury,
> Nor time prattled away, cradle of ignorance,
> Nor causeless duty, nor cumber of arrogance, . . .

> (Sidney, 'O sweet woods' 17–23)

Pastoral literature is inspired by a nostalgic yearning for a lost life of innocence, simplicity and ease – an existence comparable with the prelapsarian state in Eden and with the pagan

Golden Age. It is written from the point of view of the city man who, disenchanted with the corruption and artificiality of urban life, imagines that in the country is the ideal existence he longs for. His attitude is similar to that of the princess Elizabeth who, when she was held prisoner at Woodstock, is said to have heard a milkmaid singing and, envying her her happy carefree existence, to have wished that she were a milkmaid too. The shepherd's life is attractive because he is unaffected by the sudden changes of fortune which characterized Elizabethan political life; he knows none of the courtier's craft and guile; his mind is at peace, for he is not envious of rank nor ambitious for wealth ('Love and faith is shepherds' treasure'). These are the virtues of the pastoral life as Lodge defines them at some length in *Old Damon's Pastoral*. They fed the nostalgic fancies of the Elizabethans in the host of pastorals which proliferated after Spenser's *Shepheardes Calender*, that 'masterpiece if any', first brought the genre into popularity in 1579.

Since pastoral literature works on the assumption that rural life is idyllic, its landscapes and its people are always to a large extent idealized. The pastoral does not purport to explore or reflect the actual life of shepherds lest it destroy the very illusion on which it is founded. It is one thing to imagine the happy life of a milkmaid singing at her work, another to move closer and watch her on her knees scrubbing the dairy. The pastoral world is an imaginary one, viewed wistfully from a distance. Theocritus wrote his *Idylls*, about the rural life of his native Sicily, in the sophisticated court of Egyptian Alexandria. Virgil, for whom Sicilian fields were not sufficiently remote to carry the aura of romantic charm, placed his shepherds in the distant Arcadia in Greece, and gave it a fertility and gentleness which that harsh country never knew. Elizabethan poets followed the classical precedent: their pastoral world seems often to be near the horizon, seen but never reached. The refrain of Shakespeare's song in *As You Like It*, 'Come hither, come hither, come hither', is the alluring call of an Arcadia which we can easily imagine but to which we have no direct access. The singer of Campion's air 'I care not for these ladies', as he compared the coyness of court ladies (who were probably listening) with the wantonness of his country maid, knew, as his audience knew, that 'fresh Amaryllis, With milk and honey fed' was regrettably nothing but a delightful fancy. The pastoral world is not a flower that grows on mortal soil; it belongs to the poet and to the dreamer, and as such it is transient, insubstantial. It vanishes as swiftly as a dream on a sleeper's awakening – 'but I waked, and all was done' is the conclusion of the pleasant pastoral vision in one of Breton's poems. The spell may be broken as abruptly as Spenser's Graces in their mystic dance disappear at the boorish intrusion of Sir Calidore.

The remoteness and the mysterious imaginary quality of the pastoral world render realism, even self-consistency, unimportant. The setting of Drayton's *Ode to Beta* is English, but there are elements also of the more exotic landscape of pastoral myth. Beta's festival is celebrated on the Thames' banks near 'London's stately towers', but the shores are imagined shaded with olive trees and strewn with pearl. Beta herself (she is, of course, Queen Elizabeth) is a composite figure: she is the homely shepherds' queen bedecked with flowers as well as a majestic monarch, sitting in awesome splendour 'in purple and in pall'; she is also worshipped as a saint. The different images coalesce freely. There is little sense of incongruity in the pastoral world, where all is made ever rich and strange.

However, not all the shepherds of the pastoral are ennobled by the simple honest life and blessed with the wisdom peculiar to the Natural Man. Mantuan's lusty Eve, who is abashed at the thought of God's opinion of her prolific breeding, Greene's Doron and Carmela, who stammer out their love with unconscious malapropisms and incongruous comparisons, are clearly different people from Marlowe's eloquent Passionate Shepherd and Spenser's wise Colin Clout.

The poets were well aware that innocence can be regarded as naivete, pastoral simplicity as boorish stupidity. Country folk like the simpletons of Greene have a delightfully quaint charm, but at the same time their rusticity is gently ridiculed – and so is the idealized vision of pastoral life.

The world of the pastoral may be closer to nature, more simple and carefree than life in the city, but we are reminded again and again that it is still a part of the fallen world. Man cannot return to the Garden of Eden or to the guilt-free Golden Age, which Daniel evokes nostalgically in his translation of the Chorus from Tasso's *Aminta*. Those 'ancient happy ages' of eternal summer, peace and innocence are gone forever; one can only make a pretence at recalling them, and gather rosebuds while time permits:

> Let's love; this life of ours
> Can make no truce with time that all devours.

> (*A Pastoral* 64–5)

Behind the exultation in pastoral joys lies the sad conviction that they are fleeting, that 'nys on earth assuraunce to be sought'. After Marlowe's Passionate Shepherd has offered all the delights of spring to his beloved, Ralegh's Nymph refuses his invitation in the knowledge that his gifts will soon break, wither and be forgotten: spring's joys inevitably vanish into winter's cold, when reason and sanity expose them as mere follies. Time and death, as all pastoral elegies painfully assert, are even in Arcadia. Only in the Afterlife can the permanent joys of Eden, which are lost to mortal men, be recovered. In Heaven there are 'fieldes ay fresh, . . . grasse ay greene' for Dido, in Spenser's elegy, and the Elysian pastures of eternal summer contrast sharply with the grief-stricken autumnal world which mourns her death.

The shepherd of the Elizabethan pastoral is a contemplative figure. His life in harmony with nature brings him close to the God of nature and to an understanding of divine truths. In the solitary woods of Sidney's Arcadia

> senses do behold th' order of heav'nly host,
> And wise thoughts do behold what the Creator is.

('O sweet woods' 5-6)

Being aware of his own humble condition, 'Where the mind and store agreeth', and desiring no other, he has also come to a knowledge of himself. The shepherd's contemplative life away from the city actually endows him (paradoxically) with the wisdom necessary to teach the arts of the *civilized* life. Sidney's shepherd Philisides pipes a *Song* which is a fable on the art of civil government. Spenser's Colin Clout can explain to the knight Sir Calidore the sophisticated arts of courtesy, and Calidore, as is proved later, is more accomplished as a knight for having learned courtesy as a shepherd. So the life of contemplation ultimately serves the life of action. The pastoral ideal was seen by the Elizabethans not only as a retreat from the world which is too much with us but also as a temporary withdrawal in preparation for the fulfilment of the heroic ideal in the civilized world outside.

OVIDIAN ROMANCES

Of all the classical authors read and revered by the Elizabethans, Ovid (43 B.C.–A.D. 18) was unquestionably the most influential. From medieval times his works had inspired countless translations, commentaries and imitations. Among his best-known poems were the *Amores*, a collection of love poems, and the *Heroides*, verse epistles written (for the most part) by women of classical legend to the husbands or lovers who had deserted them. Even more popular, however, was the *Metamorphoses*, which became the great myth manual of the Renaissance. It is a spirited narration of the tales of classical mythology which involve beings whose shapes are miraculously changed. Ovid excelled in depicting the people and situations of the legends in intimate detail. He brought the gods out of the remote and misty realms of myth into the familiar domains of sunlit earth, where the Olympian deities sport and intrigue in the manner of ordinary mortal men. His scenes resemble those of a tapestry, richly elaborated with detail and colour in order to feast the senses and excite the imagination. But there is a poise and a sense of humour as well, and the sweetness never cloys. Such was the 'sweet witty soul of Ovid' which the Elizabethans admired and tried to recapture in their own narratives.

Thomas Lodge was the pioneer of the genre. His *Scylla's Metamorphosis* (1589) is a work of little poetic merit but it demonstrated the possibilities of the form to greater writers who followed. First among these was Marlowe, whose *Hero and Leander*, although left unfinished when Marlowe died in 1593, is almost universally regarded as the finest poem of its kind. All the main characteristics of the Ovidian romance are there: an erotic story, imagery which is at once delicate and rich, a luxuriousness of decoration, a narrator who, while he eagerly savours the sensual banquet he is providing, at the same time stands aloof in order to offer comments on it from a distance. Marlowe's blunt asides and deliberately obtrusive sententiae are in ironic and mocking contrast with his fantasy world of infinite richness and sweetness. For his plot Marlowe drew on a poem of Musaeus, the sixth-century Alexandrian poet, and on two epistles of Ovid's *Heroides*. In all the Ovidian romances, however, it is not the story that is of primary importance. The action of *Hero and Leander* is frequently delayed while the poet indulges delightedly in prolonged descriptions in the 'aureate' style – scanning with overt relish the bodies, clothed and unclothed, of 'Hero the fair' and 'Amorous Leander'. There is no depth of character study. It may even be considered that there is inconsistency, particularly in the portrayal of Leander as a sophisticated rhetorician and as a naive lover. Marlowe's concern is not

23

ultimately with his narrative plot nor with psychological realism, but with displaying the consummate *physical* beauty of his imagined world.

The poem is a triumphant celebration of earthly love and sensual beauty – beauty which releases all the energies and passions of nature and gives to mortal men, however briefly, the happiness of gods. Marlowe's earth shines bright with a heavenly splendour. The streets of Sestos, crowded with beautiful women, glister like the star-filled firmament. The beauty of Hero and Leander lures the very gods down from on high to seek their favour. Their love in its naivete and gentleness indeed is set in emphatic contrast with the turbulent lusts and sinister intrigues of the gods, whose 'heady riots, incest, rapes' are depicted in the crystal pavement of Venus's temple (141–4). This pavement is called Venus's 'glass', or mirror, but it does not reflect ideal love or beauty: these are now to be found not in heaven but on earth.

The lovers' world is without morals and without conscience. Hero and Leander live by no principles or laws other than their own natural instincts: their wooing and its consummation are a graceful ceremony of innocence. They are doomed not because they sin but because they are mortal. Not even Love himself can win the favour of the Destinies on their behalf, for it is not possible for earthly lovers to 'enjoy each other', *and* 'be blest'. The poem is predominantly comic in spirit, with a vigorous strain of irony and cynicism, but there is also tenderness and sympathy for the ill-fated lovers; in the celebration of mortal beauty and happiness there is an implied lament for their fragility and transience.

Shakespeare's *Venus and Adonis* was written probably in the same year as Marlowe's poem. Here the passing of beauty and the impossibility of happiness in love are thematically even more important. Adonis, the 'field's chief flower', the whole world's beauty incarnate, refuses to be 'gathered' by the importunate Venus, and his death in the boar-hunt ultimately results in the goddess's vow that sorrow hereafter

24

shall attend on love. In Ovid's *Metamorphoses* the beautiful Adonis is a willing lover; Shakespeare has changed the story so that beauty is elusive and love pleads in vain. But the poem at times also has a certain earthy humour which is totally alien to the remote and refined world of *Hero and Leander*. Venus appears neither divine nor dignified as she perspires with heat and frustration in her vain attempts to seduce Adonis, whose stubbornness (at least from Venus's point of view) is out of all proportion to his size. Shakespeare has a sympathetic understanding of a lover's feelings, but he can also appreciate and laugh at the ludicrous spectacle afforded by one whom passion has driven into a foolish predicament. The poem is in sixains and in consequence proceeds in a more leisurely way than Marlowe's. The stanza form also allows Shakespeare greater opportunity to exhibit artistry in elaborate verbal decoration. Venus's 'invitation to love', part of which is given here, is conventional in substance but dazzling in its rhetorical effect. Everywhere one sees a young poet's delight in the enthusiastic display of his ingenuity and in the happy mastery of the musical potential of his verse form.

Hero and Leander and *Venus and Adonis* both enjoyed immense popularity (indeed, notoriety) and there were many imitations. Among the best of these is Drayton's *Endymion and Phoebe* (1595). The poem is an ambitious attempt to write an Ovidian narrative of Platonic love. Phoebe is the virgin moon-goddess and Endymion, no less chaste, wins his mistress's favour by contemplating heavenly rather than earthly beauty. Unlike Marlowe and Shakespeare, Drayton is determined to avoid the erotic. There are no seductively naked bodies and no smothering kisses. The burning sun 'did hotly overlook' the feverish wooing of Shakespeare's Venus: the air of Drayton's Mount Latmos is cool and pure. Nevertheless Drayton writes best (as in the extract here) when he is nearest to his predecessors. Platonic love is later to exalt Endymion and Phoebe into the mystic regions of divine philosophy, but Drayton, like a true Ovidian, takes delight in revelling in earthly beauties. His pastoral landscapes are brilliant with colour and crowded with life. His descriptions of the lovers have the sumptuous detail of Marlowe. At times too, especially when Phoebe in her guise as a wanton nymph woos the reluctant Endymion, he catches the vivacity and humour of Shakespeare. But Drayton's poetry is uneven. His couplets, lacking the clipped rhythm of Marlowe's, tend towards a too-fluid monotony. While Drayton admired the 'air and fire' of Marlowe and the 'smooth comic vein' of Shakespeare, he was not able to sustain these qualities in his own verse. Marlowe and Shakespeare remained the acknowledged masters of the Elizabethan Ovidian romance.

SONNETS

Then have you sonnets: some think that all poems (being short) may be called sonnets, as indeed it is a diminutive word derived of *sonare*, but yet I can best allow to call those sonnets which are of fourteen lines, every line containing ten syllables. The first twelve do rhyme in staves of four lines by cross metre, and the last two rhyming together do conclude the whole.

Gascoigne, Certain Notes of Instruction, 1575

Nor is this certain limit [of rhyme] observed in sonnets any tyrannical bounding of the conceit, but rather reducing it in *gyrum* and a just form, neither too long for the shortest project nor too short for the longest, being but only employed for a present passion.

Daniel, A Defence of Rhyme, 1603

Loving in truth, and fain in verse my love to show,
That she, dear she, might take some pleasure of my pain,
Pleasure might cause her read, reading might make her
    know,
Knowledge might pity win, and pity grace obtain:
  I sought fit words to paint the blackest face of woe;
Studying inventions fine, her wits to entertain; . . .

Sidney, Astrophil and Stella (1598), 1

Armado. Assist me, some extemporal god of rhyme, for I am sure I shall turn sonnet. Devise, wit; write, pen; for I am for whole volumes in folio.

Shakespeare, Love's Labour's Lost I.ii

SIR THOMAS WYATT

Whoso list to hunt, I know where is an hind,
  But as for me, alas, I may no more:
  The vain travail hath wearied me so sore,
I am of them that farthest cometh behind;
Yet may I by no means my wearied mind   5
  Draw from the deer, but as she fleeth afore,
  Fainting I follow. I leave off therefore,
Since in a net I seek to hold the wind.
Who list her hunt, I put him out of doubt,
  As well as I, may spend his time in vain;   10
  And graven with diamonds in letters plain
There is written her fair neck round about:
  'Noli me tangere, for Caesar's I am,
  And wild for to hold, though I seem tame.'

Egerton MS. 2711

The three sonnets were written probably in the early 1530s.
They were first published in *Tottel's Miscellany*, 1557.
WHOSO LIST TO HUNT: Adapted from Petrarch, *Rime* CXC.
    (Refs. to Petrarch are to *Rime*, ed. G. Carducci and S.
    Ferrari, Florence, 1899, repr. 1957.)
13   *Noli me tangere:* 'Do not touch me'—said to have been
    inscribed on the collars of Caesar's hinds to mark them
    as his own. The phrase originates in John 20.17. Caesar
    here may be Henry VIII and the deer Anne Boleyn
    (Wyatt probably was a lover of Anne before her
    marriage to Henry in 1533).

My galley chargèd with forgetfulness
    Thorough sharp seas in winter nights doth pass
    'Tween rock and rock; and eke mine enemy, alas,
That is my lord, steereth with cruelness;
5   And every oar a thought in readiness,
    As though that death were light in such a case.
    An endless wind doth tear the sail apace,
Of forcèd sighs and trusty fearfulness;
A rain of tears, a cloud of dark disdain,
10   Hath done the wearied cords great hinderance;
    Wreathèd with error and eke with ignorance,
The stars be hid that led me to this pain;
    Drownèd is reason that should me consort,
    And I remain despairing of the port.

Egerton MS. 2711

Divers doth use, as I have heard and know,
    When that to change their ladies do begin,
    To mourn and wail and never for to lin,
Hoping thereby to pease their painful woe.
5   And some there be, that when it chanceth so
    That women change, and hate where love hath been,
    They call them false, and think with words to win
The hearts of them which otherwhere doth grow.
But as for me, though that by chance indeed
10   Change hath outworn the favour that I had,
    I will not wail, lament, nor yet be sad,
Nor call her false that falsely did me feed,
    But let it pass, and think it is of kind
    That often change doth please a woman's mind.

Devonshire MS. Add. 17492

HENRY HOWARD, EARL OF SURREY

A complaint by night of the lover not beloved

Alas, so all things now do hold their peace,
Heaven and earth disturbèd in nothing;
The beasts, the air, the birds their song do cease,
The nightè's chair the stars about doth bring;
Calm is the sea, the waves work less and less.   5
So am not I, whom love, alas, doth wring,
Bringing before my face the great increase
Of my desires, whereat I weep and sing
In joy and woe, as in a doubtful ease:
For my sweet thoughts sometime do pleasure bring, 10
But by and by the cause of my disease
Gives me a pang that inwardly doth sting,
   When that I think what grief it is again
   To live and lack the thing should rid my pain.

Tottel's Miscellany, 1557

MY GALLEY CHARGÈD: Adapted from Petrarch, *Rime* CLXXXIX.
3, 4 *enemy, lord*: i.e. Love.
8   *sighs* (Tottel): 'sights' (Egerton MS.).
12   *The stars*: i.e. the lady's eyes.

DIVERS DOTH USE:
3   *lin*: cease.
4   *pease*: appease.
12 *feed*: beguile.
13 *of kind*: by law of nature.

The two sonnets of Surrey were written in the period 1537–47.
They were first published in *Tottel's Miscellany*, 1557.
A COMPLAINT BY NIGHT: Adapted from Petrarch, *Rime*
   CLXIV. The title is not Surrey's.
3   *air*: wind.
4   *chair*: chariot.

Set me whereas the sun doth parch the green,
Or where his beams may not dissolve the ice,
In temp'rate heat, where he is felt and seen;
With proud people, in presence sad and wise;
5   Set me in base or yet in high degree,
In the long night or in the shortest day,
In clear weather or where mists thickest be,
In lost youth or when my hairs be grey;
Set me in earth, in heaven, or yet in hell,
10   In hill, in dale, or in the foaming flood;
Thrall or at large, alive whereso I dwell,
Sick or in health, in ill fame or in good:
    Yours will I be, and with that only thought
    Comfort myself, when that my hap is nought.

MS. Add. 36529

SET ME WHEREAS THE SUN: An adaptation of Petrarch, *Rime*
CXLV.
8   *lost*: 'lusty' (Tottel).

SIDNEY

SIR PHILIP SIDNEY

Leave me, O love which reachest but to dust,
And thou, my mind, aspire to higher things;
Grow rich in that which never taketh rust;
Whatever fades but fading pleasure brings.
    Draw in thy beams and humble all thy might   5
To that sweet yoke where lasting freedoms be,
Which breaks the clouds, and opens forth the light
That doth both shine, and give us sight to see.
    Oh, take fast hold, let that light be thy guide
In this small course which birth draws out to death,   10
And think how evil becometh him to slide,
Who seeketh heaven, and comes of heavenly breath.
    Then farewell, world; thy uttermost I see;
    Eternal love, maintain thy life in me.

Splendidis longum valedico nugis

Certain Sonnets, 1598

Shakespearian Pattern

LEAVE ME, O LOVE: Written probably before 1581.
3 Cf. Matt. 6.20: 'But lay up for yourselves treasures in
    heaven, where neither moth nor rust doth corrupt, . . .'.
6 Cf. Matt. 11.30: 'For my yoke is easy, and my burden is
    light.'
Motto reads 'I bid a long farewell to glittering trifles'.

From *Astrophil and Stella*, 1598

I

Loving in truth, and fain in verse my love to show,
That she, dear she, might take some pleasure of my pain,
Pleasure might cause her read, reading might make
    her know,
Knowledge might pity win, and pity grace obtain:
5   I sought fit words to paint the blackest face of woe;
Studying inventions fine, her wits to entertain;
Oft turning others' leaves to see if thence would flow
Some fresh and fruitful showers upon my sunburned
    brain.
    But words came halting forth, wanting invention's
    stay;
10 Invention, nature's child, fled step-dame study's blows,
And others' feet still seemed but strangers in my way.
Thus, great with child to speak, and helpless in my
    throes,
    Biting my truand pen, beating myself for spite,
    'Fool,' said my muse to me, 'look in thy heart, and
    write.'

ASTROPHIL AND STELLA: The sequence was probably written
1581–2; it was first published in 1591. To some extent at
least, the sonnets are based on Sidney's love for Penelope
Devereux, daughter of the Earl of Essex, who married
Robert, Lord Rich in Nov. 1581. 'Astrophil' means 'star-
lover' (with a play on Sidney's Christian name); 'Stella'
means 'star'.

SON. 1:

  9 *stay*: support.

11 *feet*: (i) tracks, ways; (ii) metrical units.

14 *heart*: i.e. the abode of Stella's image, the source of Astro-
     phil's invention.

3

Let dainty wits cry on the Sisters nine,
That bravely masked, their fancies may be told;
Or Pindar's apes, flaunt they in phrases fine,
Enam'ling with pied flowers their thoughts of gold;
   Or else let them in statelier glory shine,   5
Ennobling new-found tropes with problems old;
Or with strange similes enrich each line,
Of herbs or beasts, which Ind or Afric hold.
   For me, in sooth, no muse but one I know;
   Phrases and problems from my reach do grow,   10
And strange things cost too dear for my poor sprites.
   How then? even thus: in Stella's face I read
   What love and beauty be; then all my deed
But copying is, what in her nature writes.

SON. 3:
2   *masked*: arrayed like masquers.
3   *Pindar's apes*: imitators of the Greek lyric poet Pindar
    (c. 522–442 B.C.).
4   *Enam'ling*: embellishing.
6   *tropes*: rhetorical figures.
7–8 Such 'strange similes' were characteristic of Lyly and
    writers of the Euphuistic style.
13 *deed*: task.

5

It is most true that eyes are formed to serve
The inward light, and that the heavenly part
Ought to be king, from whose rules who do swerve,
Rebels to nature, strive for their own smart.
5   It is most true, what we call Cupid's dart
An image is, which for ourselves we carve,
And, fools, adore in temple of our heart,
Till that good god make church and churchman starve.
    True, that true beauty virtue is indeed,
10 Whereof this beauty can be but a shade,
Which elements with mortal mixture breed.
True, that on earth we are but pilgrims made,
    And should in soul up to our country move:
    True; and yet true that I must Stella love.

7

When nature made her chief work Stella's eyes,
In colour black why wrapped she beams so bright?
Would she in beamy black, like painter wise,
Frame daintiest lustre mixed of shades and light?
5   Or did she else that sober hue devise
In object best to knit and strength our sight,
Lest, if no veil these brave gleams did disguise,
They sunlike should more dazzle than delight?
    Or would she her miraculous power show,
10   That, whereas black seems beauty's contrary,
She even in black doth make all beauties flow?
Both so, and thus: she, minding Love should be
    Placed ever there, gave him this mourning weed
    To honour all their deaths who for her bleed.

15

You that do search for every purling spring
  Which from the ribs of old Parnassus flows,
  And every flower, not sweet perhaps, which grows
Near thereabouts, into your poesy wring;
You that do dictionary's method bring   5
  Into your rhymes, running in rattling rows;
  You that poor Petrarch's long-deceasèd woes
With new-born sighs and denizened wit do sing:
  You take wrong ways; those far-fet helps be such
  As do bewray a want of inward touch,   10
And sure at length stol'n goods do come to light.
  But if, both for your love and skill, your name
  You seek to nurse at fullest breasts of fame,
Stella behold, and then begin to endite.

SON. 5:
  2 *The inward light*: i.e. reason.

SON. 7:
  6 *In*: with. *knit and strength*: concentrate and strengthen.
  7 *brave*: resplendent.

SON. 15:
  1 *purling*: murmuring.
  8 *denizened*: naturalized (as an immigrant).
 10 *bewray*: betray.

31

With how sad steps, O moon, thou climb'st the skies!
  How silently, and with how wan a face!
  What, may it be that even in heavenly place
That busy archer his sharp arrows tries?
5 Sure, if that long-with-love-acquainted eyes
  Can judge of love, thou feel'st a lover's case;
  I read it in thy looks; thy languished grace
To me, that feel the like, thy state descries.
  Then, ev'n of fellowship, O moon, tell me,
10 Is constant love deemed there but want of wit?
Are beauties there as proud as here they be?
Do they above love to be loved, and yet
  Those lovers scorn whom that love doth possess?
  Do they call virtue there ungratefulness?

39

Come, sleep, O sleep, the certain knot of peace,
The baiting place of wit, the balm of woe,
The poor man's wealth, the prisoner's release,
Th' indifferent judge between the high and low;
5 With shield of proof shield me from out the prease
Of those fierce darts despair at me doth throw;
Oh, make in me those civil wars to cease:
I will good tribute pay, if thou do so.
  Take thou of me smooth pillows, sweetest bed,
10 A chamber deaf to noise and blind to light,
A rosy garland, and a weary head;
And if these things, as being thine by right,
  Move not thy heavy grace, thou shalt in me,
  Livelier than elsewhere, Stella's image see.

45

Stella oft sees the very face of woe
   Painted in my beclouded stormy face,
   But cannot skill to pity my disgrace,
Not though thereof the cause herself she know;
Yet, hearing late a fable which did show   5
   Of lovers never known a grievous case,
   Pity thereof gat in her breast such place
That, from that sea derived, tears' spring did flow.
   Alas, if fancy, drawn by imaged things,
Though false, yet with free scope, more grace doth breed 10
Than servant's wrack, where new doubts honour brings;
Then think, my dear, that you in me do read
   Of lover's ruin some sad tragedy:
   I am not I; pity the tale of me.

SON. 31:
14 *virtue there ungratefulness*: i.e. ungratefulness there a virtue.

SON. 39:
2 *baiting place*: place of rest on a journey.
5 *prease*: press.
11 *rosy garland*: i.e. garland of secrecy and silence (*sub rosa*).

SON. 45:
3 *cannot skill*: is unable.
11 I.e. than the misfortune of a (real) servant, whose honour-
ing of his beloved merely increases her disbelief in his
plight.

47

What, have I thus betrayed my liberty?
  Can those black beams such burning marks engrave
  In my free side? or am I born a slave,
Whose neck becomes such yoke of tyranny?
5 Or want I sense to feel my misery?
  Or sprite, disdain of such disdain to have?
  Who for long faith, though daily help I crave,
May get no alms, but scorn of beggary?
  Virtue, awake! Beauty but beauty is;
10 I may, I must, I can, I will, I do
Leave following that which it is gain to miss.
Let her go! Soft, but here she comes! Go to,
  Unkind, I love you not! O me, that eye
  Doth make my heart give to my tongue the lie!

53

In martial sports I had my cunning tried,
  And yet to break more staves did me address,
  While with the people's shouts, I must confess,
Youth, luck, and praise even filled my veins with pride;
5 When Cupid, having me, his slave, descried
  In Mars's livery, prancing in the press:
  'What now, sir fool!' said he (I would no less),
'Look here, I say.' I looked, and Stella spied,
  Who, hard by, made a window send forth light.
10 My heart then quaked, then dazzled were mine eyes,
One hand forgat to rule, th' other to fight;
Nor trumpet's sound I heard, nor friendly cries;
  My foe came on, and beat the air for me,
  Till that her blush taught me my shame to see.

54

Because I breathe not love to everyone,
  Nor do not use set colours for to wear,
  Nor nourish special locks of vowèd hair,
Nor give each speech a full point of a groan,
The courtly nymphs, acquainted with the moan   5
  Of them who in their lips love's standard bear:
  'What, he?' say they of me, 'now I dare swear
He cannot love; no, no, let him alone.'
  And think so still, so Stella know my mind.
Profess indeed I do not Cupid's art;   10
But you, fair maids, at length this true shall find,
That his right badge is but worn in the heart;
  Dumb swans, not chatt'ring pies, do lovers prove;
  They love indeed who quake to say they love.

SON. 47:
  2 *black beams*: i.e. Stella's eyes. *burning marks*: brands of slavery.
  4 *becomes*: befits.
 12 *go* (1591): 'do' (1598).

SON. 53: Sidney participated in several tournaments 1579–84.
  2 *staves*: tilting lances.
  6 *press*: throng.
  7 *I would no less*: I would have said no less.
 11 *rule*: control the horse.
 12 *trumpet's sound*: signal for the tilt to begin.

SON. 54:
  2 *set colours*: i.e. those of his lady.
  4 *full point*: full stop.
 12 *but worn*: worn only.
 13 *pies*: magpies.

71

Who will in fairest book of nature know
   How virtue may best lodged in beauty be,
   Let him but learn of love to read in thee,
Stella, those fair lines which true goodness show.
5   There shall he find all vices' overthrow,
   Not by rude force, but sweetest sovereignty
   Of reason, from whose light those night-birds fly,
That inward sun in thine eyes shineth so.
   And, not content to be perfection's heir
10   Thyself, dost strive all minds that way to move,
Who mark in thee what is in thee most fair;
So while thy beauty draws the heart to love,
   As fast thy virtue bends that love to good.
   But ah, desire still cries, 'Give me some food!'

74

I never drank of Aganippe well,
Nor ever did in shade of Tempe sit;
And muses scorn with vulgar brains to dwell;
Poor layman I, for sacred rites unfit.
5   Some do I hear of poets' fury tell,
But, God wot, wot not what they mean by it;
And this I swear, by blackest brook of hell,
I am no pick-purse of another's wit.
   How falls it then, that with so smooth an ease
10   My thoughts I speak, and what I speak doth flow
In verse, and that my verse best wits doth please?
Guess we the cause: 'What, is it thus?' Fie, no.
   'Or so?' Much less. 'How then?' Sure thus it is:
   My lips are sweet, inspired with Stella's kiss.

103

O happy Thames, that didst my Stella bear!
I saw thyself, with many a smiling line
Upon thy cheerful face, joy's livery wear,
While those fair planets on thy streams did shine.
   The boat for joy could not to dance forbear,   5
While wanton winds, with beauties so divine
Ravished, stayed not, till in her golden hair
They did themselves (O sweetest prison!) twine.
   And fain those Aeol's youth there would their stay
Have made; but forced by nature still to fly,   10
First did with puffing kiss those locks display.
She, so dishevelled, blushed; from window I
   With sight thereof cried out, 'Oh, fair disgrace!
   Let honour's self to thee grant highest place!'

SON. 71:
  7 *those night-birds*: i.e. 'all vices', which avoid the 'sun' of
    reason.

SON. 74:
  1 *Aganippe well*: fountain sacred to the Muses.
  2 *Tempe*: vale in Thessaly, haunt of Apollo.
  7 *by . . . hell*: The most solemn oath of the gods was by the
    river Styx.

SON. 103:
  4 *fair planets*: i.e. Stella's eyes.
  9 *Aeol's youth*: sons of Aeolus, breezes.
 13 *disgrace*: disarray.

FULKE GREVILLE

From *Caelica*, 1633

Fie, foolish earth, think you the heaven wants glory,
Because your shadows do yourself benight?
All's dark unto the blind, let them be sorry;
The heavens in themselves are ever bright.
5   Fie, fond desire, think you that love wants glory,
Because your shadows do yourself benight?
The hopes and fears of lust may make men sorry,
But love still in herself finds her delight.
Then, earth, stand fast; the sky that you benight
10   Will turn again and so restore your glory;
Desire, be steady; hope is your delight,
An orb wherein no creature can be sorry;
    Love being placed above these middle regions,
    Where every passion wars itself with legions.

The nurse-life wheat, within his green husk growing,
Flatters our hope and tickles our desire,
Nature's true riches in sweet beauties showing,
Which set all hearts, with labour's love, on fire.
5   No less fair is the wheat when golden ear
Shows unto hope the joys of near enjoying:
Fair and sweet is the bud, more sweet and fair
The rose, which proves that time is not destroying.
    Caelica, your youth, the morning of delight,
10   Enamelled o'er with beauties white and red,
All sense and thoughts did to belief invite
That love and glory there are brought to bed;
    And your ripe years' love-noon (he goes no higher)
    Turns all the spirits of man into desire.

SAMUEL DANIEL

From *Delia*, 1601

I once may see when years shall wreck my wrong,
  When golden hairs shall change to silver wire,
  And those bright rays that kindle all this fire
Shall fail in force, their working not so strong:
Then beauty, now the burden of my song,   5
  Whose glorious blaze the world doth so admire,
  Must yield up all to tyrant time's desire;
Then fade those flowers that decked her pride so long.
  When if she grieve to gaze her in her glass,
Which then presents her winter-withered hue,   10
  Go you, my verse, go tell her what she was,
For what she was she best shall find in you;
  Your fiery heat lets not her glory pass,
But phoenix-like shall make her live anew.

CAELICA: These two sonnets were written probably before
  1586.
FIE, FOOLISH EARTH:
13 *these middle regions*: earth, between heaven and hell.
14 *legions*: multitudes (of other passions).

THE NURSE-LIFE WHEAT:
13 *he*: i.e. the morning sun (from l. 9).

I ONCE MAY SEE: First published 1591.
 1 *wreck*: wreak.

These plaintive verse, the posts of my desire,
Which haste for succour to her slow regard,
Bear not report of any slender fire,
Forging a grief to win a fame's reward.
5   Nor are my passions limned for outward hue,
For that no colours can depaint my sorrows;
Delia herself and all the world may view
Best in my face where cares have tilled deep furrows.
     No bays I seek to deck my mourning brow,
10   O clear-eyed Rector of the holy Hill:
My humble accents bear the olive bough
Of intercession, but to move her will.
     These lines I use t' unburden mine own heart;
     My love affects no fame, nor 'steems of art.

Fair is my love, and cruel as she's fair:
Her brow shades frowns, although her eyes are sunny;
Her smiles are lightning, though her pride despair,
And her disdains are gall, her favours honey.
5   A modest maid, decked with a blush of honour,
Whose feet do tread green paths of youth and love;
The wonder of all eyes that look upon her,
Sacred on earth, designed a saint above.
     Chastity and beauty, which were deadly foes,
10   Live reconcilèd friends within her brow;
And had she pity to conjoin with those,
Then who had heard the plaints I utter now?
     For had she not been fair, and thus unkind,
     My muse had slept, and none had known my mind.

THESE PLAINTIVE VERSE: This and succeeding sonnets were
    first published in 1592.
1 *posts*: messengers.
5 *limned . . . hue*: tricked out for the superficial appearance.
10 *Rector of the holy Hill*: Apollo, ruler of Parnassus.

Look, Delia, how w' esteem the half-blown rose,
The image of thy blush and summer's honour,
Whilst yet her tender bud doth undisclose
That full of beauty time bestows upon her.
   No sooner spreads her glory in the air   5
But straight her wide-blown pomp comes to decline;
She then is scorned that late adorned the fair:
So fade the roses of those cheeks of thine.
   No April can revive thy withered flowers,
Whose springing grace adorns thy glory now;   10
Swift speedy time, feathered with flying hours,
Dissolves the beauty of the fairest brow.
    Then do not thou such treasure waste in vain,
    But love now, whilst thou mayst be loved again.

When winter snows upon thy sable hairs,
And frost of age hath nipped thy beauties near,
When dark shall seem thy day that never clears,
And all lies withered that was held so dear;
   Then take this picture which I here present thee,   5
Limnèd with a pencil not all unworthy;
Here see the gifts that God and nature lent thee,
Here read thyself, and what I suffered for thee.
   This may remain thy lasting monument,
Which happily posterity may cherish;   10
These colours with thy fading are not spent,
These may remain when thou and I shall perish.
    If they remain, then thou shalt live thereby;
    They will remain, and so thou canst not die.

WHEN WINTER SNOWS:
6 *Limnèd*: described.

Let others sing of knights and paladins
In agèd accents and untimely words,
Paint shadows in imaginary lines,
Which well the reach of their high wits records;
5   But I must sing of thee, and those fair eyes
Authentic shall my verse in time to come,
When yet th' unborn shall say, 'Lo, where she lies,
Whose beauty made him speak that else was dumb.'
       These are the arks, the trophies I erect,
10   That fortify thy name against old age;
And these thy sacred virtues must protect
Against the dark and time's consuming rage.
       Though th' error of my youth in them appear,
       Suffice they show I lived and loved thee dear.

GILES FLETCHER

From *Licia*, 1593

In time the strong and stately turrets fall,
In time the rose and silver lilies die,
In time the monarchs captives are, and thrall,
In time the sea and rivers are made dry;
5   The hardest flint in time doth melt asunder;
Still-living fame in time doth fade away;
The mountains proud we see in time come under;
And earth, for age, we see in time decay.
       The sun in time forgets for to retire
10   From out the East, where he was wont to rise;
The basest thoughts we see in time aspire,
And greedy minds in time do wealth despise.
       Thus all, sweet fair, in time must have an end,
       Except thy beauty, virtues, and thy friend.

48

EDMUND SPENSER

From *Amoretti*, 1595

13

In that proud port, which her so goodly graceth,
    whiles her faire face she reares up to the skie:
    and to the ground her eie lids low embaseth,
    most goodly temperature ye may descry,
Myld humblesse mixt with awfull majesty.   5
    For looking on the earth whence she was borne,
    her minde remembreth her mortalitie,
    what so is fayrest shall to earth returne.
But that same lofty countenance seemes to scorne
    base thing, and thinke how she to heaven may clime: 10
    treading downe earth as lothsome and forlorne,
    that hinders heavenly thoughts with drossy slime.
Yet lowly still vouchsafe to looke on me,
    such lowlinesse shall make you lofty be.

LET OTHERS SING:
1-4 Referring principally to Spenser and *The Faerie Queene*.
    paladins: heroes of chivalry.
9 *trophies*: memorials.

IN TIME THE STRONG: Adapted from *De suo amore aeterno*, a
    sonnet by Hieronymus Angerianus (fl. 1520).

AMORETTI: The sequence was published together with the
    Epithalamion, Spenser's ode written in celebration of his
    marriage in June 1594 to Elizabeth Boyle. 'Amoretti' is
    Italian, meaning 'little loves'.
SON. 13:
1 *port*: carriage.
4 *temperature*: proportion.

15

Ye tradefull Merchants, that with weary toyle,
   do seeke most pretious things to make your gain;
   and both the Indias of their treasures spoile,
   what needeth you to seeke so farre in vaine?
5 For loe my love doth in her selfe containe
   all this worlds riches that may farre be found,
   if Saphyres, loe her eies be Saphyres plaine,
   if Rubies, loe hir lips be Rubies sound:
If Pearles, hir teeth be pearles both pure and round;
10 if Yvorie, her forhead yvory weene;
   if Gold, her locks are finest gold on ground;
   if silver, her faire hands are silver sheene.
But that which fairest is, but few behold,
   her mind adornd with vertues manifold.

23

Penelope for her *Ulisses* sake,
   Deviz'd a Web her wooers to deceave:
   in which the worke that she all day did make
   the same at night she did againe unreave.
5 Such subtile craft my Damzell doth conceave,
   th' importune suit of my desire to shonne:
   for all that I in many dayes doo weave,
   in one short houre I find by her undonne.
So when I thinke to end that I begonne,
10 I must begin and never bring to end:
   for with one looke she spils that long I sponne,
   and with one word my whole years work doth rend.
Such labour like the Spyders web I fynd,
   whose fruitlesse worke is broken with least wynd.

54

Of this worlds Theatre in which we stay,
  My love lyke the Spectator ydly sits
beholding me that all the pageants play,
  disguysing diversly my troubled wits.
Sometimes I joy when glad occasion fits,   5
  and mask in myrth lyke to a Comedy:
soone after when my joy to sorrow flits,
  I waile and make my woes a Tragedy.
Yet she beholding me with constant eye,
  delights not in my merth nor rues my smart: 10
but when I laugh she mocks, and when I cry
  she laughes, and hardens evermore her hart.
What then can move her? if nor merth nor mone,
  she is no woman, but a sencelesse stone.

SON. 15: Adapted from Desportes, *Diane* 1.32. Cf. *Epithalamion* 167–203, and Song Sol. 4–7.
3 *Indias*: i.e. the East and West Indies.
10 *weene*: think.
12 *sheene*: fair.

SON. 23:
6 *importune*: persistent.
11 *spils*: destroys.

SON. 54:
3 *pageants*: roles.
6 *mask*: masquerade.

63

After long stormes and tempests sad assay,
  Which hardly I endurèd heretofore:
  in dread of death and daungerous dismay,
  with which my silly barke was tossèd sore:
5 I doe at length descry the happy shore,
  in which I hope ere long for to arryve;
  fayre soyle it seemes from far and fraught with store
  of all that deare and daynty is alyve.
Most happy he that can at last atchyve
10 the joyous safety of so sweet a rest:
  whose least delight sufficeth to deprive
  remembrance of all paines which him opprest.
All paines are nothing in respect of this,
  all sorrowes short that gaine eternall blisse.

67

Lyke as a huntsman after weary chace,
  Seeing the game from him escapt away,
  sits downe to rest him in some shady place,
  with panting hounds beguilèd of their pray:
5 So after long pursuit and vaine assay,
  when I all weary had the chace forsooke,
  the gentle deare returnd the selfe-same way,
  thinking to quench her thirst at the next brooke.
There she beholding me with mylder looke,
10 sought not to fly, but fearelesse still did bide:
  till I in hand her yet halfe trembling tooke,
  and with her owne goodwill hir fyrmely tyde.
Strange thing me seemd to see a beast so wyld,
  so goodly wonne with her owne will beguyld.

68

Most glorious Lord of lyfe, that on this day,
   Didst make thy triumph over death and sin:
   and having harrowd hell, didst bring away
   captivity thence captive us to win:
This joyous day, deare Lord, with joy begin,   5
   and grant that we for whom thou diddest dye
   being with thy deare blood clene washt from sin,
   may live for ever in felicity.
And that thy love we weighing worthily,
   may likewise love thee for the same againe: 10
   and for thy sake that all lyke deare didst buy,
   with love may one another entertayne.
So let us love, deare love, lyke as we ought,
   love is the lesson which the Lord us taught.

SON. 63:
  1 *assay*: ordeal.
  2 *hardly*: with difficulty.
  4 *silly*: helpless.

SON. 67:
  5 *assay*: attempt.

SON. 68: The sonnet recalls many biblical passages; e.g. 1 Cor.
    15.55-7, Eph. 4.8, Rev. 1.5, John 15.12.
  1 *this day*: i.e. Easter Sunday.

71

I joy to see how in your drawen work,
    Your selfe unto the Bee ye doe compare;
    and me unto the Spyder that doth lurke,
    in close awayt to catch her unaware.
5   Right so your selfe were caught in cunning snare
    of a deare foe, and thrallèd to his love:
    in whose streight bands ye now captivèd are
    so firmely, that ye never may remove.
But as your worke is woven all above,
10   with woodbynd flowers and fragrant Eglantine:
    so sweet your prison you in time shall prove,
    with many deare delights bedeckèd fyne.
And all thensforth eternall peace shall see,
    betweene the Spyder and the gentle Bee.

75

One day I wrote her name upon the strand,
    but came the waves and washèd it away:
    agayne I wrote it with a second hand,
    but came the tyde, and made my paynes his pray.
5   'Vayne man,' sayd she, 'that doest in vaine assay,
    a mortall thing so to immortalize,
    for I my selve shall lyke to this decay,
    and eek my name bee wypèd out lykewize.'
'Not so,' quod I, 'let baser things devize
10   to dy in dust, but you shall live by fame:
    my verse your vertues rare shall eternize,
    and in the hevens wryte your glorious name.
Where whenas death shall all the world subdew,
    our love shall live, and later life renew.'

79

Men call you fayre, and you doe credit it,
   For that your selfe ye dayly such doe see:
   but the trew fayre, that is the gentle wit,
   and vertuous mind, is much more praysd of me.
For all the rest, how ever fayre it be,   5
   shall turne to nought and loose that glorious hew:
   but onely that is permanent and free
   from frayle corruption, that doth flesh ensew.
That is true beautie: that doth argue you
   to be divine and borne of heavenly seed: 10
   deriv'd from that fayre Spirit, from whom al true
   and perfect beauty did at first proceed.
He onely fayre, and what he fayre hath made,
   all other fayre lyke flowres untymely fade.

SON. 71:
  1 *drawen work*: tapestry.
  4 *awayt*: ambush.
  7 *streight*: tight.
  9 *above*: 'about' (1595).
 11 *prove*: find.

SON. 75:
  2 *away* (1611): 'a way' (1595).
  4 *pray*: prey.

SON. 79:
  8 *ensew*: follow, succeed.
 11 *that fayre Spirit*: the Holy Spirit, source of heavenly beauty.

BARNABE BARNES

From *A Divine Century of Spiritual Sonnets*, 1595

The world's bright comforter, whose beamsome light
    Poor creatures cheereth, mounting from the deep,
    His course doth in prefixèd compass keep;
    And, as courageous giant, takes delight
5 To run his race and exercise his might,
    Till him, down galloping the mountain's steep,
    Clear Hesperus, smooth messenger of sleep,
    Views; and the silver ornament of night
    Forth brings, with stars past number in her train,
10 All which with sun's long-borrowed splendour shine.
The seas, with full tide swelling, ebb again;
All years to their old quarters new resign;
    The winds forsake their mountain chambers wild,
    And all in all things with God's virtue filled.

THE WORLD'S BRIGHT COMFORTER:
7 *Hesperus*: the evening star.
12 *quarters*: fourfold divisions.

MICHAEL DRAYTON

From *Idea*, 1619

To nothing fitter can I thee compare
Than to the son of some rich penny-father,
Who, having now brought on his end with care,
Leaves to his son all he had heaped together;
    This new-rich novice, lavish of his chest,   5
To one man gives, doth on another spend,
Then here he riots; yet amongst the rest
Haps to lend some to one true honest friend.
    Thy gifts thou in obscurity dost waste:
False friends thy kindness, born but to deceive thee;   10
Thy love, that is on the unworthy placed;
Time hath thy beauty, which with age will leave thee.
    Only that little which to me was lent
    I give thee back, when all the rest is spent.

IDEA: Idea was Drayton's name for Anne Goodere, daughter
of his patron Sir Henry Goodere. She married Henry
Rainsford of Clifford Chambers, Glos., in 1595. The first
four sonnets printed here first appeared in 1599.
TO NOTHING FITTER:
  2 *penny-father*: miser.

An evil spirit, your beauty, haunts me still,
Wherewith, alas, I have been long possessed,
Which ceaseth not to tempt me to each ill,
Nor gives me once but one poor minute's rest;
5   In me it speaks, whether I sleep or wake,
And when by means to drive it out I try,
With greater torments then it me doth take,
And tortures me in most extremity;
    Before my face it lays down my despairs,
10 And hastes me on unto a sudden death,
Now tempting me to drown myself in tears,
And then in sighing to give up my breath.
    Thus am I still provoked to every evil
    By this good wicked spirit, sweet angel devil.

To the Critic.

Methinks I see some crooked mimic jeer,
And tax my muse with this fantastic grace:
Turning my papers, asks, 'What have we here?'
Making withal some filthy antic face.
5   I fear no censure, nor what thou canst say,
Nor shall my spirit one jot of vigour lose.
Think'st thou my wit shall keep the pack-horse way
That ev'ry dudgeon low invention goes?
    Since sonnets thus in bundles are impressed,
10 And ev'ry drudge doth dull our satiate ear,
Think'st thou my love shall in those rags be dressed
That ev'ry dowdy, ev'ry trull doth wear?
    Up to my pitch no common judgement flies,
    I scorn all earthly dung-bred scarabies.

METHINKS I SEE:
8   *dudgeon*: contemptible.
9   *impressed*: printed.
14 *scarabies*: beetles.

Whilst thus my pen strives to eternize thee,
Age rules my lines with wrinkles in my face,
Where, in the map of all my misery,
Is modelled out the world of my disgrace.
    Whilst in despite of tyrannizing times,   5
Medea-like I make thee young again;
Proudly thou scorn'st my world-outwearing rhymes,
And murder'st virtue with thy coy disdain;
    And though in youth my youth untimely perish
To keep thee from oblivion and the grave,   10
Ensuing ages yet my rhymes shall cherish,
Where I, entombed, my better part shall save;
    And though this earthly body fade and die,
    My name shall mount upon eternity.

Dear, why should you command me to my rest,
When now the night doth summon all to sleep?
Methinks this time becometh lovers best;
Night was ordained together friends to keep.
    How happy are all other living things,   5
Which, though the day disjoin by sev'ral flight,
The quiet ev'ning yet together brings,
And each returns unto his love at night!
    O thou that art so courteous else to all,
Why shouldst thou, night, abuse me only thus,   10
That ev'ry creature to his kind dost call,
And yet 'tis thou dost only sever us?
    Well could I wish it would be ever day,
    If, when night comes, you bid me go away.

WHILST THUS MY PEN:
  6 *Medea-like*: Medea by her magic restored Jason's father
    Aeson to youth.

DEAR, WHY SHOULD YOU COMMAND: First published 1602

To Time.

> Stay, speedy time; behold, before thou pass,
> From age to age what thou hast sought to see:
> One in whom all the excellencies be,
> In whom heaven looks itself as in a glass.
> 5   Time, look thou too in this tralucent glass,
> And thy youth past in this pure mirror see,
> As the world's beauty in his infancy,
> What it was then, and thou before it was.
>   Pass on, and to posterity tell this,
> 10   Yet see thou tell but truly what hath been;
> Say to our nephews that thou once hast seen
> In perfect human shape all heavenly bliss;
>   And bid them mourn, nay more, despair with thee,
>   That she is gone, her like again to see.

> How many paltry, foolish, painted things,
> That now in coaches trouble ev'ry street,
> Shall be forgotten, whom no poet sings,
> Ere they be well wrapped in their winding sheet!
> 5   Where I to thee eternity shall give,
> When nothing else remaineth of these days,
> And queens hereafter shall be glad to live
> Upon the alms of thy superfluous praise;
>   Virgins and matrons, reading these my rhymes,
> 10   Shall be so much delighted with thy story
> That they shall grieve they lived not in these times,
> To have seen thee, their sex's only glory.
>   So shalt thou fly above the vulgar throng,
>   Still to survive in my immortal song.

Since there's no help, come, let us kiss and part —
Nay, I have done: you get no more of me;
And I am glad, yea, glad with all my heart
That thus so cleanly I myself can free;
   Shake hands forever, cancel all our vows,   5
And when we meet at any time again,
Be it not seen in either of our brows
That we one jot of former love retain.
   Now at the last gasp of love's latest breath,
When, his pulse failing, passion speechless lies,   10
When faith is kneeling by his bed of death,
And innocence is closing up his eyes, —
   Now if thou wouldst, when all have given him over,
   From death to life thou mightst him yet recover.

STAY, SPEEDY TIME: Published in early form 1594; exten-
sively revised before 1619.
8 *and*: 'what' (1600).
11 *nephews*: descendants.

HOW MANY PALTRY: First published 1619.

SINCE THERE'S NO HELP: First published 1619.

SONNETS

WILLIAM SHAKESPEARE

From *Sonnets*, 1609

I

From fairest creatures we desire increase,
That thereby beauty's rose might never die,
But as the riper should by time decease,
His tender heir might bear his memory.
5   But thou, contracted to thine own bright eyes,
Feed'st thy light's flame with self-substantial fuel,
Making a famine where abundance lies,
Thyself thy foe, to thy sweet self too cruel.
Thou that art now the world's fresh ornament
10   And only herald to the gaudy spring,
Within thine own bud buriest thy content
And, tender churl, mak'st waste in niggarding.
Pity the world, or else this glutton be —
To eat the world's due, by the grave and thee.

SONNETS: Most, if not all, of Shakespeare's sonnets were
written in the 1590s; the exact date is not known.
SON. I:
5 *contracted*: betrothed (cf. Narcissus, who was consumed
with love for his own reflection).
6 *self-substantial*: of its own substance.
11 *content*: (i) contents, i.e. seed; (ii) satisfaction.
12 *churl*: miser.

12

When I do count the clock that tells the time,
And see the brave day sunk in hideous night;
When I behold the violet past prime,
And sable curls all silvered o'er with white;
   When lofty trees I see barren of leaves,   5
Which erst from heat did canopy the herd,
And summer's green all girded up in sheaves,
Borne on the bier with white and bristly beard;
   Then of thy beauty do I question make,
That thou among the wastes of time must go,   10
Since sweets and beauties do themselves forsake,
And die as fast as they see others grow;
   And nothing 'gainst time's scythe can make defence
   Save breed, to brave him when he takes thee hence.

SON. 12:
  2 *brave*: resplendent.
  4 *all*: 'or' (1609).
  8 *bier*: i.e. harvest cart.
 10 *wastes of time*: things despoiled by time.
 11 *themselves forsake*: surrender themselves to change.
 14 *breed*: offspring.

15

When I consider everything that grows
Holds in perfection but a little moment,
That this huge stage presenteth nought but shows
Whereon the stars in secret influence comment;
5   When I perceive that men as plants increase,
Cheered and checked even by the selfsame sky,
Vaunt in their youthful sap, at height decrease,
And wear their brave state out of memory;
       Then the conceit of this inconstant stay
10   Sets you most rich in youth before my sight,
Where wasteful time debateth with decay
To change your day of youth to sullied night;
       And all in war with time for love of you,
       As he takes from you, I engraft you new.

SON. 15:
6 *sky*: (i) weather, which affects ('cheers' and 'checks')
   plants' growth; (ii) stars, whose influence similarly
   affects men's lives.
8 *out of memory*: i.e. until their splendour is forgotten.
9 *conceit of this inconstant stay*: idea of this transience in nature's
   course.
11 *debateth*: conspires (or perhaps 'contends').
14 *engraft you new*: i.e. give you new life in my poetry (as new
   graft is inserted into old stock). There is a pun on 'en-
   grave'.

16

But wherefore do not you a mightier way
Make war upon this bloody tyrant, time?
And fortify yourself in your decay
With means more blessèd than my barren rhyme?
   Now stand you on the top of happy hours,   5
And many maiden gardens, yet unset,
With virtuous wish would bear your living flowers
Much liker than your painted counterfeit;
   So should the lines of life that life repair,
Which this (time's pencil or my pupil pen)   10
Neither in inward worth nor outward fair,
Can make you live yourself in eyes of men.
   To give away yourself keeps yourself still;
   And you must live drawn by your own sweet skill.

SON. 16:

6 *unset*: unsown.

8 *counterfeit*: portrait.

9 *lines of life*: i.e. children of your lineage (as living portraits of you, in contrast with the wrinkled portrait drawn by 'time's pencil' and the lines of verse written by 'my pupil pen').

10 *pupil*: inexpert.

13 *To give away yourself*: i.e. by producing children.

18

Shall I compare thee to a summer's day?
Thou art more lovely and more temperate.
Rough winds do shake the darling buds of May,
And summer's lease hath all too short a date;
5   Sometime too hot the eye of heaven shines,
And often is his gold complexion dimmed;
And every fair from fair sometime declines,
By chance or nature's changing course untrimmed;
     But thy eternal summer shall not fade,
10   Nor lose possession of that fair thou ow'st;
Nor shall death brag thou wand'rest in his shade,
When in eternal lines to time thou grow'st.
     So long as men can breathe or eyes can see,
     So long lives this, and this gives life to thee.

19

Devouring time, blunt thou the lion's paws,
And make the earth devour her own sweet brood;
Pluck the keen teeth from the fierce tiger's jaws,
And burn the long-lived phoenix in her blood;
5   Make glad and sorry seasons as thou fleet'st,
And do whate'er thou wilt, swift-footed time,
To the wide world and all her fading sweets;
But I forbid thee one most heinous crime:
     Oh, carve not with thy hours my love's fair brow,
10   Nor draw no lines there with thine antique pen;
Him in thy course untainted do allow,
For beauty's pattern to succeeding men.
     Yet, do thy worst, old time: despite thy wrong,
     My love shall in my verse ever live young.

23

As an unperfect actor on the stage,
Who with his fear is put besides his part,
Or some fierce thing replete with too much rage,
Whose strength's abundance weakens his own heart;
   So I, for fear of trust, forget to say   5
The perfect ceremony of love's rite,
And in mine own love's strength seem to decay,
O'ercharged with burden of mine own love's might.
   Oh, let my books be then the eloquence
And dumb presagers of my speaking breast,   10
Who plead for love, and look for recompense
More than that tongue that more hath more expressed.
   Oh, learn to read what silent love hath writ;
   To hear with eyes belongs to love's fine wit.

SON. 18:
  4 *date*: duration.
  5 *eye of heaven*: sun.
  8 *untrimmed*: stripped of its finery.
 10 *ow'st*: ownest.
 12 *to . . . grow'st*: you are grafted to (i.e. incorporated into) time.

SON. 19:
  4 *long-lived phoenix*: The phoenix was fabled to live for over 500 years before dying in the flames from which she was reborn. *in her blood*: i.e. alive.
 10 *antique*: (i) antic, grotesque; (ii) old.
 11 *untainted*: i.e. untouched by decay.

SON. 23:
  2 *besides*: out of.
  4 *heart*: capacity for action.
  5 *for fear of trust*: i.e. in distrust of myself and of my reception.
5–6 *say . . . rite*: say my lines perfectly in love's ritual.
  9 *books*: some eds. emend to 'looks'.
 10 *presagers*: spokesmen.
 12 *more expressed*: more fully (or more often) expressed.
 14 *wit*: perception.

29

When, in disgrace with fortune and men's eyes,
I all alone beweep my outcast state,
And trouble deaf heaven with my bootless cries,
And look upon myself, and curse my fate;
5   Wishing me like to one more rich in hope,
Featured like him, like him with friends possessed,
Desiring this man's art, and that man's scope,
With what I most enjoy contented least;
Yet in these thoughts myself almost despising,
10   Haply I think on thee, and then my state,
Like to the lark at break of day arising
From sullen earth, sings hymns at heaven's gate;
For thy sweet love remembered such wealth brings
That then I scorn to change my state with kings.

30

When to the sessions of sweet silent thought
I summon up remembrance of things past,
I sigh the lack of many a thing I sought,
And with old woes new wail my dear time's waste.
5   Then can I drown an eye, unused to flow,
For precious friends hid in death's dateless night,
And weep afresh love's long since cancelled woe,
And moan th' expense of many a vanished sight.
Then can I grieve at grievances foregone,
10   And heavily from woe to woe tell o'er
The sad account of fore-bemoanèd moan,
Which I new pay as if not paid before.
But if the while I think on thee, dear friend,
All losses are restored, and sorrows end.

33

Full many a glorious morning have I seen
Flatter the mountain tops with sovereign eye,
Kissing with golden face the meadows green,
Gilding pale streams with heavenly alchemy;
   Anon permit the basest clouds to ride   5
With ugly rack on his celestial face,
And from the forlorn world his visage hide,
Stealing unseen to west with this disgrace.
   Even so my sun one early morn did shine
With all-triumphant splendour on my brow;   10
But out, alack! he was but one hour mine;
The region cloud hath masked him from me now.
   Yet him for this my love no whit disdaineth;
   Suns of the world may stain, when heaven's sun
      staineth.

SON. 29:
1 *in disgrace*: out of favour.
3 *bootless*: profitless.
6 *him . . . him*: this person . . . that person.
7 *scope*: versatility.
10 *state*: frame of mind, spirits.
12 *sullen*: dark, melancholy.

SON. 30:
1 *sessions*: court sittings.
4 *new*: anew.
6 *dateless*: endless.
7 *cancelled*: paid in full.
8 *expense*: loss.
9 *foregone*: past.
10 *tell*: reckon.

SON. 33:
2 *Flatter*: cheer, brighten (as a sovereign bestowing his favours).
5 *Anon*: in a short while. *basest*: (i) darkest; (ii) meanest.
6 *rack*: drifting cloud mass.
8 *disgrace*: (i) disfigurement; (ii) dishonour.
12 *region*: of the upper air.
14 *stain*: lose brightness.

34

Why didst thou promise such a beauteous day,
And make me travel forth without my cloak,
To let base clouds o'ertake me in my way,
Hiding thy brav'ry in their rotten smoke?
5   'Tis not enough that through the cloud thou break
To dry the rain on my storm-beaten face,
For no man well of such a salve can speak
That heals the wound, and cures not the disgrace.
       Nor can thy shame give physic to my grief;
10   Though thou repent, yet I have still the loss;
Th' offender's sorrow lends but weak relief
To him that bears the strong offence's cross.
       Ah, but those tears are pearl which thy love sheds,
       And they are rich, and ransom all ill deeds.

35

No more be grieved at that which thou hast done;
Roses have thorns, and silver fountains mud;
Clouds and eclipses stain both moon and sun,
And loathsome canker lives in sweetest bud.
5   All men make faults, and even I in this,
Authorizing thy trespass with compare,
Myself corrupting, salving thy amiss,
Excusing thy sins more than thy sins are:
       For to thy sensual fault I bring in sense —
10   Thy adverse party is thy advocate —
And 'gainst myself a lawful plea commence:
Such civil war is in my love and hate
       That I an accessary needs must be
       To that sweet thief which sourly robs from me.

53

What is your substance, whereof are you made,
That millions of strange shadows on you tend?
Since every one hath, every one, one shade,
And you, but one, can every shadow lend.
   Describe Adonis, and the counterfeit   5
Is poorly imitated after you;
On Helen's cheek all art of beauty set,
And you in Grecian tires are painted new;
   Speak of the spring and foison of the year:
The one doth shadow of your beauty show,   10
The other as your bounty doth appear,
And you in every blessèd shape we know.
   In all external grace you have some part,
   But you like none, none you, for constant heart.

SON. 34:
3 *base*: See note to Son. 33, l. 5.
4 *brav'ry*: finery. *rotten smoke*: foul mist.
8 *disgrace*: See note to Son. 33, l. 8.
12 *cross*: 'loss' (1609).

SON. 35:
3 *stain*: darken.
4 *canker*: caterpillar.
6 *Authorizing*: vindicating. *with compare*: by comparisons (i.e.
    those of ll. 2–4).
7 *salving*: mitigating, smoothing over.
8 Making more excuses for your sins than the extent of
    them warrants. *thy . . . thy*: 'their . . . their' (1609).
9 *I bring in sense*: I introduce reason (thus adding to my own
    faults).
11 *lawful plea*: lawsuit.

SON. 53:
2 *strange*: alien. *shadows* (3 *shade*; 4, 10 *shadow*): the words pun
    on (i) image cast by the body intercepting light; (ii)
    reflection or symbol of the Platonic form. *tend*: attend.
4 And you, although but one person, can cast any number
    of shadows (i.e. images of beauty).
5 *counterfeit*: portrait.
8 *tires*: attire.
9 *foison*: abundant harvest.

55

Not marble nor the gilded monuments
Of princes shall outlive this powerful rhyme;
But you shall shine more bright in these contents
Than unswept stone, besmeared with sluttish time.
5   When wasteful war shall statues overturn,
And broils root out the work of masonry,
Nor Mars his sword nor war's quick fire shall burn
The living record of your memory.
    'Gainst death and all oblivious enmity
10   Shall you pace forth; your praise shall still find room
Even in the eyes of all posterity
That wear this world out to the ending doom.
    So, till the judgement that yourself arise,
    You live in this, and dwell in lovers' eyes.

57

Being your slave, what should I do but tend
Upon the hours and times of your desire?
I have no precious time at all to spend,
Nor services to do, till you require.
5   Nor dare I chide the world-without-end hour,
Whilst I, my sovereign, watch the clock for you,
Nor think the bitterness of absence sour,
When you have bid your servant once adieu;
    Nor dare I question with my jealous thought
10   Where you may be, or your affairs suppose,
But, like a sad slave, stay and think of nought
Save where you are how happy you make those.
    So true a fool is love that in your will,
    Though you do anything, he thinks no ill.

65

Since brass, nor stone, nor earth, nor boundless sea,
But sad mortality o'ersways their power,
How with this rage shall beauty hold a plea,
Whose action is no stronger than a flower?
    Oh, how shall summer's honey breath hold out   5
Against the wrackful siege of batt'ring days,
When rocks impregnable are not so stout,
Nor gates of steel so strong, but time decays?
    Oh, fearful meditation! Where, alack,
Shall time's best jewel from time's chest lie hid?   10
Or what strong hand can hold his swift foot back?
Or who his spoil of beauty can forbid?
    Oh, none, unless this miracle have might,
    That in black ink my love may still shine bright.

SON. 55:
1 *monuments*: 'monument' (1609).
4 *Than unswept stone*: i.e. than your neglected memorial stone
   (whose inscription in time will be obliterated).
5 *wasteful*: devastating.
6 *broils*: turmoils.
7 *Nor Mars his sword*: i.e. neither the sword of Mars (shall
   destroy). *quick*: fierce.
9 *all oblivious enmity*: all the enemy force of oblivion.
12 *wear*: last (with a sense also of 'wear away').
13 *judgement*: Judgement Day. *that*: when.

SON. 57:
5 *world-without-end*: endlessly tedious.
10 *suppose*: guess at.
13 *true*: (i) faithful; (ii) real. *will*: (i) desire; (ii) wilfulness;
   (iii) lust (there may also be a pun on 'William').

SON. 65:
3 *rage*: destructive violence.
4 *action*: (i) force, power; (ii) lawcase.
6 *wrackful*: destructive.
10 *chest*: (i) jewel-box; (ii) coffin.
12 *spoil*: marring (with a pun on 'booty'). *of*: 'or' (1609).

71

No longer mourn for me when I am dead
Than you shall hear the surly sullen bell
Give warning to the world that I am fled
From this vile world, with vildest worms to dwell.
5   Nay, if you read this line, remember not
The hand that writ it, for I love you so
That I in your sweet thoughts would be forgot,
If thinking on me then should make you woe.
    Oh, if, I say, you look upon this verse
10 When I perhaps compounded am with clay,
Do not so much as my poor name rehearse,
But let your love even with my life decay;
      Lest the wise world should look into your moan,
      And mock you with me after I am gone.

73

That time of year thou mayst in me behold
When yellow leaves, or none, or few, do hang
Upon those boughs which shake against the cold,
Bare ruined choirs where late the sweet birds sang.
5   In me thou seest the twilight of such day
As after sunset fadeth in the West,
Which by and by black night doth take away,
Death's second self, that seals up all in rest.
    In me thou seest the glowing of such fire
10 That on the ashes of his youth doth lie,
As the death-bed whereon it must expire,
Consumed with that which it was nourished by.
      This thou perceiv'st, which makes thy love more
        strong
      To love that well which thou must leave ere long.

74

94

They that have power to hurt and will do none,
That do not do the thing they most do show,
Who, moving others, are themselves as stone,
Unmovèd, cold, and to temptation slow —
    They rightly do inherit heaven's graces,   5
And husband nature's riches from expense;
They are the lords and owners of their faces,
Others but stewards of their excellence.
    The summer's flower is to the summer sweet,
Though to itself it only live and die;   10
But if that flower with base infection meet,
The basest weed outbraves his dignity.
    For sweetest things turn sourest by their deeds;
    Lilies that fester smell far worse than weeds.

SON. 71:
13 *wise*: coolly judging.
14 *with*: on account of (or perhaps 'as well as').

SON. 73:
 4 *choirs*: part of a church or monastery where divine service
    is sung.
10 *his*: its.
12 I.e. the glowing fire is being stifled by the ashes which
    were once the fuel which fed it.
14 *leave*: relinquish.

SON. 94:
 1 *will*: desire to.
 2 *show*: i.e. show capacity for doing (or 'appear to do').
 5 *rightly*: indeed (or perhaps 'by right').
 6 *expense*: waste.
 8 *stewards*: distributors (stewards were officials who managed
    their lord's estates). *their*: refers to *They* (l. 1).
12 *outbraves his dignity*: i.e. surpasses the flower in worth.

102

My love is strengthened, though more weak in seeming;
I love not less, though less the show appear;
That love is merchandized whose rich esteeming
The owner's tongue doth publish everywhere.
5   Our love was new, and then but in the spring,
When I was wont to greet it with my lays;
As Philomel in summer's front doth sing,
And stops her pipe in growth of riper days.
     Not that the summer is less pleasant now
10 Than when her mournful hymns did hush the night,
But that wild music burdens every bough,
And sweets grown common lose their dear delight.
     Therefore, like her, I sometime hold my tongue,
     Because I would not dull you with my song.

104

To me, fair friend, you never can be old,
For as you were when first your eye I eyed,
Such seems your beauty still. Three winters cold
Have from the forests shook three summers' pride,
5   Three beauteous springs to yellow autumn turned,
In process of the seasons have I seen;
Three April perfumes in three hot Junes burned,
Since first I saw you fresh, which yet are green.
     Ah, yet doth beauty, like a dial hand,
10 Steal from his figure, and no pace perceived;
So your sweet hue, which methinks still doth stand,
Hath motion, and mine eye may be deceived,—
     For fear of which, hear this, thou age unbred:
     Ere you were born was beauty's summer dead.

116

Let me not to the marriage of true minds
Admit impediments: love is not love
Which alters when it alteration finds,
Or bends with the remover to remove.
   Oh no! it is an ever-fixèd mark,   5
That looks on tempests and is never shaken;
It is the star to every wand'ring bark,
Whose worth's unknown, although his height be taken.
   Love's not time's fool, though rosy lips and cheeks
Within his bending sickle's compass come;   10
Love alters not with his brief hours and weeks,
But bears it out even to the edge of doom.
   If this be error and upon me proved,
   I never writ, nor no man ever loved.

SON. 102:
1 *seeming*: appearance.
3 *merchandized*: treated like saleable goods. *esteeming*: value.
7 *Philomel*: the nightingale. *front*: beginning.
8 *her*: 'his' (1609).
11 *wild*: unrestrained.
14 *dull*: cloy, weary.

SON. 104:
7 I.e. thrice have spring's fragrances been consumed by summer's heat.
9 *dial*: clock or sundial.
10 *his figure*: the numeral on the dial (and perhaps the Friend's appearance).
11 *hue*: features. *stand*: stay constant.

SON. 116:
1–2 *Let . . . impediments*: echoes the Church of England marriage service.
4 Or inclines to inconstancy when the beloved is inconstant.
5 *mark*: sea-mark.
8 *worth*: influence, value. *height be taken*: altitude be determined.
11 *his*: i.e. time's.
12 *bears it out*: endures.
13 *upon*: against.

121

'Tis better to be vile than vile esteemed,
When not to be receives reproach of being,
And the just pleasure lost, which is so deemed
Not by our feeling, but by others' seeing.
5   For why should others' false adulterate eyes
Give salutation to my sportive blood?
Or on my frailties why are frailer spies,
Which in their wills count bad what I think good?
    No: I am that I am, and they that level
10 At my abuses reckon up their own;
I may be straight though they themselves be bevel;
By their rank thoughts my deeds must not be shown,—
    Unless this general evil they maintain:
    All men are bad and in their badness reign.

SON. 121:
3 *just*: legitimate. *so deemed*: i.e. deemed vile.
4 *feeling*: experience (of the pleasure).
5 *adulterate*: lascivious.
6 I.e. hail my amorous activities as akin to their own.
8 *in their wills*: wilfully (or perhaps 'because of their own lust').
9 *level*: take aim.
11 *bevel*: oblique, crooked.
14 *reign*: exercise authority (as judges); or possibly 'flourish'.

127

In the old age black was not counted fair,
Or if it were, it bore not beauty's name;
But now is black beauty's successive heir,
And beauty slandered with a bastard shame;
　　For since each hand hath put on nature's power,　5
Fairing the foul with art's false borrowed face,
Sweet beauty hath no name, no holy bower,
But is profaned, if not lives in disgrace.
　　Therefore my mistress' brows are raven black,
Her eyes so suited, and they mourners seem　　10
At such who, not born fair, no beauty lack,
Sland'ring creation with a false esteem.
　　Yet so they mourn, becoming of their woe,
　　That every tongue says beauty should look so.

SON. 127:
1　*In the old age*: formerly. *fair*: (i) beautiful; (ii) blonde.
3　*successive*: by succession.
4　*a bastard shame*: the shame of being a bastard.
5　*put on*: assumed.
6　*art's . . . face*: i.e. cosmetics.
7　*Sweet beauty*: i.e. natural blonde beauty.
8　*disgrace*: discredit.
9　*brows*: 'eyes' (1609).
10　*so suited*: (i) matching; (ii) so clad (i.e. in mourning).
11　*no beauty lack*: i.e. due to their use of cosmetics.
12　*creation*: nature. *esteem*: value.
13　*becoming of*: gracing.

128

How oft, when thou, my music, music play'st
Upon that blessèd wood whose motion sounds
With thy sweet fingers, when thou gently sway'st
The wiry concord that mine ear confounds,
5   Do I envy those jacks that nimble leap
To kiss the tender inward of thy hand,
Whilst my poor lips, which should that harvest reap,
At the wood's boldness by thee blushing stand!
    To be so tickled, they would change their state
10   And situation with those dancing chips
O'er whom thy fingers walk with gentle gait,
Making dead wood more blest than living lips.
    Since saucy jacks so happy are in this,
    Give them thy fingers, me thy lips to kiss.

129

Th' expense of spirit in a waste of shame
Is lust in action; and till action, lust
Is perjured, murd'rous, bloody, full of blame,
Savage, extreme, rude, cruel, not to trust;
5   Enjoyed no sooner but despisèd straight;
Past reason hunted, and no sooner had,
Past reason hated, as a swallowed bait
On purpose laid to make the taker mad;
    Mad in pursuit, and in possession so;
10   Had, having, and in quest to have, extreme;
A bliss in proof, and proved, a very woe;
Before, a joy proposed; behind, a dream.
    All this the world well knows; yet none knows well
    To shun the heaven that leads men to this hell.

130

My mistress' eyes are nothing like the sun;
Coral is far more red than her lips' red;
If snow be white, why then her breasts are dun;
If hairs be wires, black wires grow on her head.
    I have seen roses damasked, red and white,   5
But no such roses see I in her cheeks;
And in some perfumes is there more delight
Than in the breath that from my mistress reeks.
    I love to hear her speak, yet well I know
That music hath a far more pleasing sound;   10
I grant I never saw a goddess go,—
My mistress when she walks treads on the ground.
    And yet by heaven I think my love as rare
    As any she belied with false compare.

SON. 128:
2   *wood*: keys of the virginal (as *chips*, l. 10).
3   *sway'st*: governest.
4   *confounds*: amazes.
5   *jacks*: here the keys, though properly applied to wooden
    uprights fixed to the key-levers of the virginal. There is a
    pun on *jacks* meaning 'knaves'.
11 *thy*: 'their' (1609).
14 *thy fingers*: 'their fingers' (1609).

SON. 129:
1   *spirit*: vital energy. *waste of shame*: shameful squandering.
3   *perjured*: treacherous.
4   *rude*: brutal.
9   *Mad*: 'Made' (1609).
11 *in proof*: in the experiencing. *proved*: experienced. *a very woe*:
    'and very woe' (1609).

SON. 130:
4   *If hairs be wires*: This, like the other comparisons which
    the poet disparages, was a conventional conceit among
    earlier sonneteers.
5   *damasked*: pink.
8   *reeks*: is exhaled.
13 *love*: mistress.
14 *she*: woman.

138

When my love swears that she is made of truth,
I do believe her, though I know she lies,
That she might think me some untutored youth,
Unlearnèd in the world's false subtleties.
5   Thus vainly thinking that she thinks me young,
Although she knows my days are past the best,
Simply I credit her false-speaking tongue;
On both sides thus is simple truth suppressed.
But wherefore says she not she is unjust?
10 And wherefore say not I that I am old?
Oh, love's best habit is in seeming trust,
And age in love loves not t' have years told.
Therefore I lie with her, and she with me,
And in our faults by lies we flattered be.

141

In faith, I do not love thee with mine eyes,
For they in thee a thousand errors note;
But 'tis my heart that loves what they despise,
Who in despite of view is pleased to dote;
5   Nor are mine ears with thy tongue's tune delighted,
Nor tender feeling to base touches prone;
Nor taste nor smell desire to be invited
To any sensual feast with thee alone.
But my five wits nor my five senses can
10 Dissuade one foolish heart from serving thee,
Who leaves unswayed the likeness of a man,
Thy proud heart's slave and vassal wretch to be.
Only my plague thus far I count my gain,
That she that makes me sin awards me pain.

146

Poor soul, the centre of my sinful earth,
Foiled by these rebel powers that thee array,
Why dost thou pine within and suffer dearth,
Painting thy outward walls so costly gay?
    Why so large cost, having so short a lease,   5
Dost thou upon thy fading mansion spend?
Shall worms, inheritors of this excess,
Eat up thy charge? Is this thy body's end?
    Then, soul, live thou upon thy servant's loss,
And let that pine to aggravate thy store;   10
Buy terms divine in selling hours of dross;
Within be fed, without be rich no more:
    So shalt thou feed on death, that feeds on men,
    And death once dead, there's no more dying then.

SON. 138:
  1 *truth*: faithfulness (with a play on 'veracity').
  5 *vainly thinking*: i.e. in self-deception pretending to think.
  7 *Simply*: with assumed naïveté.
  9 *unjust*: unfaithful.
  11 *habit*: guise.
  12 *told*: reckoned.
  13 *lie with*: (i) lie to; (ii) sleep with.

SON. 141:
  6 *to . . . prone*: eager for your sensual touches.
  8 *alone*: above all others.
  9 *five wits*: the mental faculties.
  11 I.e. the heart deserts the body it should rule, leaving it
     ungoverned and a man in appearance only.
  13 To this extent only do I consider my affliction a benefit.

SON. 146:
  1 *earth*: i.e. body.
  2 *Foiled by*: 'My sinful earth' (1609). *rebel powers*: i.e. fleshly
     desires. *array*: (i) afflict; (ii) clothe; (iii) defile.
  6 *fading*: deteriorating.
  8 *charge*: i.e. the body, on which much has been spent.
  9 *thy servant's*: i.e. the body's.
  10 *aggravate*: increase.
  11 *terms divine*: eternal ages.

SIR JOHN DAVIES

From 'Gulling Sonnets'

The lover, under burden of his mistress' love,
Which like to Aetna did his heart oppress,
Did give such piteous groans that he did move
The heavens at length to pity his distress.
5   But for the Fates, in their high court above,
Forbade to make the grievous burden less,
The gracious powers did all conspire to prove
If miracle this mischief might redress;
Therefore, regarding that the load was such
10   As no man might with one man's might sustain,
And that mild patience imported much
To him that should endure an endless pain,
By their decree he soon transformèd was
Into a patient burden-bearing ass.

Chetham MS. 8012

GULLING SONNETS: Davies wrote nine sonnets parodying the
sonneteering conventions of the 1590s. They were written
some time after 1596.
THE LOVER, UNDER BURDEN:
2 *like to Aetna*: The volcanic rumblings of Mount Aetna
were said to be the groans of the giant Enceladus buried
beneath.

The sacred muse that first made Love divine
Hath made him naked and without attire;
But I will clothe him with this pen of mine,
That all the world his fashion shall admire:
   His hat of hope, his band of beauty fine,   5
His cloak of craft, his doublet of desire;
Grief, for a girdle, shall about him twine;
His points of pride, his eyelet-holes of ire,
   His hose of hate, his codpiece of conceit,
His stockings of stern strife, his shirt of shame,   10
His garters of vainglory gay and slight,
His pantofles of passions I will frame;
   Pumps of presumption shall adorn his feet,
   And socks of sullenness exceeding sweet.

Chetham MS. 8012

THE SACRED MUSE:
  8 *points*: laces fastening doublet to breeches.
  9 *hose*: breeches.
 12 *pantofles*: overshoes.

LYRICS

THE POWER OF MUSIC AND POETRY
Animals and trees gather to hear the
music of Orpheus, from N. Reusner,
Emblemata, Frankfort, 1581.
(Folger Shakespeare Library).

Our Poet . . . cometh to you with words set in delightful proportion, either accompanied with, or prepared for, the well-enchanting skill of music.

Sidney, *An Apology for Poetry*, 1595

Others who more delighted to write songs or ballads of pleasure to be sung with the voice, and to the harp, lute, or citheron, and such other musical instruments, they were called melodious poets (*melici*), or, by a more common name, lyric poets.

Puttenham, *The Art of English Poesy*, 1589

It is now time to handle such verses as are fit for ditties or odes; which we may call lyrical, because they are apt to be sung to an instrument, if they were adorned with convenient notes.

Campion, *Observations in the Art of English Poesy*, 1602

Short airs, if they be skilfully framed and naturally expressed, are like quick and good epigrams in poesy, many of them showing as much artifice, and breeding as great difficulty, as a larger poem.

Campion, ' To the Reader', in *Two Books of Airs, c.* 1613

SIR THOMAS WYATT

They flee from me that sometime did me seek,
  With naked foot stalking in my chamber;
I have seen them gentle, tame, and meek,
  That now are wild and do not remember
  That sometime they put themself in danger   5
    To take bread at my hand; and now they range,
    Busily seeking with a continual change.

Thanked be fortune, it hath been otherwise
  Twenty times better; but once in special,
In thin array, after a pleasant guise,   10
  When her loose gown from her shoulders did fall,
  And she me caught in her arms long and small,
    Therewithal sweetly did me kiss,
    And softly said, 'Dear heart, how like you this?'

It was no dream; I lay broad waking.   15
  But all is turnèd, thorough my gentleness,
Into a strange fashion of forsaking;
  And I have leave to go, of her goodness,
  And she also to use newfangleness.
    But since that I so kindely am served,   20
    I would fain know what she hath deserved.

Egerton MS. 2711

Wyatt's lyrics were first published in *Tottel's Miscellany*, 1557.
THEY FLEE FROM ME:
  5 *in danger*: (i) in (my) power; (ii) in peril.
 16 *thorough*: through.
 19 *newfangleness*: fickleness.
 20 *kindely*: (i) by the law of nature; (ii) tenderly.

Once, as methought, fortune me kissed
  And bade me ask what I thought best,
And I should have it as me list,
  Therewith to set my heart in rest.

5   I askèd nought but my dear heart
  To have for evermore mine own:
Then at an end were all my smart,
  Then should I need no more to moan.

Yet, for all that, a stormy blast
10   Had overturned this goodly day,
And fortune seemèd at the last
  That to her promise she said nay.

But like as one out of despair,
  To sudden hope revivèd I:
15   Now fortune showeth herself so fair
  That I content me wonderly.

My most desire my hand may reach,
  My will is alway at my hand;
Me need not long for to beseech
20   Her that hath power me to command.

What earthly thing more can I crave?
  What would I wish more at my will?
Nothing on earth more would I have,
  Save that I have to have it still.

ONCE, AS METHOUGHT:
  8 *to moan* (Devonshire MS. Add. 17492): 'moan' (Egerton MS.).

For fortune hath kept her promise   25
   In granting me my most desire;
Of my sufferance I have redress,
   And I content me with my hire.

Egerton MS. 2711

My lute, awake! perform the last
Labour that thou and I shall waste,
   And end that I have now begun;
For when this song is sung and past,
   My lute, be still, for I have done.   5

As to be heard where ear is none,
As lead to grave in marble stone,
   My song may pierce her heart as soon.
Should we then sigh, or sing, or moan?
   No, no, my lute, for I have done.   10

The rocks do not so cruelly
Repulse the waves continually
   As she my suit and affection,
So that I am past remedy,
   Whereby my lute and I have done.   15

Proud of the spoil that thou hast got
Of simple hearts, thorough Love's shot,
   By whom, unkind, thou hast them won,
Think not he hath his bow forgot,
   Although my lute and I have done.   20

28 *hire*: reward.
MY LUTE, AWAKE:
7 *grave*: engrave.

Vengeance shall fall on thy disdain,
That makest but game on earnest pain;
   Think not alone under the sun
Unquit to cause thy lovers plain,
25   Although my lute and I have done.

Perchance thee lie withered and old,
The winter night that are so cold,
   Plaining in vain unto the moon:
Thy wishes then dare not be told;
30   Care then who list, for I have done.

And then may chance thee to repent
The time that thou hast lost and spent
   To cause thy lovers sigh and swoon;
Then shalt thou know beauty but lent,
35   And wish and want as I have done.

Now cease, my lute; this is the last
Labour that thou and I shall waste,
   And ended is that we begun;
Now is this song both sung and past;
40   My lute, be still, for I have done.

Egerton MS. 2711

In eternum I was once determed
For to have lovèd, and my mind affirmed
That with my heart it should be confirmed
    In eternum.

24 You will not be paid back for causing your lovers to
lament.
IN ETERNUM:
1 *determed* (Egerton MS.): 'determined' (Devonshire MS.).

92

Forthwith I found the thing that I might like,   5
And sought with love to warm her heart alike,
For, as methought, I should not see the like
      In eternum.

To trace this dance I put myself in press;
Vain hope did lead, and bade I should not cease   10
To serve, to suffer, and still to hold my peace
      In eternum.

With this first rule I furthered me apace,
That, as methought, my truth had taken place
With full assurance to stand in her grace   15
      In eternum.

It was not long ere I by proof had found
That feeble building is on feeble ground;
For in her heart this word did never sound:
      In eternum.   20

In eternum then from my heart I kest
That I had first determined for the best;
Now in the place another thought doth rest
      In eternum.

Devonshire MS. Add. 17492

9 *in press*: into the endeavour.
21 *kest*: cast.

With serving still
   This have I won,
For my goodwill
   To be undone;

5   And for redress
   Of all my pain,
Disdainfulness
   I have again;

And for reward
10   Of all my smart,
Lo, thus unheard
   I must depart!

Wherefore all ye
   That after shall
15   By fortune be,
   As I am, thrall,

Example take
   What I have won,
Thus for her sake
20   To be undone.

Devonshire MS. Add. 17492

HENRY HOWARD, EARL OF SURREY

Complaint of the absence of her lover being upon the sea

O happy dames, that may embrace
The fruit of your delight,
Help to bewail the woeful case
And eke the heavy plight
Of me, that wonted to rejoice   5
The fortune of my pleasant choice;
Good ladies, help to fill my mourning voice.

In ship, freight with remembrance
Of thoughts and pleasures past,
He sails that hath in governance   10
My life while it will last;
With scalding sighs, for lack of gale,
Furthering his hope, that is his sail,
Toward me, the sweet port of his avail.

Alas, how oft in dreams I see   15
Those eyes that were my food,
Which sometime so delighted me
That yet they do me good;
Wherewith I wake with his return,
Whose absent flame did make me burn;   20
But when I find the lack, Lord, how I mourn!

When other lovers in arms across
Rejoice their chief delight,
Drowned in tears, to mourn my loss
I stand the bitter night   25
In my window, where I may see
Before the winds how the clouds flee.
Lo, what a mariner love hath made me!

COMPLAINT OF THE ABSENCE: Written c. 1545. Title is not
Surrey's. A sixteenth-century musical setting survives in MS.
14 *avail*: disembarking.

95

And in green waves when the salt flood
30   Doth rise by rage of wind,
A thousand fancies in that mood
Assail my restless mind:
Alas, now drencheth my sweet foe,
That with the spoil of my heart did go,
35   And left me; but, alas, why did he so?

And when the seas wax calm again
To chase fro me annoy,
My doubtful hope doth cause me plain;
So dread cuts off my joy.
40   Thus is my wealth mingled with woe,
And of each thought a doubt doth grow:
Now he comes! will he come? alas, no, no!

Tottel's Miscellany, 1557

A praise of his love,
wherein he reproveth them that compare their ladies with his

Give place, ye lovers, here before
That spent your boasts and brags in vain;
My lady's beauty passeth more
The best of yours, I dare well sayn,
5   Than doth the sun the candle-light,
Or brightest day the darkest night;

And thereto hath a troth as just
As had Penelope the fair;
For what she saith, ye may it trust
10   As it by writing sealèd were;
And virtues hath she many mo
Than I with pen have skill to show.

A PRAISE OF HIS LOVE: Written in the years 1537–47. Title is
    not Surrey's.
  7   *thereto*: moreover. *troth as just*: faith as true.

96

I could rehearse, if that I would,
The whole effect of nature's plaint,
When she had lost the perfect mould,   15
The like to whom she could not paint;
With wringing hands how she did cry,
And what she said, I know it, I.

I know she swore with raging mind:
Her kingdom only set apart,   20
There was no loss by law of kind
That could have gone so near her heart;
And this was chiefly all her pain:
She could not make the like again.

Sith nature thus gave her the praise   25
To be the chiefest work she wrought,
In faith, methink, some better ways
On your behalf might well be sought
Than to compare, as ye have done,
To match the candle with the sun.   30

Tottel's Miscellany, 1557

GEORGE GASCOIGNE

Gascoigne's Arraignment

At Beauty's bar as I did stand,
When False Suspect accusèd me,
'George,' quoth the judge, 'hold up thy hand;
Thou art arraigned of Flattery.
Tell therefore how thou wilt be tried: 5
Whose judgement here wilt thou abide?'

21 *by . . . kind*: in the natural course of things.

    'My lord,' quoth I, 'this lady here,
Whom I esteem above the rest,
Doth know my guilt, if any were;
10   Wherefore her doom shall please me best.
Let her be judge and juror both,
To try me, guiltless, by mine oath.'

    Quoth Beauty, 'No, it fitteth not
A prince herself to judge the cause:
15   Here is our justice, well you wot,
Appointed to discuss our laws;
If you will guiltless seem to go,
God and your country quit you so.'

    Then Craft, the crier, called a quest,
20   Of whom was Falsehood foremost fere;
A pack of pickthanks were the rest,
Which came false witness for to bear.
The jury such, the judge unjust,
Sentence was said I should be trussed.

25   Jealous, the jailer, bound me fast,
To hear the verdict of the bill;
'George,' quoth the judge, 'now thou art cast,
Thou must go hence to Heavy Hill,
And there be hanged, all but the head;
30   God rest thy soul when thou art dead.'

GASCOIGNE'S ARRAIGNMENT:
10 *doom*: judgement.
15 *wot*: know.
19 *quest*: jury.
20 *fere*: confederate.
24 *trussed*: 'strung up'.
27 *cast*: condemned.
28 *Heavy Hill*: Tyburn Hill.

Down fell I then upon my knee,
All flat before Dame Beauty's face,
And cried, 'Good lady, pardon me,
Which here appeal unto your grace;
You know, if I have been untrue,   35
It was in too much praising you.

'And though this judge do make such haste
To shed with shame my guiltless blood,
Yet let your pity first be placed,
To save the man that meant you good;   40
So shall you show yourself a queen,
And I may be your servant seen.'

Quoth Beauty, 'Well, because I guess
What thou dost mean henceforth to be,
Although thy faults deserve no less   45
Than justice here hath judgèd thee,
Wilt thou be bound to stint all strife,
And be true prisoner all thy life?'

'Yea, madam,' quoth I, 'that I shall;
Lo, Faith and Truth my sureties.'   50
'Why, then,' quoth she, 'come when I call;
I ask no better warrantise.'
Thus am I Beauty's bounden thrall,
At her command when she doth call.

A Hundred Sundry Flowers, 1573

SIR PHILIP SIDNEY

My true love hath my heart and I have his,
By just exchange one for another given;
I hold his dear, and mine he cannot miss,
There never was a better bargain driven.
5 My true love hath my heart and I have his.

His heart in me keeps him and me in one,
My heart in him his thoughts and senses guides.
He loves my heart, for once it was his own;
I cherish his, because in me it bides.
10 My true love hath my heart and I have his.

Puttenham, *The Art of English Poesy,* 1589

Why dost thou haste away,
O Titan fair, the giver of the day?
Is it to carry news
To Western wights, what stars in East appear?
5 Or dost thou think that here
Is left a sun whose beams thy place may use?
Yet stay, and well peruse
What be her gifts that make her equal thee;
Bend all thy light to see

MY TRUE LOVE HATH MY HEART: This lyric appeared in
earlier form as a sonnet in Sidney's *Old Arcadia,* written
probably 1577–80.
6 *His (Old Arcadia)*: 'My' (Puttenham).

In earthly clothes enclosed a heavenly spark.   10
Thy running course cannot such beauties mark;
No, no, thy motions be
Hastened from us with bar of shadow dark,
Because that thou, the author of our sight,
Disdain'st we see thee stained with other's light.   15

The Countess of Pembroke's Arcadia, 1593

The nightingale, as soon as April bringeth
Unto her rested sense a perfect waking,
While late bare earth, proud of new clothing, springeth,
Sings out her woes, a thorn her song-book making;
   And mournfully bewailing,   5
   Her throat in tunes expresseth
   What grief her breast oppresseth
For Tereus' force on her chaste will prevailing.
   O Philomela fair, O take some gladness,
   That here is juster cause of plaintful sadness: 10
   Thine earth now springs, mine fadeth;
   Thy thorn without, my thorn my heart invadeth.

WHY DOST THOU HASTE AWAY: One of the earliest English
   madrigals; written probably 1577–80.
15 *stained*: eclipsed.
THE NIGHTINGALE: Written probably before 1581, to an
   Italian tune. There is another setting by T. Bateson, *The
   First Set of English Madrigals,* 1604. Philomela was ravished by
   her brother-in-law Tereus, who cut out her tongue to
   prevent her disclosing his crime. She was transformed
   into a nightingale, a bird which is said to press against a
   thorn when singing its sweet melancholy song.
4 *song-book*: book of prick-song, with music written down,
   or 'pricked'.

Alas, she hath no other cause of anguish
But Tereus' love, on her by strong hand wroken;
15 Wherein she, suff'ring all her spirits' languish,
Full woman-like, complains her will was broken.
But I, who daily craving
Cannot have to content me,
Have more cause to lament me,
20 Since wanting is more woe than too much having.
O Philomela fair, O take some gladness,
That here is juster cause of plaintful sadness:
Thine earth now springs, mine fadeth;
Thy thorn without, my thorn my heart invadeth.

Certain Sonnets, 1598

From *Astrophil and Stella*, 1598

First Song

Doubt you to whom my muse these notes intendeth,
Which now my breast, o'ercharged, to music lendeth?
To you, to you, all song of praise is due;
Only in you my song begins and endeth.

5 Who hath the eyes which marry state with pleasure?
Who keeps the key of nature's chiefest treasure?
To you, to you, all song of praise is due;
Only for you the heaven forgat all measure.

Who hath the lips where wit in fairness reigneth?
10 Who womankind at once both decks and staineth?
To you, to you, all song of praise is due;
Only by you Cupid his crown maintaineth.

14 *wroken*: wreaked.
Both these songs from *Astrophil and Stella* were written probably
in 1581–2.

102

Who hath the feet whose step all sweetness planteth?
Who else for whom fame worthy trumpets wanteth?
To you, to you, all song of praise is due;   15
Only to you her sceptre Venus granteth.

Who hath the breast whose milk doth passions nourish?
Whose grace is such that when it chides doth cherish?
To you, to you, all song of praise is due;
Only through you the tree of life doth flourish.   20

Who hath the hand which without stroke subdueth?
Who long-dead beauty with increase reneweth?
To you, to you, all song of praise is due;
Only at you all envy hopeless rueth.

Who hath the hair which, loosest, fastest tieth?   25
Who makes a man live, then glad when he dieth?
To you, to you, all song of praise is due;
Only of you the flatterer never lieth.

Who hath the voice which soul from senses sunders?
Whose force but yours the bolts of beauty thunders?   30
To you, to you, all song of praise is due;
Only with you not miracles are wonders.

Doubt you to whom my muse these notes intendeth,
Which now my breast, o'ercharged, to music lendeth?
To you, to you, all song of praise is due;   35
Only in you my song begins and endeth.

FIRST SONG:
13   *all* (1591): 'of' (1598).
32   *not miracles are wonders*: i.e. wonders are not miracles.

Fourth Song

Only joy, now here you are,
Fit to hear and ease my care;
Let my whispering voice obtain
Sweet reward for sharpest pain;
5   Take me to thee, and thee to me.
'No, no, no, no, my dear, let be.'

Night hath closed all in her cloak,
Twinkling stars love-thoughts provoke;
Danger hence good care doth keep,
10   Jealousy itself doth sleep;
Take me to thee, and thee to me.
'No, no, no, no, my dear, let be.'

Better place no wit can find,
Cupid's yoke to loose or bind;
15   These sweet flowers on fine bed too
Us in their best language woo;
Take me to thee, and thee to me.
'No, no, no, no, my dear, let be.'

This small light the moon bestows
20   Serves thy beams but to disclose,
So to raise my hap more high;
Fear not else, none can us spy;
Take me to thee, and thee to me.
'No, no, no, no, my dear, let be.'

FOURTH SONG: Set to music by Henry Youll, *Canzonets to Three Voices*, 1608.

That you heard was but a mouse,   25
Dumb sleep holdeth all the house;
Yet asleep, methinks, they say,
Young folks, take time while you may;
Take me to thee, and thee to me.
'No, no, no, no, my dear, let be.'   30

Niggard time threats, if we miss
This large offer of our bliss,
Long stay ere he grant the same;
Sweet, then, while each thing doth frame,
Take me to thee, and thee to me.   35
'No, no, no, no, my dear, let be.'

Your fair mother is abed,
Candles out, and curtains spread;
She thinks you do letters write;
Write, but let me first endite: 40
Take me to thee, and thee to me.
'No, no, no, no, my dear, let be.'

Sweet, alas, why strive you thus?
Concord better fitteth us;
Leave to Mars the force of hands,   45
Your power in your beauty stands;
Take me to thee, and thee to me.
'No, no, no, no, my dear, let be.'

Woe to me, and do you swear
Me to hate but I forbear?   50
Cursèd be my destines all,
That brought me so high, to fall;
Soon with my death I will please thee.
'No, no, no, no, my dear, let be.'

34 *doth frame*: is favourable.
47 *me to thee, and thee to me* (1591): 'thee to me, and me to thee'
    (1598).
50 *but*: unless.

FULKE GREVILLE

From *Caelica*, 1633

You little stars that live in skies,
And glory in Apollo's glory,
In whose aspects conjoinèd lies
The heavens' will, and nature's story,
5   Joy to be likened to those eyes,
Which eyes make all eyes glad, or sorry;
    For when you force thoughts from above,
    These overrule your force by love.

And thou, O Love, which in these eyes
10   Hast married reason with affection,
And made them saints of beauty's skies,
Where joys are shadows of perfection,
Lend me thy wings that I may rise
Up, not by worth but thy election;
15   For I have vowed, in strangest fashion,
    To love, and never seek compassion.

When all this All doth pass from age to age,
And revolution in a circle turn,
Then heavenly justice doth appear like rage,
The caves do roar, the very seas do burn,
5   Glory grows dark, the sun becomes a night,
    And makes this great world feel a greater might.

These three lyrics from Greville's poetic miscellany, *Caelica*,
1633, were probably written in the period 1577–86.
YOU LITTLE STARS: Set to music by M. Peerson, *Motets or
Grave Chamber Music*, 1630.
2 *Apollo's*: i.e. the sun's.
3 *aspects conjoinèd*: relative positions.
WHEN ALL THIS ALL:
1–6 The end of each Great Year, or complete stellar cycle,
was thought to be marked by terrible upheavals in
nature.

When love doth change his seat from heart to heart,
And worth about the wheel of fortune goes,
Grace is diseased, desert seems overthwart,
Vows are forlorn, and truth doth credit lose;   10
   Chance then gives law, desire must be wise,
   And look more ways than one, or lose her eyes.

My age of joy is past, of woe begun,
Absence my presence is, strangeness my grace;
With them that walk against me, is my sun: 15
The wheel is turned, I hold the lowest place;
   What can be good to me, since my love is,
   To do me harm, content to do amiss?

You that seek what life is in death,
Now find it air that once was breath,
New names unknown, old names gone,
Till time end bodies, but souls none.
   Reader! then make time, while you be,   5
   But steps to your eternity.

---

15 *sun*: i.e. mistress (the poet is cast into the shade by his rivals).

YOU THAT SEEK: Part of an epitaph, possibly intended to be Greville's own.

Chorus Sacerdotum

Oh, wearisome condition of humanity!
Born under one law, to another bound;
Vainly begot, and yet forbidden vanity;
Created sick, commanded to be sound.
5   What meaneth nature by these diverse laws?
Passion and reason self-division cause:
Is it the mark or majesty of power
To make offences that it may forgive?
Nature herself doth her own self deflower,
10   To hate those errors she herself doth give.
For how should man think that, he may not do,
If nature did not fail, and punish too?
Tyrant to others, to herself unjust,
Only commands things difficult and hard,
15   Forbids us all things which it knows is lust,
Makes easy pains, unpossible reward.
If nature did not take delight in blood,
She would have made more easy ways to good.
We that are bound by vows, and by promotion,
20   With pomp of holy sacrifice and rites,
To teach belief in good, and still devotion,
To preach of heaven's wonders and delights,—
Yet, when each of us in his own heart looks,
He finds the God there far unlike his books.

Mustapha (1633), Act V

CHORUS SACERDOTUM: Written probably 1594–6; first pub-
lished 1609. Title means 'Chorus of Priests'.
2 *one law*: i.e. natural law. *another*: i.e. divine law.
21 *still*: instil.

JOHN LYLY

Song by Apelles

Cupid and my Campaspe played
At cards for kisses; Cupid paid.
He stakes his quiver, bow, and arrows,
His mother's doves and team of sparrows;
Loses them too; then down he throws   5
The coral of his lip, the rose
Growing on 's cheek (but none knows how),
With these the crystal of his brow,
And then the dimple of his chin:
All these did my Campaspe win.   10
At last he set her both his eyes;
She won, and Cupid blind did rise.
  O Love, has she done this to thee?
  What shall, alas, become of me?

Campaspe (1632), III.v

ROBERT GREENE

In time we see that silver drops
  The craggy stones make soft;
The slowest snail in time, we see,
  Doth creep and climb aloft.

SONG BY APELLES: This song from the play *Campaspe* may
not be by Lyly. The play, without the song, was first pub-
lished in 1584.

5 With feeble puffs the tallest pine
  In tract of time doth fall;
 The hardest heart in time doth yield
  To Venus' luring call.

 Where chilling frost alate did nip,
10 There flasheth now a fire;
 Where deep disdain bred noisome hate,
  There kindleth now desire.

 Time causeth hope to have his hap;
  What care in time not eased?
15 In time I loathed that now I love,
  In both content and pleased.

Arbasto, 1584

 When gods had framed the sweet of women's face,
 And locked men's looks within their golden hair,
 That Phoebus blushed to see their matchless grace,
 And heavenly gods on earth did make repair;
5 To quip fair Venus' overweening pride,
  Love's happy thoughts to jealousy were tied.

 Then grew a wrinkle on fair Venus' brow;
 The amber sweet of love was turned to gall;
 Gloomy was heaven: bright Phoebus did avow
10 He could be coy and would not love at all,
  Swearing no greater mischief could be wrought
  Than love united to a jealous thought.

Ciceronis Amor, 1589

WHEN GODS HAD FRAMED:
quip: chastise.

CHIDIOCK TICHBORNE

Tichborne's Elegy,
written with his own hand in the Tower
before his execution

My prime of youth is but a frost of cares,
My feast of joy is but a dish of pain,
My crop of corn is but a field of tares,
And all my good is but vain hope of gain;
The day is past, and yet I saw no sun,   5
And now I live, and now my life is done.

My tale was heard and yet it was not told,
My fruit is fall'n and yet my leaves are green,
My youth is spent and yet I am not old,
I saw the world and yet I was not seen;   10
My thread is cut and yet it is not spun,
And now I live, and now my life is done.

I sought my death and found it in my womb,
I looked for life and saw it was a shade,
I trod the earth and knew it was my tomb,   15
And now I die, and now I was but made;
My glass is full, and now my glass is run,
And now I live, and now my life is done.

Anon., *Verses of Praise and Joy Written upon*
Her Majesty's Preservation, 1586

TICHBORNE'S ELEGY: Tichborne was executed Sept. 1586, at
28, for his part in the Babington plot against the Queen.
The lyric was set to music by J. Mundy (1594), M. East
(1604), and R. Alison (1606).

ROBERT SOUTHWELL

Look Home

Retirèd thoughts enjoy their own delights,
As beauty doth in self-beholding eye;
Man's mind a mirror is of heavenly sights,
A brief wherein all marvels summèd lie:
5   Of fairest forms and sweetest shapes the store,
Most graceful all, yet thought may grace them more.

The mind a creature is, yet can create,
To nature's patterns adding higher skill;
Of finest works wit better could the state,
10   If force of wit had equal power of will.
Device of man in working hath no end,
What thought can think, another thought can mend.

Man's soul of endless beauties image is,
Drawn by the work of endless skill and might;
15   This skilful might gave many sparks of bliss,
And to discern this bliss, a native light;
To frame God's image as his worths required
His might, his skill, his word, and will conspired.

All that he had his image should present,
20   All that it should present he could afford;
To that he could afford his will was bent,
His will was followed with performing word.
Let this suffice, by this conceive the rest:
He should, he could, he would, he did the best.

Saint Peter's Complaint, with Other Poems, 1595

Southwell's poems were written 1586–92.
LOOK HOME:
  4 *brief*: summary, epitome.
  9 I.e. wit could better the state of finest works.
20 *afford*: accomplish.

Upon the Image of Death

Before my face the picture hangs
That daily should put me in mind
Of those cold qualms and bitter pangs
That shortly I am like to find;
   But yet, alas, full little I   5
   Do think hereon that I must die.

I often look upon a face
Most ugly, grisly, bare, and thin;
I often view the hollow place
Where eyes and nose had sometimes been;   10
   I see the bones across that lie,
   Yet little think that I must die.

I read the label underneath,
That telleth me whereto I must;
I see the sentence eke that saith   15
'Remember, man, that thou art dust!'
   But yet, alas, but seldom I
   Do think indeed that I must die.

Continually at my bed's head
A hearse doth hang, which doth me tell   20
That I ere morning may be dead,
Though now I feel myself full well;
   But yet, alas, for all this, I
   Have little mind that I must die.

UPON THE IMAGE OF DEATH:
  3 *qualms* (reading in Simon Wastell, *Microbiblion*, 1629, where
    the poem was reprinted): 'names' (1595).
 20 *hearse*: funeral pall.

25 The gown which I do use to wear,
The knife wherewith I cut my meat,
And eke that old and ancient chair
Which is my only usual seat:
    All those do tell me I must die,
30   And yet my life amend not I.

My ancestors are turned to clay,
And many of my mates are gone;
My youngers daily drop away,
And can I think to 'scape alone?
35   No, no, I know that I must die,
    And yet my life amend not I.

Not Solomon, for all his wit,
Nor Samson, though he were so strong,
No king nor parson ever yet
40 Could 'scape, but death laid him along;
    Wherefore I know that I must die,
    And yet my life amend not I.

Though all the East did quake to hear
Of Alexander's dreadful name,
45 And all the West did likewise fear
To hear of Julius Caesar's fame,
    Yet both by death in dust now lie.
    Who then can 'scape, but he must die?

If none can 'scape death's dreadful dart,
50 If rich and poor his beck obey,
If strong, if wise, if all do smart,
Then I to 'scape shall have no way.
    Oh, grant me grace, O God, that I
    My life may mend, sith I must die.

Maeoniae, 1595

ANONYMOUS

I joy not in no earthly bliss;
   I force not Croesus' wealth a straw;
For care I know not what it is;
   I fear not fortune's fatal law.
My mind is such as may not move   5
For beauty bright, nor force of love.

I wish but what I have at will;
   I wander not to seek for more;
I like the plain, I climb no hill;
   In greatest storms I sit on shore,   10
And laugh at them that toil in vain
To get what must be lost again.

I kiss not where I wish to kill;
   I feign not love where most I hate;
I break no sleep to win my will;   15
   I wait not at the mighty's gate.
I scorn no poor, nor fear no rich;
I feel no want, nor have too much.

The court and cart I like nor loathe;
   Extremes are counted worst of all;   20
The golden mean between them both
   Doth surest sit and fear no fall.
This is my choice, for why I find
No wealth is like the quiet mind.

W. Byrd, *Psalms, Sonnets, and Songs*, 1588

I JOY NOT IN NO EARTHLY BLISS:
  2 *force not*: care not for.
  23 *for why*: because.

ANONYMOUS

A Sonnet

His golden locks time hath to silver turned;
Oh, time too swift, oh, swiftness never ceasing!
His youth 'gainst time and age hath ever spurned,
But spurned in vain; youth waneth by increasing:
5   Beauty, strength, youth are flowers but fading seen;
    Duty, faith, love are roots, and ever green.

His helmet now shall make a hive for bees,
And lover's sonnets turned to holy psalms;
A man-at-arms must now serve on his knees,
10   And feed on prayers, which are age his alms;
    But though from court to cottage he depart,
    His saint is sure of his unspotted heart.

And when he saddest sits in homely cell,
He'll teach his swains this carol for a song:
15   'Blest be the hearts that wish my sovereign well,
    Curst be the souls that think her any wrong.'
    Goddess, allow this agèd man his right,
    To be your beadsman now, that was your knight.

Peele, *Polyhymnia*, 1590

A SONNET: Sung at the tournament held on Accession Day,
17 Nov. 1590, which is celebrated in George Peele's *Polyhym-
nia*. At the tilt the Queen's Champion, Sir Henry Lee, at
the age of 57 resigned the office he had held since 1559. This
song may have been written by Lee himself. There is a
musical setting by John Dowland, *The First Book of Songs or
Airs*, 1597.

THOMAS CAMPION

Hark, all you ladies that do sleep!
  The fairy queen Proserpina
Bids you awake, and pity them that weep.
  You may do in the dark
What the day doth forbid;   5
  Fear not the dogs that bark,
        Night will have all hid.

But if you let your lovers moan,
  The fairy queen Proserpina
Will send abroad her fairies ev'ry one,   10
  That shall pinch black and blue
Your white hands and fair arms,
  That did not kindly rue
        Your paramours' harms.

In myrtle arbours on the downs,   15
  The fairy queen Proserpina,
This night by moonshine leading merry rounds,
  Holds a watch with sweet love,
Down the dale, up the hill;
  No plaints or groans may move   20
        Their holy vigil.

All you that will hold watch with love,
  The fairy queen Proserpina
Will make you fairer than Dione's dove;
  Roses red, lilies white,   25
And the clear damask hue,

HARK, ALL YOU LADIES: First published in Sidney's *Astrophil
and Stella*, 1591. For musical setting, see *Works of Thomas
Campion*, ed. W. R. Davis, 1969, p. 45.
24 *Dione's*: Venus's.
26 *damask*: rose-pink.

Shall on your cheeks alight;
    Love will adorn you.

All you that love, or loved before,
30   The fairy queen Proserpina
Bids you increase that loving humour more;
    They that yet have not fed
On delight amorous,
    She vows that they shall lead
35   Apes in Avernus.

                              A Book of Airs, 1601

When to her lute Corinna sings,
Her voice revives the leaden strings,
And doth in highest notes appear
As any challenged echo clear;
5   But when she doth of mourning speak,
Ev'n with her sighs the strings do break.

And as her lute doth live or die,
Led by her passion, so must I;
For when of pleasure she doth sing,
10   My thoughts enjoy a sudden spring;
But if she doth of sorrow speak,
Ev'n from my heart the strings do break.

                              A Book of Airs, 1601

34–5 To lead apes in hell was proverbially the fate of old
    maids.
WHEN TO HER LUTE: Musical setting in Davis, p. 29.
  2 *leaden*: inert.
  4 *challenged*: aroused.

Follow your saint, follow with accents sweet;
Haste you, sad notes, fall at her flying feet.
There, wrapped in cloud of sorrow, pity move,
And tell the ravisher of my soul I perish for her love.
But if she scorns my never-ceasing pain,   5
Then burst with sighing in her sight, and ne'er
     return again.

All that I sung still to her praise did tend;
Still she was first, still she my songs did end.
Yet she my love and music both doth fly,
The music that her echo is, and beauty's sympathy.   10
Then let my notes pursue her scornful flight;
It shall suffice that they were breathed, and died
     for her delight.

A Book of Airs, 1601

The man of life upright,
   Whose guiltless heart is free
From all dishonest deeds,
   Or thought of vanity:

The man whose silent days   5
   In harmless joys are spent,
Whom hopes cannot delude,
   Nor sorrow discontent:

That man needs neither towers
   Nor armour for defence,   10
Nor secret vaults to fly
   From thunder's violence.

He only can behold
With unaffrighted eyes
15   The horrors of the deep
And terrors of the skies.

Thus, scorning all the cares
That fate or fortune brings,
He makes the heaven his book,
20   His wisdom heavenly things,

Good thoughts his only friends,
His wealth a well-spent age,
The earth his sober inn
And quiet pilgrimage.

A Book of Airs, 1601

When thou must home to shades of underground,
And there arrived, a new admirèd guest,
The beauteous spirits do engirt thee round,
White Iope, blithe Helen, and the rest,
5   To hear the stories of thy finished love
From that smooth tongue whose music hell can move;

Then wilt thou speak of banqueting delights,
Of masques and revels which sweet youth did make,
Of tourneys and great challenges of knights,
10 And all these triumphs for thy beauty's sake.
When thou hast told these honours done to thee,
Then tell, O tell, how thou didst murder me.

A Book of Airs, 1601

WHEN THOU MUST HOME: Musical setting in Davis, p. 47.
  4 *Iope*: Cassiope, who accounted herself more beautiful
    than the Nereids.

Come, let us sound with melody the praises
Of the kings' King, th' omnipotent Creator,
Author of number, that hath all the world in
   Harmony framèd.

Heav'n is his throne perpetually shining,   5
His divine power and glory thence he thunders,
One in All, and All still in One abiding,
   Both Father and Son.

O sacred Sprite, invisible, eternal,
Ev'rywhere, yet unlimited, that all things   10
Canst in one moment penetrate, revive me,
   O holy Spirit.

Rescue, O rescue me from earthly darkness,
Banish hence all these elemental objects,
Guide my soul that thirsts to the lively fountain   15
   Of thy divineness.

Cleanse my soul, O God, thy bespotted image,
Alterèd with sin so that heav'nly pureness
Cannot acknowledge me but in thy mercies,
   O Father of grace.   20

But when once thy beams do remove my darkness,
Oh, then I'll shine forth as an angel of light,
And record, with more than an earthly voice, thy
   Infinite honours.

A Book of Airs, 1601

COME, LET US SOUND: A poem in the quantitative metre of
 classical poetry. In quantitative verse, rhythm was dic-
tated not by stress or accent (as in English verse) but by
'quantity'; i.e. each syllable was regarded as long (—) or
short (◡) according to the length of time taken to pro-
nounce it. In English poetry duration of individual

THOMAS NASHE

Song

Spring, the sweet spring, is the year's pleasant king;
Then blooms each thing, then maids dance in a ring,
Cold doth not sting, the pretty birds do sing:
    Cuckoo, jug-jug, pu-we, to-witta-woo!

5   The palm and may make country houses gay,
Lambs frisk and play, the shepherds pipe all day,
And we hear ay birds tune this merry lay:
    Cuckoo, jug-jug, pu-we, to-witta-woo!

The fields breathe sweet, the daisies kiss our feet,
10   Young lovers meet, old wives a-sunning sit;
In every street these tunes our ears do greet:
    Cuckoo, jug-jug, pu-we, to-witta-woo!
    Spring, the sweet spring!

Summer's Last Will and Testament, 1600

---

syllables is often important, but since length of syllable cannot be defined *consistently*, quantitative metres have never been employed with complete success. This poem is written in the Sapphic metre (from the Greek poetess Sappho [seventh century B.C.]). Its scansion is:

— ∪ — — — ∪ ∪ — ∪ — — (3 lines)
— ∪ ∪ — — (1 line).

The musical setting is reproduced in Davis, p. 49.
SONG: SPRING, THE SWEET SPRING: Written 1592.
5 *palm*: willow.

122

Song

Adieu, farewell earth's bliss,
This world uncertain is;
Fond are life's lustful joys,
Death proves them all but toys,
None from his darts can fly.   5
I am sick, I must die.
   Lord, have mercy on us!

Rich men, trust not in wealth,
Gold cannot buy you health;
Physic himself must fade,   10
All things to end are made.
The plague full swift goes by.
I am sick, I must die.
   Lord, have mercy on us!

Beauty is but a flower   15
Which wrinkles will devour;
Brightness falls from the air,
Queens have died young and fair,
Dust hath closed Helen's eye.
I am sick, I must die.   20
   Lord, have mercy on us!

Strength stoops unto the grave,
Worms feed on Hector brave,
Swords may not fight with fate,
Earth still holds ope her gate;   25

SONG: ADIEU, FAREWELL: Sung in Nashe's play, *Summer's Last Will and Testament*, at the request of Summer for 'some doleful ditty to the lute That may complain my near-approaching death.' The plague was raging in 1592, when the song was written.
3 *Fond*: foolish.
12 *by*: 'high' (1600).

'Come! come!' the bells do cry.
I am sick, I must die.
   Lord, have mercy on us!

Wit with his wantonness
30   Tasteth death's bitterness;
Hell's executioner
Hath no ears for to hear
What vain art can reply.
I am sick, I must die.
35   Lord, have mercy on us!

Haste, therefore, each degree,
To welcome destiny:
Heaven is our heritage,
Earth but a player's stage;
40   Mount we unto the sky.
I am sick, I must die.
   Lord, have mercy on us!

Summer's Last Will and Testament, 1600

EDWARD DE VERE, EARL OF OXFORD

What cunning can express
The favour of her face,
To whom in this distress
I do appeal for grace?
5   A thousand cupids fly
   About her gentle eye;

From whence each throws a dart
That kindleth soft sweet fire
Within my sighing heart,
Possessèd by desire.   10
  No sweeter life I try
  Than in her love to die.

The lily in the field,
That glories in his white,
For pureness now must yield   15
And render up his right.
  Heaven pictured in her face
  Doth promise joy and grace.

Fair Cynthia's silver light,
That beats on running streams,   20
Compares not with her white,
Whose hairs are all sunbeams.
  Her virtues so do shine,
  As day unto mine ey'n.

With this there is a red   25
Exceeds the damask rose,
Which in her cheeks is spread,
Whence every favour grows.
  In sky there is no star
  That she surmounts not far.   30

When Phoebus from the bed
Of Thetis doth arise,
The morning blushing red
In fair carnation wise,
  He shows it in her face,   35
  As queen of every grace.

WHAT CUNNING CAN EXPRESS:
11 *try*: may experience.

This pleasant lily-white,
This taint of roseate red,
This Cynthia's silver light,
40   This sweet fair Dea spread,
      These sunbeams in mine eye:
      These beauties make me die.

The Phoenix Nest, 1593

SIR WALTER RALEGH

Praised be Diana's fair and harmless light,
Praised be the dews wherewith she moists the ground,
Praised be her beams, the glory of the night,
Praised be her power, by which all powers abound.

5   Praised be her nymphs, with whom she decks the woods,
Praised be her knights, in whom true honour lives,
Praised be that force by which she moves the floods;
Let that Diana shine, which all these gives.

In heaven queen she is among the spheres,
10   In ay she mistress-like makes all things pure,
Eternity in her oft change she bears;
She beauty is, by her the fair endure.

Time wears her not: she doth his chariot guide,
Mortality below her orb is placed;
15   By her the virtue of the stars down slide,
In her is virtue's perfect image cast.
    A knowledge pure it is her worth to know;
    With Circes let them dwell that think not so.

The Phoenix Nest, 1593

40 *Dea*: goddess.
PRAISED BE DIANA'S: Probably written in praise of Queen
Elizabeth.

Nature, that washed her hands in milk
  And had forgot to dry them,
Instead of earth took snow and silk,
  At love's request to try them,
If she a mistress could compose   5
To please love's fancy out of those.

Her eyes he would should be of light,
  A violet breath, and lips of jelly;
Her hair not black, nor over-bright,
  And of the softest down her belly;   10
As for her inside, he 'ld have it
Only of wantonness and wit.

At love's entreaty such a one
  Nature made, but with her beauty
She hath framed a heart of stone;   15
  So as love, by ill destiny,
Must die for her whom nature gave him,
Because her darling would not save him.

But time (which nature doth despise,
  And rudely gives her love the lie,   20
Makes hope a fool, and sorrow wise)
  His hands do neither wash nor dry;
But being made of steel and rust,
Turns snow, and silk, and milk to dust.

The light, the belly, lips, and breath,   25
  He dims, discolours, and destroys;
With those he feeds, but fills not death,
  Which sometimes were the food of joys.
Yea, time doth dull each lively wit,
And dries all wantonness with it.   30

NATURE, THAT WASHED HER HANDS:
26 *discolours* (MS. Add. 25707): 'discovers' (Harleian MS.).

Oh, cruel time! which takes in trust
  Our youth, our joys, and all we have,
And pays us but with age and dust;
  Who in the dark and silent grave,
35 When we have wandered all our ways,
Shuts up the story of our days.

Harleian MS. 6917

What is our life? a play of passion,
Our mirth the music of division;
Our mothers' wombs the tiring-houses be,
Where we are dressed for this short comedy;
5 Heaven the judicious, sharp spectator is,
That sits and marks still who doth act amiss;

31–6 These lines, slightly changed, were printed as an epitaph
in a collection by R. Brathwait, *Remains after Death*, 1618.
The first line begins 'Even such is time . . .'. A final couplet
is added:
    And from which earth, and grave, and dust,
    The Lord will raise me up, I trust.
The poem is headed 'By Sir W. R., which he writ the
night before his execution'. If this claim is correct,
Ralegh in 1618 must have recast and expanded the original
lines, which were probably written much earlier.
WHAT IS OUR LIFE?:
2 *division*: a florid melodic phrase.

Our graves that hide us from the searching sun
Are like drawn curtains when the play is done.
Thus march we, playing, to our latest rest;
Only we die in earnest, that's no jest.   10

Orlando Gibbons, *The First Set of*
Madrigals and Motets, 1612

GEORGE PEELE

Song

Hot sun, cool fire, tempered with sweet air,
Black shade, fair nurse, shadow my white hair.
Shine, sun; burn, fire; breathe, air, and ease me;
Black shade, fair nurse, shroud me and please me;
Shadow, my sweet nurse, keep me from burning,   5
Make not my glad cause cause of mourning.
   Let not my beauty's fire
   Inflame unstaid desire,
   Nor pierce any bright eye
   That wand'reth lightly.   10

The Love of King David and Fair Bethsabe, 1599

9   *latest*: last.
SONG: HOT SUN, COOL FIRE: Peele's play *The Love of King
David and Fair Bethsabe* was written in or before 1594. The
song is sung by Bethsabe (Bathsheba), wife of Urias, as
she bathes at a spring; King David watches her unseen.

EDMUND SPENSER

Epithalamion

Ye learnèd sisters which have oftentimes
Beene to me ayding, others to adorne:
Whom ye thought worthy of your gracefull rymes,
That even the greatest did not greatly scorne
5   To heare theyr names sung in your simple layes,
But joyèd in theyr prayse.
And when ye list your owne mishaps to mourne,
Which death, or love, or fortunes wreck did rayse,
Your string could soone to sadder tenor turne,
10   And teach the woods and waters to lament
Your dolefull dreriment.
Now lay those sorrowfull complaints aside,
And having all your heads with girland crownd,
Helpe me mine owne loves prayses to resound,
15   Ne let the same of any be envide:
So Orpheus did for his owne bride,

EPITHALAMION: Written by Spenser in celebration of his
marriage in 1594 to Elizabeth Boyle. It was published with
the *Amoretti*, the sonnet sequence and the marriage hymn
forming a more or less continuous narrative of courtship
and marriage. 'Epithalamion' in Greek means 'Upon the
bridal chamber'. The numerological basis of the poem has
been fully expounded in A. K. Hieatt, *Short Time's Endless
Monument*, N. Y., 1960.
1 *learnèd sisters*: i.e. the Muses.
2–6 Spenser had sung the 'prayse' of Queen Elizabeth (*The
Faerie Queene*, 1590), Ralegh (*Colin Clout*, 1595), and Sidney
(*Astrophel*, 1595).
7–8 The Muses lament the state of poetry and learning in
Spenser's *The Teares of the Muses*, 1591.
15 *of*: by.
16 *Orpheus*: legendary musician whose playing tamed beasts
and charmed trees and stones. When his wife Eurydice
died, Orpheus played to Pluto and Persephone in Hades,
winning their consent for the return of his wife to the
upper world.

So I unto my selfe alone will sing,
The woods shall to me answer and my Eccho ring.

Early before the worlds light giving lampe,
His golden beame upon the hils doth spred,   20
Having disperst the nights unchearefull dampe,
Doe ye awake, and with fresh lusty hed,
Go to the bowre of my belovèd love,
My truest turtle dove,
Bid her awake; for Hymen is awake,   25
And long since ready forth his maske to move,
With his bright Tead that flames with many a flake,
And many a bachelor to waite on him,
In theyr fresh garments trim.
Bid her awake therefore and soone her dight,   30
For lo the wishèd day is come at last,
That shall for al the paynes and sorrowes past,
Pay to her usury of long delight:
And whylest she doth her dight,
Doe ye to her of joy and solace sing,   35
That all the woods may answer and your eccho ring.

Bring with you all the Nymphes that you can heare
Both of the rivers and the forrests greene:
And of the sea that neighbours to her neare,
Al with gay girlands goodly wel beseene.   40
And let them also with them bring in hand,
Another gay girland
For my fayre love, of lillyes and of roses,
Bound truelove wize with a blew silke riband.

22 *lusty hed*: vigour.
25 *Hymen*: god of marriage.
26 *maske*: wedding procession.
27 *Tead*: torch. *flake*: flash.
30 *dight*: dress.
35 *solace*: delight.
37 *you can heare*: i.e. can hear you.
40 *beseene*: apparelled.

45   And let them make great store of bridale poses,
     And let them eeke bring store of other flowers
     To deck the bridale bowers.
     And let the ground whereas her foot shall tread,
     For feare the stones her tender foot should wrong
50   Be strewed with fragrant flowers all along,
     And diapred lyke the discolored mead.
     Which done, doe at her chamber dore awayt,
     For she will waken strayt,
     The whiles doe ye this song unto her sing,
55   The woods shall to you answer and your Eccho ring.

     Ye Nymphes of Mulla which with carefull heed,
     The silver scaly trouts doe tend full well,
     And greedy pikes which use therein to feed,
     (Those trouts and pikes all others doo excell)
60   And ye likewise which keepe the rushy lake,
     Where none doo fishes take,
     Bynd up the locks the which hang scatterd light,
     And in his waters which your mirror make,
     Behold your faces as the christall bright,
65   That when you come whereas my love doth lie,
     No blemish she may spie.
     And eke ye lightfoot mayds which keepe the deere,
     That on the hoary mountayne use to towre,
     And the wylde wolves which seeke them to devoure,
70   With your steele darts doo chace from comming neer
     Be also present heere,
     To helpe to decke her and to help to sing,
     That all the woods may answer and your eccho ring.

51 *diapred*: variegated. *discolored mead*: diversely coloured
    meadow.
56 *Mulla*: the river Awbeg near Kilcolman, Spenser's Irish
    estate.
67 *deere*: 'dore' (1595).
68 *towre*: climb aloft.
69 *wylde wolves*: Wolves were common in Ireland at the time.

Wake, now my love, awake; for it is time,
The Rosy Morne long since left Tithones bed,   75
All ready to her silver coche to clyme,
And Phoebus gins to shew his glorious hed.
Hark how the cheerefull birds do chaunt theyr laies
And carroll of loves praise.
The merry Larke hir mattins sings aloft,   80
The thrush replyes, the Mavis descant playes,
The Ouzell shrills, the Ruddock warbles soft,
So goodly all agree with sweet consent,
To this dayes merriment.
Ah my deere love why doe ye sleepe thus long,   85
When meeter were that ye should now awake,
T' awayt the comming of your joyous make,
And hearken to the birds lovelearnèd song,
The deawy leaves among.
For they of joy and pleasance to you sing,   90
That all the woods them answer and theyr eccho ring.

My love is now awake out of her dreame,
And her fayre eyes like stars that dimmèd were
With darksome cloud, now shew theyr goodly beams
More bright then Hesperus his head doth rere.   95
Come now ye damzels, daughters of delight,
Helpe quickly her to dight.
But first come ye fayre houres which were begot
In Joves sweet paradice, of Day and Night,
Which doe the seasons of the yeare allot,   100
And al that ever in this world is fayre
Doe make and still repayre.

74 Cf. Song Sol. 2. 10–13.
75 *Tithones bed*: Tithonus was the husband of Aurora, the
   dawn.
81 *Mavis*: song-thrush.
82 *Ouzell*: blackbird. *Ruddock*: robin.
87 *make*: mate.
95 *Hesperus*: the evening star.
98–102 The classical Hours (Horae) were daughters of Jupiter

And ye three handmayds of the Cyprian Queene,
The which doe still adorne her beauties pride,
105 Helpe to addorne my beautifullest bride:
And as ye her array, still throw betweene
Some graces to be seene,
And as ye use to Venus, to her sing,
The whiles the woods shal answer and your eccho ring.

110 Now is my love all ready forth to come,
Let all the virgins therefore well awayt,
And ye fresh boyes that tend upon her groome
Prepare your selves; for he is comming strayt.
Set all your things in seemely good aray
115 Fit for so joyfull day,
The joyfulst day that ever sunne did see.
Faire Sun, shew forth thy favourable ray,
And let thy lifull heat not fervent be
For feare of burning her sunshyny face,
120 Her beauty to disgrace.
O fayrest Phoebus, father of the Muse,
If ever I did honour thee aright,
Or sing the thing, that mote thy mind delight,
Doe not thy servants simple boone refuse,
125 But let this day let this one day be myne,

---

and Themis; they conducted in the seasons and gave justice and peace. Here they are daughters of Day (Jupiter) and Night, and thus their influence over the phases of earthly mutability is extended.

103 *three ... Queene*: i.e. the three Graces, attendants of Venus; see *The Dance of the Graces*, from *The Faerie Queene*, ll. 91–6, 146–80.
106 *betweene*: now and then.
108 *use*: are wont.
118 *lifull*: life-giving.
120 *disgrace*: disfigure.
121 *Phoebus*: Apollo, god of the sun (auspicious on a wedding day), and of poetry. He is usually the companion rather than the father of the Muses.

Let all the rest be thine.
Then I thy soverayne prayses loud wil sing,
That all the woods shal answer and theyr eccho ring.

Harke how the Minstrels gin to shrill aloud
Their merry Musick that resounds from far,   130
The pipe, the tabor, and the trembling Croud,
That well agree withouten breach or jar.
But most of all the Damzels doe delite,
When they their tymbrels smyte,
And thereunto doe daunce and carrol sweet,   135
That all the sences they doe ravish quite,
The whyles the boyes run up and downe the street,
Crying aloud with strong confusèd noyce,
As if it were one voyce.
'Hymen io Hymen, Hymen,' they do shout,   140
That even to the heavens theyr shouting shrill
Doth reach, and all the firmament doth fill,
To which the people standing all about,
As in approvance doe thereto applaud
And loud advaunce her laud,   145
And evermore they 'Hymen Hymen' sing,
That al the woods them answer and theyr eccho ring.

Loe where she comes along with portly pace
Lyke Phoebe from her chamber of the East,
Arysing forth to run her mighty race,   150
Clad all in white, that seemes a virgin best.
So well it her beseemes that ye would weene
Some angell she had beene.
Her long loose yellow locks lyke golden wyre,

131 *tabor*: small drum. *Croud*: fiddle.
134 *tymbrels*: tambourines.
148 *portly*: dignified.
149 *Phoebe*: virgin moon-goddess.
151 *seemes*: befits.

155 Sprinckled with perle, and perling flowres a tweene,
Doe lyke a golden mantle her attyre,
And being crownèd with a girland greene,
Seeme lyke some mayden Queene.
Her modest eyes abashèd to behold
160 So many gazers, as on her do stare,
Upon the lowly ground affixèd are.
Ne dare lift up her countenance too bold,
But blush to heare her prayses sung so loud,
So farre from being proud.
165 Nathlesse doe ye still loud her prayses sing.
That all the woods may answer and your eccho ring.
Tell me ye merchants daughters did ye see
So fayre a creature in your towne before,
So sweet, so lovely, and so mild as she,
170 Adornd with beautyes grace and vertues store,
Her goodly eyes lyke Saphyres shining bright,
Her forehead yvory white,
Her cheekes lyke apples which the sun hath rudded,
Her lips lyke cherryes charming men to byte,
175 Her brest like to a bowle of creame uncrudded,
Her paps lyke lyllies budded,
Her snowie necke lyke to a marble towre,
And all her body like a pallace fayre,
Ascending uppe with many a stately stayre,
180 To honors seat and chastities sweet bowre.
Why stand ye still ye virgins in amaze,
Upon her so to gaze,
Whiles ye forget your former lay to sing,

155 *perling*: winding.
158 Perhaps referring to Queen Elizabeth in conventional
   pastoral guise.
171–80 Cf. Song Sol. 4–7, and *Amoretti* 15. This blazon of the
   bride's beauties owes much also to classical and medieval
   convention.
175 *uncrudded*: uncurdled.
180 I.e. to her 'mind adornd with vertues manifold' (*Am.* 15).

To which the woods did answer and your eccho ring.
But if ye saw that which no eyes can see,   185
The inward beauty of her lively spright,
Garnisht with heavenly guifts of high degree,
Much more then would ye wonder at that sight,
And stand astonisht lyke to those which red
Medusaes mazeful hed.   190
There dwels sweet love and constant chastity,
Unspotted fayth and comely womanhood,
Regard of honour and mild modesty,
There vertue raynes as Queene in royal throne,
And giveth lawes alone.   195
The which the base affections doe obay,
And yeeld theyr services unto her will,
Ne thought of thing uncomely ever may
Thereto approch to tempt her mind to ill.
Had ye once seene these her celestial threasures,   200
And unrevealèd pleasures,
Then would ye wonder and her prayses sing,
That al the woods should answer and your echo ring.

Open the temple gates unto my love,
Open them wide that she may enter in,   205
And all the postes adorne as doth behove,
And all the pillours deck with girlands trim,
For to recyve this Saynt with honour dew,
That commeth in to you.
With trembling steps and humble reverence,   210
She commeth in, before th' almighties vew,

189 *red*: saw.
190 The power of Medusa to turn to stone all who looked on
      her snake-covered head was interpreted as the power of
      chaste beauty to enchant the onlooker. *mazeful*: be-
      wildering, confounding.
198 *uncomely*: unbecoming.
206 *the postes adorne*: i.e. deck the doorposts with boughs of
      trees (as was the custom for Roman weddings).

Of her ye virgins learne obedience,
When so ye come into those holy places,
To humble your proud faces:
215 Bring her up to th' high altar, that she may
The sacred ceremonies there partake,
The which do endlesse matrimony make,
And let the roring Organs loudly play
The praises of the Lord in lively notes,
220 The whiles with hollow throates
The Choristers the joyous Antheme sing,
That al the woods may answere and their eccho ring.

Behold whiles she before the altar stands
Hearing the holy priest that to her speakes
225 And blesseth her with his two happy hands,
How the red roses flush up in her cheekes,
And the pure snow with goodly vermill stayne,
Like crimsin dyde in grayne,
That even th' Angels which continually,
230 About the sacred Altare doe remaine,
Forget their service and about her fly,
Ofte peeping in her face that seemes more fayre,
The more they on it stare.
But her sad eyes still fastened on the ground,
235 Are governèd with goodly modesty,
That suffers not one looke to glaunce awry,
Which may let in a little thought unsownd.
Why blush ye love to give to me your hand,
The pledge of all our band?
240 Sing ye sweet Angels, Alleluya sing,
That all the woods may answere and your eccho ring.

Now al is done; bring home the bride againe,

227 *vermill*: vermilion.
228 *in grayne*: in fast colour.
234 *sad*: sober.
239 *band*: bond.

Bring home the triumph of our victory,
Bring home with you the glory of her gaine,
With joyance bring her and with jollity. 245
Never had man more joyfull day then this,
Whom heaven would heape with blis.
Make feast therefore now all this live long day,
This day for ever to me holy is,
Poure out the wine without restraint or stay, 250
Poure not by cups, but by the belly full,
Poure out to all that wull,
And sprinkle all the postes and wals with wine,
That they may sweat, and drunken be withall.
Crowne ye God Bacchus with a coronall, 255
And Hymen also crowne with wreathes of vine,
And let the Graces daunce unto the rest;
For they can doo it best:
The whiles the maydens doe theyr carroll sing,
To which the woods shal answer and theyr eccho ring. 260

Ring ye the bels, ye yong men of the towne,
And leave your wonted labors for this day:
This day is holy; doe ye write it downe,
That ye for ever it remember may.
This day the sunne is in his chiefest hight, 265
With Barnaby the bright,
From whence declining daily by degrees,
He somewhat loseth of his heat and light,
When once the Crab behind his back he sees.
But for this time it ill ordainèd was, 270
To chose the longest day in all the yeare,
And shortest night, when longest fitter weare:

244 *of her gaine*: of having gained her.
252 *wull*: will.
253 A custom at Roman wedding feasts.
265–6 I.e. it is the summer solstice which (in Spenser's time)
      was St. Barnabas' Day, 11 June.
269 I.e. when the sun leaves the zodiacal sign of Cancer.

Yet never day so long, but late would passe.
Ring ye the bels, to make it weare away,
275 And bonefiers make all day,
And daunce about them, and about them sing:
That all the woods may answer, and your eccho ring.

Ah when will this long weary day have end,
And lende me leave to come unto my love?
280 How slowly do the houres theyr numbers spend!
How slowly does sad Time his feathers move!
Hast thee O fayrest Planet to thy home
Within the Westerne fome:
Thy tyrèd steedes long since have need of rest.
285 Long though it be, at last I see it gloome,
And the bright evening star with golden creast
Appeare out of the East.
Fayre childe of beauty, glorious lampe of love
That all the host of heaven in rankes doost lead,
290 And guydest lovers through the nights dread,
How chearefully thou lookest from above,
And seemst to laugh atweene thy twinkling light
As joying in the sight
Of these glad many which for joy doe sing,
295 That all the woods them answer and their echo ring.

Now ceasse ye damsels your delights forepast;
Enough is it, that all the day was youres:
Now day is doen, and night is nighing fast:
Now bring the Bryde into the brydall boures.
300 Now night is come, now soone her disaray,
And in her bed her lay;
Lay her in lillies and in violets,
And silken courteins over her display,

273 *late*: finally.
282 *fayrest Planet*: i.e. the sun.
303 *display*: spread.

And odourd sheetes, and Arras coverlets.
Behold how goodly my faire love does ly   305
In proud humility;
Like unto Maia, when as Jove her tooke,
In Tempe, lying on the flowry gras,
Twixt sleepe and wake, after she weary was,
With bathing in the Acidalian brooke.   310
Now it is night, ye damsels may be gon,
And leave my love alone,
And leave likewise your former lay to sing:
The woods no more shal answere, nor your echo ring.

Now welcome night, thou night so long expected,   315
That long daies labour doest at last defray,
And all my cares, which cruell love collected,
Hast sumd in one, and cancellèd for aye:
Spread thy broad wing over my love and me,
That no man may us see,   320
And in thy sable mantle us enwrap,
From feare of perrill and foule horror free.
Let no false treason seeke us to entrap,
Nor any dread disquiet once annoy
The safety of our joy: 325
But let the night be calme and quietsome,
Without tempestuous storms or sad afray:
Lyke as when Jove with fayre Alcmena lay,

304 *Arras*: tapestry.
307 *Maia*: the most beautiful of the Pleïades, daughters of Atlas.
308 *Tempe*: beautiful vale in Thessaly. Spenser changes the setting from Maia's cave on Mount Cyllene in Arcadia.
310 *Acidalian brooke*: normally associated with Venus and the Graces; it is actually in Boeotia.
327 *sad afray*: grievous alarm.
328 When Jove slept with Alcmena he miraculously prolonged the night to prevent the return of her husband Amphitryon.

When he begot the great Tirynthian groome:
330   Or lyke as when he with thy selfe did lie,
And begot Majesty.
And let the mayds and yongmen cease to sing:
Ne let the woods them answer, nor theyr eccho ring.

Let no lamenting cryes, nor dolefull teares,
335   Be heard all night within nor yet without:
Ne let false whispers, breeding hidden feares,
Breake gentle sleepe with misconceivèd dout.
Let no deluding dreames, nor dreadful sights
Make sudden sad affrights;
340   Ne let housefyres, nor lightnings helpelesse harmes,
Ne let the Pouke, nor other evill sprights,
Ne let mischivous witches with theyr charmes,
Ne let hob Goblins, names whose sence we see not,
Fray us with things that be not.
345   Let not the shriech Oule, nor the Storke be heard:
Nor the night Raven that still deadly yels,
Nor damnèd ghosts cald up with mighty spels,
Nor griesly vultures make us once affeard:
Ne let th' unpleasant Quyre of Frogs still croking
350   Make us to wish theyr choking.
Let none of these theyr drery accents sing;
Ne let the woods them answer, nor theyr eccho ring.

But let stil Silence trew night watches keepe,
That sacred peace may in assurance rayne,

329   *Tirynthian groome*: i.e. Hercules of Tiryns.
330-1 *he . . . Majesty*: In Ovid Majesty is the daughter of Honour
     and Reverence (*Fasti* V.23-6), not of Jove and Night,
     which is Spenser's invention.
341   *the Pouke*: i.e. Puck (here a satanic figure rather than a
     tricksy spirit).
343   *names . . . not*: Hobgoblins were given names such as Flib-
     bertigibbet, Hobbididence.
344   *Fray*: frighten.

And tymely sleep, when it is tyme to sleepe,　　　355
May poure his limbs forth on your pleasant playne,
The whiles an hundred little wingèd loves,
Like divers fethered doves,
Shall fly and flutter round about your bed,
And in the secret darke, that none reproves,　　　360
Their prety stealthes shal worke, and snares shal spread
To filch away sweet snatches of delight,
Conceald through covert night.
Ye sonnes of Venus, play your sports at will,
For greedy pleasure, carelesse of your toyes,　　　365
Thinks more upon her paradise of joyes,
Then what ye do, albe it good or ill.
All night therefore attend your merry play,
For it will soone be day:
Now none doth hinder you, that say or sing,　　　370
Ne will the woods now answer, nor your Eccho ring.

Who is the same, which at my window peepes?
Or whose is that faire face, that shines so bright?
Is it not Cinthia, she that never sleepes,
But walkes about high heaven al the night?　　　375
O fayrest goddesse, do thou not envy
My love with me to spy:
For thou likewise didst love, though now unthought,
And for a fleece of woll, which privily,
The Latmian shephard once unto thee brought,　　　380
His pleasures with thee wrought.
Therefore to us be favorable now;
And sith of wemens labours thou hast charge,
And generation goodly dost enlarge,
Encline thy will t' effect our wishfull vow,　　　385

378-81 Cynthia, the virgin moon-goddess, loved Endymion, a
　　　　shepherd on Mount Latmos. *unthought*: forgotten.
383　Cynthia was goddess of childbirth.
385　*thy* (1611): 'they' (1595).

And the chast wombe informe with timely seed,
That may our comfort breed:
Till which we cease our hopefull hap to sing,
Ne let the woods us answere, nor our Eccho ring.

390 And thou great Juno, which with awful might
The lawes of wedlock still dost patronize,
And the religion of the faith first plight
With sacred rites hast taught to solemnize:
And eeke for comfort often callèd art
395 Of women in their smart,
Eternally bind thou this lovely band,
And all thy blessings unto us impart.
And thou glad Genius, in whose gentle hand,
The bridale bowre and geniall bed remaine,
400 Without blemish or staine,
And the sweet pleasures of theyr loves delight
With secret ayde doest succour and supply,
Till they bring forth the fruitfull progeny,
Send us the timely fruit of this same night.
405 And thou fayre Hebe, and thou Hymen free,
Grant that it may so be.
Til which we cease your further prayse to sing,
Ne any woods shal answer, nor your Eccho ring.

And ye high heavens, the temple of the gods,
410 In which a thousand torches flaming bright
Doe burne, that to us wretched earthly clods,
In dreadful darknesse lend desirèd light;
And all ye powers which in the same remayne,

390 *Juno*: guardian of the sanctity of marriage and, with
        Cynthia, patroness of childbirth.
396 *lovely*: loving.
398 *Genius*: Roman household god of birth and generation.
399 *geniall bed*: marriage bed.
405 *Hebe*: goddess of youth, with powers of rejuvenation.
413 *powers*: deities (stars) with influence on men's lives.

More then we men can fayne,
Poure out your blessing on us plentiously,   415
And happy influence upon us raine,
That we may raise a large posterity,
Which from the earth, which they may long possesse,
With lasting happinesse,
Up to your haughty pallaces may mount,   420
And for the guerdon of theyr glorious merit
May heavenly tabernacles there inherit,
Of blessèd Saints for to increase the count.
So let us rest, sweet love, in hope of this,
And cease till then our tymely joyes to sing,   425
The woods no more us answer, nor our eccho ring.

Song made in lieu of many ornaments,
With which my love should duly have bene dect,
Which cutting off through hasty accidents,
Ye would not stay your dew time to expect,   430
But promist both to recompens,
Be unto her a goodly ornament,
And for short time an endlesse moniment.

Amoretti and Epithalamion, 1595

WILLIAM SHAKESPEARE

Song

Sigh no more, ladies, sigh no more,
    Men were deceivers ever,
One foot in sea and one on shore,
    To one thing constant never.

414 *fayne*: imagine.
420 *haughty*: lofty, dignified.
421 *guerdon*: reward.
427–33 The full meaning of the envoy is obscure. For a
    plausible interpretation see A. K. Hieatt, op. cit.

5   Then sigh not so, but let them go,
       And be you blithe and bonny,
     Converting all your sounds of woe
       Into Hey nonny, nonny.
     Sing no more ditties, sing no mo
10   Of dumps so dull and heavy;
     The fraud of men was ever so,
       Since summer first was leavy.
     Then sigh not so, but let them go,
       And be you blithe and bonny,
15   Converting all your sounds of woe
       Into Hey nonny, nonny.

Much Ado About Nothing (1623), II [iii]

     O mistress mine, where are you roaming?
     Oh, stay and hear; your true love's coming,
       That can sing both high and low.
     Trip no further, pretty sweeting;
5   Journeys end in lovers meeting,
       Every wise man's son doth know.

     What is love? 'Tis not hereafter;
     Present mirth hath present laughter;
       What's to come is still unsure.
10   In delay there lies no plenty,
     Then come kiss me, sweet and twenty;
       Youth's a stuff will not endure.

Twelfth Night (1623), II.iii

SONG: SIGH NO MORE: Written *c.* 1598.
11 *was*: 'were' (1623).
O MISTRESS MINE: This and the following lyric were written
  c. 1600. Evidence suggests that the song was written to a
  popular tune already existing, a version of which appears
  in Thomas Morley, *The First Book of Consort Lessons*, 1599.

When that I was and a little tiny boy,
  With hey, ho, the wind and the rain,
A foolish thing was but a toy,
  For the rain it raineth every day.

But when I came to man's estate,   5
  With hey, ho, the wind and the rain,
'Gainst knaves and thieves men shut their gate,
  For the rain it raineth every day.

But when I came, alas! to wive,
  With hey, ho, the wind and the rain,   10
By swaggering could I never thrive,
  For the rain it raineth every day.

But when I came unto my beds,
  With hey, ho, the wind and the rain,
With tosspots still had drunken heads,   15
  For the rain it raineth every day.

A great while ago the world begun,
  With hey, ho, the wind and the rain,
But that's all one, our play is done,
  And we'll strive to please you every day.   20

Twelfth Night (1623), V.i

WHEN THAT I WAS: Sung by the clown Feste at the end of
  Twelfth Night.
15 *tosspots*: drunkards.

THOMAS DEKKER

Song

Virtue's branches wither, virtue pines,
  Oh, pity, pity, and alack the time!
Vice doth flourish, vice in glory shines,
  Her gilded boughs above the cedar climb.

5 Vice hath golden cheeks, oh, pity, pity!
  She in every land doth monarchize;
Virtue is exiled from every city,
  Virtue is a fool, vice only wise.

Oh, pity, pity! virtue weeping dies;
10 Vice laughs to see her faint, alack the time!
This sinks, with painted wings the other flies;
  Alack, that best should fall, and bad should climb!

Oh, pity, pity, pity! mourn, not sing!
  Vice is a saint, virtue an underling;
15 Vice doth flourish, vice in glory shines,
  Virtue's branches wither, virtue pines.

Old Fortunatus, 1600

SONG: VIRTUE'S BRANCHES WITHER: The song appears in
  Dekker's play *Old Fortunatus*, where it is sung by a priest
  while the trees of Virtue and Vice are planted. Virtue's
  tree has 'green and withered leaves mingled together, and
  little fruit on it'; Vice's is a 'fair tree of gold with apples
  on it'.

Song

Golden slumbers kiss your eyes,
Smiles awake you when you rise;
Sleep, pretty wantons, do not cry,
And I will sing a lullaby;
Rock them, rock them, lullaby.   5

Care is heavy, therefore sleep you,
You are care, and care must keep you;
Sleep, pretty wantons, do not cry,
And I will sing a lullaby;
Rock them, rock them, lullaby.   10

Patient Grissill, 1603

NICHOLAS BRETON

Say that I should say I love ye,
    Would you say 'tis but a saying?
But if love in prayers move ye,
    Will you not be moved with praying?

Think I think that love should know ye,   5
    Will you think 'tis but a thinking?
But if love the thought do show ye,
    Will ye lose your eyes with winking?

Write that I do write you blessèd,
    Will you write 'tis but a writing?   10
But if truth and love confess it,
    Will ye doubt the true enditing?

SONG: GOLDEN SLUMBERS: This song from the play *Patient Grissill* is a lullaby sung to Grissill's children before they are cruelly abducted by order of her husband, the marquis.

No; I say, and think, and write it,
   Write, and think, and say your pleasure;
15 Love, and truth, and I endite it,
   You are blessèd out of measure.

England's Helicon, 1600

ANONYMOUS

Love winged my hopes and taught me how to fly
Far from base earth, but not to mount too high;
   For true pleasure
   Lives in measure,
5   Which, if men forsake,
Blinded they into folly run, and grief for pleasure take.

But my vain hopes, proud of their new-taught flight,
Enamoured, sought to woo the sun's fair light,
   Whose rich brightness
10   Moved their lightness
   To aspire so high,
That, all scorched and consumed with fire, now
     drowned in woe they lie.

And none but love their woeful hap did rue,
For love did know that their desires were true;
15   Though fate frownèd,
   And now drownèd
   They in sorrow dwell,
It was the purest light of heaven for whose fair love
     they fell.

R. Jones, *The Second Book of Songs and Airs*, 1601

LOVE WINGED MY HOPES: First published in Thomas Morley, *The First Book of Airs*, 1600. The imagery refers to the legend of Icarus's flight (Ovid, *Met.* VIII. 183–235).

A. W.

To Time

Eternal time, that wastest without waste,
That art and art not, diest and livest still;
Most slow of all and yet of greatest haste;
Both ill and good, and neither good nor ill:
   How can I justly praise thee or dispraise?   5
   Dark are thy nights, but bright and clear thy days.

Both free and scarce, thou giv'st and tak'st again;
Thy womb, that all doth breed, is tomb to all;
Whatso by thee hath life, by thee is slain;
From thee do all things rise, by thee they fall;   10
   Constant, inconstant, moving, standing still;
   Was, Is, Shall be, do thee both breed and kill.

I lose thee while I seek to find thee out;
The farther off, the more I follow thee;
The faster hold, the greater cause of doubt;   15
Was, Is, I know; but *Shall* I cannot see.
   All things by thee are measured; thou, by none;
   All are in thee; thou, in thyself alone.

F. Davison, *A Poetical Rhapsody*, 1602

TO TIME: The poet A. W. has not been identified.
  7 *free*: liberal. *scarce*: niggardly.

LYRICS

ANONYMOUS

A Madrigal

My love in her attire doth show her wit,
    It doth so well become her;
For ev'ry season she hath dressings fit,
    For winter, spring, and summer.
5   No beauty she doth miss,
    When all her robes are on;
But beauty's self she is,
    When all her robes are gone.

F. Davison, *A Poetical Rhapsody,* 1602

ANONYMOUS

Weep you no more, sad fountains;
    What need you flow so fast?
Look how the snowy mountains
    Heaven's sun doth gently waste.
5   But my sun's heavenly eyes
    View not your weeping,
    That now lies sleeping
Softly, now softly lies
    Sleeping.

10   Sleep is a reconciling,
    A rest that peace begets.
Doth not the sun rise smiling
    When fair at ev'n he sets?
    Rest you then, rest, sad eyes,
15   Melt not in weeping,
    While she lies sleeping
Softly, now softly lies
    Sleeping.

J. Dowland, *The Third and Last Book of Songs or Airs,* 1603

BEN JONSON

On My First Daughter

Here lies, to each her parents' ruth,
Mary, the daughter of their youth;
Yet, all heaven's gifts being heaven's due,
It makes the father less to rue.
At six months' end she parted hence,   5
With safety of her innocence;
Whose soul heaven's Queen (whose name she bears)
In comfort of her mother's tears,
Hath placed amongst her virgin-train;
Where, while that severed doth remain,   10
This grave partakes the fleshly birth;
Which cover lightly, gentle earth.

Epigrams, 1616

Song

Slow, slow, fresh fount, keep time with my salt tears;
    Yet slower yet, oh, faintly, gentle springs;
List to the heavy part the music bears,
    Woe weeps out her division when she sings.

ON MY FIRST DAUGHTER: Written *c.* 1598.
1 *ruth*: sorrow.
10 *that*: i.e. the soul, which will ultimately be reunited with
    the body at the Resurrection.
SONG: SLOW, SLOW, FRESH FOUNT: Written 1600–1. Set to
    music by Henry Youll, *Canzonets to Three Voices*, 1608. Sung
    in the play *Cynthia's Revels* by Echo, grieving at the spring
    where her beloved Narcissus, pining from self-love, died
    and was changed into a daffodil.
4 *division*: florid run of music.

5
        Droop herbs and flowers,
        Fall grief in showers;
        Our beauties are not ours;
           Oh, I could still,
    Like melting snow upon some craggy hill,

10
         Drop, drop, drop, drop,
    Since nature's pride is now a withered daffodil.

Cynthia's Revels (1616), I.ii

Song

      Oh, that joy so soon should waste!
        Or so sweet a bliss
        As a kiss
      Might not forever last!

5
      So sugared, so melting, so soft, so delicious!
        The dew that lies on roses
      When the morn herself discloses,
        Is not so precious.
      Oh, rather than I would it smother,

10
      Were I to taste such another,
        It should be my wishing
        That I might die kissing.

Cynthia's Revels (1616), IV.iii

Hymn

      Queen and huntress, chaste and fair,
      Now the sun is laid to sleep,
      Seated in thy silver chair,
      State in wonted manner keep;

5
        Hesperus entreats thy light,
        Goddess excellently bright.

SONG: OH, THAT JOY: Set to music by Henry Lawes.
HYMN: Intended as a compliment to Queen Elizabeth.
  5 *Hesperus*: the evening star.

Earth, let not thy envious shade
Dare itself to interpose;
Cynthia's shining orb was made
Heaven to clear, when day did close;   10
  Bless us then with wishèd sight,
  Goddess excellently bright.

Lay thy bow of pearl apart,
And thy crystal-shining quiver;
Give unto the flying hart   15
Space to breathe, how short soever,
  Thou that mak'st a day of night,
  Goddess excellently bright.

Cynthia's Revels (1616), V.vi

Song

[*Crispinus.*]

If I freely may discover
What would please me in my lover:
  I would have her fair, and witty,
  Savouring more of court than city;
  A little proud, but full of pity;   5
  Light and humorous in her toying,
  Oft building hopes and soon destroying;
  Long, but sweet, in the enjoying;
Neither too easy, nor too hard,
All extremes I would have barred.   10

10 *clear*: brighten.
SONG: IF I FREELY MAY DISCOVER: Written 1601. Set to music
  by Henry Lawes.

[*Hermogenes.*]
>She should be allowed her passions,
>So they were but used as fashions:
>>Sometimes froward, and then frowning,
>>Sometimes sickish, and then swowning,
15>>Every fit with change still crowning;
>>Purely jealous I would have her,
>>Then only constant when I crave her,
>>'Tis a virtue should not save her.
>Thus, nor her delicates would cloy me,
20>Neither her peevishness annoy me.

The Poetaster (1616), II.ii

On My First Son

Farewell, thou child of my right hand, and joy;
>My sin was too much hope of thee, loved boy.
Seven years thou wert lent to me, and I thee pay,
>Exacted by thy fate, on the just day.
5Oh, could I lose all father now! For why
>Will man lament the state he should envy?
To have so soon 'scaped world's and flesh's rage,
>And, if no other misery, yet age!
Rest in soft peace, and asked, say, Here doth lie
10>Ben Jonson his best piece of poetry—
For whose sake, henceforth, all his vows be such,
>As what he loves may never like too much.

Epigrams, 1616

ON MY FIRST SON: Written 1603, when Jonson's seven-year-old
>son died of the plague.
1 *child of my right hand*: the meaning in Hebrew of Benjamin.
12 A translation of Martial's line 'Quidquid ames, cupias non
>placuisse nimis' (*Epigrams* VI.xxix.8): 'Whatever you love,
>desire that it may not please you too much'.

Song: That Women are but Men's Shadows

Follow a shadow, it still flies you;
   Seem to fly it, it will pursue:
So court a mistress, she denies you;
   Let her alone, she will court you.
Say, are not women truly, then,   5
   Styled but the shadows of us men?
At morn and even shades are longest,
   At noon they are or short or none:
So men at weakest, they are strongest,
   But grant us perfect, they're not known.   10
Say, are not women truly, then,
   Styled but the shadows of us men?

The Forest, 1616

SONG: THAT WOMEN ARE BUT MEN'S SHADOWS: 'Pembroke
and his Lady discoursing, the Earl said that women were
men's shadows, and she maintained them; both appealing
to Jonson, he affirmed it true, for which my Lady gave a
penance to prove it in verse—hence his epigram' (Jonson's
Conversations with Drummond 364–7). The poem is an adaptation
of Barthélemi Aneau's 'Mulier Umbra Viri', 1552.
Of the lyrics by Donne printed here all but the last were
probably written before 1600. Their titles may not be Donne's.

JOHN DONNE

Song

Go and catch a falling star,
  Get with child a mandrake root,
Tell me where all past years are,
  Or who cleft the devil's foot,
Teach me to hear mermaids singing,
Or to keep off envy's stinging,
      And find
      What wind
Serves to advance an honest mind.

If thou be'st born to strange sights,
  Things invisible to see,
Ride ten thousand days and nights,
  Till age snow white hairs on thee,
Thou, when thou return'st, wilt tell me
All strange wonders that befell thee,
      And swear
      Nowhere
Lives a woman true, and fair.

If thou find'st one, let me know;
  Such a pilgrimage were sweet,—
Yet do not: I would not go,
  Though at next door we might meet;
Though she were true when you met her,
And last till you write your letter,
      Yet she
      Will be
False, ere I come, to two or three.

Poems, 1633

SONG: GO AND CATCH: Probably written to an already existing tune; for one musical setting see *Elegies and The Songs and Sonnets,* ed. Helen Gardner, Oxford, 1965, p. 241.
2 *mandrake*: plant whose forked root resembles the human form.

Song

Sweetest love, I do not go
    For weariness of thee,
Nor in hope the world can show
    A fitter love for me;
      But since that I   5
Must die at last, 'tis best
To use myself in jest—
    Thus by feigned deaths to die.

Yesternight the sun went hence,
    And yet is here today;   10
He hath no desire nor sense,
    Nor half so short a way;
      Then fear not me,
But believe that I shall make
Speedier journeys, since I take   15
    More wings and spurs than he.

Oh, how feeble is man's power,
    That if good fortune fall,
Cannot add another hour,
    Nor a lost hour recall!   20
      But come bad chance,
And we join to it our strength,
And we teach it art and length,
    Itself o'er us to advance.

SONG: SWEETEST LOVE: Probably written to an already existing tune; for one musical setting, see Gardner, p. 240.
8 *feigned deaths*: i.e. absences.

25   When thou sigh'st, thou sigh'st not wind,
    But sigh'st my soul away;
  When thou weep'st, unkindly kind,
    My life's blood doth decay.
      It cannot be
30 That thou lov'st me, as thou say'st,
  If in thine my life thou waste;
    Thou art the best of me.

  Let not thy divining heart
    Forethink me any ill:
35 Destiny may take thy part,
    And may thy fears fulfil;
      But think that we
  Are but turned aside to sleep;
  They who one another keep
40   Alive, ne'er parted be.

Poems, 1633

Break of Day

  'Tis true, 'tis day; what though it be?
  Oh, wilt thou therefore rise from me?
  Why should we rise because 'tis light?
  Did we lie down because 'twas night?
5 Love, which in spite of darkness brought us hither,
  Should in despite of light keep us together.

32 *best of me*: i.e. my 'soul' and 'life's blood'.
BREAK OF DAY: An aubade, or complaint of lovers parting
  at dawn. The speaker is a woman. Set to music by W.
  Corkine, *The Second Book of Airs*, 1612; see Gardner, p. 243.

Light hath no tongue, but is all eye;
If it could speak as well as spy,
This were the worst that it could say,
That, being well, I fain would stay,   10
And that I loved my heart and honour so,
That I would not from him, that had them, go.

Must business thee from hence remove?
Oh, that's the worst disease of love;
The poor, the foul, the false, love can   15
Admit, but not the busied man.
He which hath business, and makes love, doth do
Such wrong as when a married man doth woo.

Poems, 1633

Woman's Constancy

Now thou hast loved me one whole day,
Tomorrow when thou leav'st, what wilt thou say?
Wilt thou then antedate some new-made vow?
    Or say that now
We are not just those persons which we were?   5
Or, that oaths made in reverential fear
Of love and his wrath, any may forswear?
Or, as true deaths true marriages untie,
So lovers' contracts, images of those,
Bind but till sleep, death's image, them unloose?   10
    Or, your own end to justify,
For having purposed change and falsehood, you
Can have no way but falsehood to be true?
Vain lunatic, against these scapes I could
    Dispute and conquer, if I would;   15
    Which I abstain to do,
For by tomorrow I may think so too.

Poems, 1633

WOMAN'S CONSTANCY:
14 *lunatic*: (i) fool; (ii) inconstant person. *scapes*: (i) excuses;
(ii) sins.

The Apparition

When by thy scorn, O murd'ress, I am dead,
And that thou thinkst thee free
From all solicitation from me,
Then shall my ghost come to thy bed,
5   And thee, feigned vestal, in worse arms shall see;
Then thy sick taper will begin to wink,
And he whose thou art then, being tired before,
Will, if thou stir, or pinch to wake him, think
      Thou call'st for more,
10   And in false sleep will from thee shrink;
And then, poor aspen wretch, neglected thou
Bathed in a cold quicksilver sweat wilt lie,
      A verier ghost than I.
What I will say, I will not tell thee now,
15   Lest that preserve thee; and since my love is spent,
I had rather thou shouldst painfully repent,
Than by my threat'nings rest still innocent.

Poems, 1633

THE APPARITION: Set to music by William Lawes.
6 Indicating the presence of a ghost.
11 *aspen*: quivering.
16–17 I.e. I had rather you be forced into painful repentance
    of your crimes later, than be dissuaded from committing
    them because of my threatenings now.

The Broken Heart

He is stark mad, whoever says
   That he hath been in love an hour,
Yet not that love so soon decays,
   But that it can ten in less space devour.
Who will believe me if I swear   5
That I have had the plague a year?
   Who would not laugh at me if I should say
   I saw a flask of powder burn a day?

Ah, what a trifle is a heart,
   If once into love's hands it come!   10
All other griefs allow a part
   To other griefs, and ask themselves but some;
They come to us, but us love draws,
He swallows us, and never chaws;
   By him, as by chained shot, whole ranks do die,   15
   He is the tyrant pike, our hearts the fry.

If 'twere not so, what did become
   Of my heart when I first saw thee?
I brought a heart into the room,
   But from the room I carried none with me.   20
If it had gone to thee, I know
Mine would have taught thine heart to show
   More pity unto me; but love, alas,
   At one first blow did shiver it as glass.

THE BROKEN HEART:
 8 *flask*: 'flash' (1635).
14 *chaws*: chews.
15 *chained shot*: cannon-balls chained together.
16 *fry*: small fish.

25   Yet nothing can to nothing fall,
        Nor any place be empty quite;
    Therefore I think my breast hath all
        Those pieces still, though they be not unite;
    And now as broken glasses show
30   A hundred lesser faces, so
        My rags of heart can like, wish, and adore,
        But after one such love, can love no more.

Poems, 1633

The Good-Morrow

    I wonder, by my troth, what thou and I
        Did till we loved? were we not weaned till then,
    But sucked on country pleasures childishly?
        Or snorted we in the Seven Sleepers' den?
5   'Twas so; but this, all pleasures fancies be;
    If ever any beauty I did see,
Which I desired, and got, 'twas but a dream of thee.

    And now good morrow to our waking souls,
        Which watch not one another out of fear;
10   For love all love of other sights controls,
        And makes one little room an everywhere.
    Let sea-discoverers to new worlds have gone,
    Let maps to other, worlds on worlds have shown,
Let us possess our world: each hath one, and is one.

THE GOOD-MORROW:
3   *country pleasures*: unrefined, immature love affairs.
4   *the Seven Sleepers' den*: Seven Christian youths of Ephesus, fleeing Roman persecution, were walled up in a cave, where they slept for two centuries; they awoke to find Christianity flourishing.
5   *but*: except for.
13   *other*: other people.
14   *our world* (MSS.): 'one world' (1633).

My face in thine eye, thine in mine appears,   15
   And true plain hearts do in the faces rest;
Where can we find two better hemispheres,
   Without sharp North, without declining West?
Whatever dies was not mixed equally;
   If our two loves be one, or thou and I   20
Love so alike that none do slacken, none can die.

Poems, 1633

17 *hemispheres*: i.e. (i) the lovers' eyes; (ii) by extension, the
    lovers, who together comprise one 'world'.
18 I.e. without the risk of love either cooling or abating.
19 *not mixed equally*: i.e. composed of elements in unequal
    proportions (and hence subject to decay).

SATIRES

THE DANCE OF THE SATYRS
Part of the title page of Richard Brathwait,
Nature's Embassy, or The Wild Man's Measures, 1625.
(Bodleian Library, Oxford)

The satiric [poet] ... sportingly never leaveth until he make a man laugh at folly, and at length, ashamed, to laugh at himself, which he cannot avoid without avoiding the folly.

Sidney, *An Apology for Poetry*, 1595

There was yet another kind of poet, who intended to tax the common abuses and vice of the people in rough and bitter speeches, and their invectives were called satires, and themselves satirics.

Puttenham, *The Art of English Poesy*, 1589

The satyr should be like the porcupine,
That shoots sharp quills out in each angry line,
And wounds the blushing cheek and fiery eye
Of him that hears and readeth guiltily.

Hall, *Virgidemiarum* (1597), V.iii

In serious jest, and jesting seriousness,
I strive to scourge polluting beastliness.

Marston, *The Scourge of Villainy* (1598), Bk. III, Proemium

SIR THOMAS WYATT

Of the courtier's life, written to John Poyntz

Mine own John Poyntz, since ye delight to know
   The cause why that homeward I me draw
   And flee the press of courts, whereso they go,
Rather than to live thrall under the awe
   Of lordly looks, wrapped within my cloak,   5
   To will and lust learning to set a law:
It is not for because I scorn or mock
   The power of them to whom fortune hath lent
   Charge over us, of right to strike the stroke;
But true it is that I have always meant   10
   Less to esteem them than the common sort,
   Of outward things that judge in their intent
Without regard what doth inward resort.
   I grant sometime that of glory the fire
   Doth touch my heart. Me list not to report   15
Blame by honour, and honour to desire;
   But how may I this honour now attain,
   That cannot dye the colour black a liar?
My Poyntz, I cannot frame my tune to feign,

OF THE COURTIER'S LIFE: Probably written in 1536, when
   Wyatt was banished from court to his father's estate,
   Allington Castle, in Kent. The poem is adapted from the
   tenth Satire of the Italian poet Alamanni (1495–1556),
   which is also in *terza rima*.

     The text is taken from Egerton MS. 2711 (E), except for
   ll. 1–51, which are missing from that MS. Ll. 1–27, 31–51 are
   from Devonshire MS. Add. 17492 (D); ll. 28–30 are from
   Parker MS. 168 (P).

     The title is taken from *Tottel's Miscellany*, 1557, in which
   the poem was first published. John Poyntz, of whom little
   is known, was a friend of Wyatt at court.

3 *press*: crowd.
18 *dye . . . liar*: i.e. paint the obvious truth with false colours.
19 *frame my tune*: 'frame my tongue' (P); 'from me tune' (D).

20 To cloak the truth for praise without desert
  Of them that list all vice for to retain.
I cannot honour them that sets their part
  With Venus and Bacchus all their life long;
  Nor hold my peace of them, although I smart.
25 I cannot crouch nor kneel to do so great a wrong
  To worship them like God on earth alone,
  That are as wolves these silly lambs among.
I cannot with my word complain and moan
  And suffer nought, nor smart without complaint,
30 Nor turn the word that from my mouth is gone.
I cannot speak and look like a saint,
  Use wiles for wit, and make deceit a pleasure;
  And call craft counsel, for profit still to paint.
I cannot wrest the law to fill the coffer;
35 With innocent blood to feed myself fat;
  And do most hurt where most help I offer.
I am not he that can allow the state
  Of high Caesar, and damn Cato to die,
  That with his death did 'scape out of the gate
40 From Caesar's hands, if Livy do not lie,
  And would not live where liberty was lost,
  So did his heart the common weal apply.
I am not he such eloquence to boast
  To make the crow singing as the swan,
45 Nor call the lion of coward beasts the most,
That cannot take a mouse as the cat can;

20 *without desert*: undeserved.
27 *silly*: innocent.
30 *turn*: call back.
33 *paint*: feign.
37 *allow the state*: approve the status.
38–42 Cato of Utica fought on the side of political freedom against Julius Caesar at Thapsus (46 B.C.), and on his defeat committed suicide. *Livy*: Roman historian (59 B.C.–A.D. 17). Cato's death is recounted in his *History* CXIV.
38 *high* (Arundel MS.): 'him' (D).
45 *coward* (P): 'cowards' (D).

And he that dieth for hunger of the gold,
    Call him Alexander, and say that Pan
Passeth Apollo in music manifold;
    Praise Sir Thopas for a noble tale,   50
    And scorn the story that the Knight told;
Praise him for counsel that is drunk of ale;
    Grin when he laugheth that beareth all the sway,
    Frown when he frowneth, and groan when he is pale;
On others' lust to hang both night and day.   55
    None of these points would ever frame in me;
    My wit is nought: I cannot learn the way.
And much the less of things that greater be,
    That asken help of colours of device
    To join the mean with each extremity;   60
With the nearest virtue to cloak alway the vice.
    And as to purpose likewise it shall fall,
    To press the virtue that it may not rise;
As drunkenness good fellowship to call;
    The friendly foe with his double face,   65
    Say he is gentle and courteous therewithal;
And say that favel hath a goodly grace
    In eloquence; and cruelty to name
    Zeal of justice; and change in time and place;
And he that suff'reth offence without blame,   70
    Call him pitiful, and him true and plain

47 *he . . . gold*: i.e. King Midas.
48–9 *say that Pan . . . manifold*: The foolish Midas judged Pan's
      rustic music to be superior to that of Apollo.
50 *Sir Thopas*: in Chaucer's *Canterbury Tales*, a mock chivalric
      romance written in doggerel.
51 *the story . . . told*: Chaucer's *Knight's Tale*, a courtly romance
      in the *Canterbury Tales*.
54 *he is* (D): 'is' (E).
55 *hang*: depend.
56 *frame*: succeed.
59 *colours of device*: subtle deceptions.
67 *favel*: flattery (or perhaps 'duplicity').
71 *pitiful*: compassionate.

That raileth reckless to every man's shame;
Say he is rude that cannot lie and feign;
　The lecher a lover, and tyranny
75　To be the right of a prince's reign.
I cannot, I; no, no, it will not be.
　This is the cause that I could never yet
　Hang on their sleeves that weigh, as thou mayst see,
A chip of chance more than a pound of wit.
80　This maketh me at home to hunt and to hawk,
　And in foul weather at my book to sit,
In frost and snow then with my bow to stalk.
　No man doth mark whereso I ride or go.
　In lusty leas at liberty I walk,
85　And of these news I feel nor weal nor woe,
　Save that a clog doth hang yet at my heel.
　No force for that, for it is ordered so
That I may leap both hedge and dyke full well.
　I am not now in France, to judge the wine,
90　With sav'ry sauce the delicates to feel;
Nor yet in Spain where one must him incline,
　Rather than to be, outwardly to seem:
　I meddle not with wits that be so fine;
Nor Flanders' cheer letteth not my sight to deem
95　Of black and white, nor taketh my wit away
　With beastliness, they beasts do so esteem;
Nor I am not where Christ is given in prey
　For money, poison, and treason, at Rome
　A common practice, usèd night and day.

85　*news*: novelties.
86　*clog . . . heel*: block is still fettered to my heel. (Wyatt was
　　not permitted to leave his father's estate.)
90　*feel*: smell and taste.
94　*Flanders' cheer*: strong Flemish liquor. *letteth*: hinders.
94–5 *to deem Of black and white*: from telling black from white.
96　*they beasts do so esteem*: i.e. the Flemish hold beasts in such
　　high regard that they readily become like beasts them-
　　selves.

But here I am in Kent and Christendom,   100
   Among the muses, where I read and rhyme;
    Where if thou list, my Poyntz, for to come,
Thou shalt be judge how I do spend my time.

Egerton MS. 2711

GEORGE GASCOIGNE

[*Avarice and Self-advancement*]
from *The Steel Glass*

How live the Moors, which spurn at glist'ring pearl,
And scorn the costs, which we do hold so dear?
How? how but well! and wear the precious pearl
Of peerless truth, amongst them publishèd,
Which we enjoy and never weigh the worth.   5
They would not then the same (like us) despise,
Which though they lack, they live in better wise
Than we, which hold the worthless pearl so dear.
But glitt'ring gold, which many years lay hid,
Till greedy minds gan search the very guts   10
Of earth and clay to find out sundry moulds
(As red and white, which are by melting made
Bright gold and silver, metals of mischief),
Hath now inflamed the noblest princes' hearts
With foulest fire of filthy avarice;   15
And seldom seen that kings can be content
To keep their bounds, which their forefathers left.
What causeth this, but greedy gold to get?
Even gold, which is the very cause of wars,

100 *in Kent and Christendom*: Kent was reputedly one of the last
     areas in England to be Christianized, hence this saying.
     The Wyatt family estate was of course in Kent.
AVARICE AND SELF-ADVANCEMENT:
2 *costs*: costly goods.
17 *left*: bequeathed.

20 The nest of strife, and nourice of debate,
The bar of heaven, and open way to hell.

But is this strange? when lords, when knights,
    and squires,
Which ought defend the state of commonwealth,
Are not afraid to covet like a king?
25 Oh, blind desire! Oh, high aspiring hearts!
The country squire doth covet to be knight,
The knight a lord, the lord an earl or a duke,
The duke a king, the king would monarch be,
And none content with that which is his own.
30 Yet none of these can see in crystal glass,
Which glistereth bright, and blears their gazing eyes,
How every life bears with him his disease.
But in my glass, which is of trusty steel,
I can perceive how kingdoms breed but care,
35 How lordship lives with lots of less delight
(Though cap and knee do seem a reverence,
And courtlike life is thought another heaven)
Than common people find in every coast.

The gentleman, which might in country keep
40 A plenteous board, and feed the fatherless
With pig and goose, with mutton, beef, and veal,
Yea, now and then a capon and a chick,
Will break up house, and dwell in market towns
A loit'ring life, and like an epicure.

20 *nourice*: nurse.
30 *crystal glass*: i.e. the looking-glass which shows the perfect
    pattern of things, and which consequently flatters those
    who look in it.
33 *glass . . . steel*: i.e. the looking-glass which reflects the truth
    and does not flatter.
35 *lots*: fortunes.
44 *loit'ring*: idle.

But who meanwhile defends the commonwealth?   45
Who rules the flock when shepherds so are fled?
Who stays the staff which should uphold the state?
Forsooth, good sir, the lawyer leapeth in,
Nay, rather leaps both over hedge and ditch,
And rules the roast; but few men rule by right.   50

O knights, O squires, O gentle bloods yborn,
You were not born all only for yourselves:
Your country claims some part of all your pains;
There should you live, and therein should you toil
To hold up right and banish cruel wrong;   55
To help the poor, to bridle back the rich,
To punish vice, and virtue to advance,
To see God served, and Belzebub suppressed.
You should not trust lieutenants in your room,
And let them sway the sceptre of your charge,   60
Whiles you meanwhile know scarcely what is done,
Nor yet can yield account, if you were called.

The Steel Glass (1576) [380–441]

JOHN DONNE

Satire I

Away, thou fondling motley humorist!
Leave me, and in this standing wooden chest,
Consorted with these few books, let me lie

47   *stays*: supports.
50   *rules the roast*: i.e. commands absolutely.
SATIRE I: Probably written 1593–4.
1   *fondling motley humorist*: foolish, capricious, fantastical
person. The humorist may represent that part of the
satirist's being, his body, which is susceptible to fleshly
temptations and whose continual urgings for material
satisfaction are a distraction to the contemplative man.
2   *standing wooden chest*: i.e. study, likened to a coffin.

In prison, and here be coffined when I die.

5 Here are God's conduits, grave divines; and here
Nature's secretary, the Philosopher;
And jolly statesmen, which teach how to tie
The sinews of a city's mystic body;
Here gathering chroniclers, and by them stand
10 Giddy fantastic poets of each land.
Shall I leave all this constant company,
And follow headlong, wild uncertain thee?
First swear by thy best love in earnest
(If thou which lov'st all, canst love any best)
15 Thou wilt not leave me in the middle street,
Though some more spruce companion thou dost
   meet;
Not though a captain do come in thy way,
Bright parcel gilt, with forty dead men's pay;
Not though a brisk, perfumed, pert courtier
20 Deign with a nod thy courtesy to answer;
Nor come a velvet Justice with a long
Great train of blue-coats, twelve or fourteen strong,
Wilt thou grin or fawn on him, or prepare
A speech to court his beauteous son and heir.
25 For better or worse take me, or leave me:
To take and leave me is adultery.
Oh, monstrous, superstitious puritan,
Of refined manners, yet ceremonial man,
That when thou meet'st one, with inquiring eyes

---

6   *the Philosopher*: i.e. Aristotle (but possibly generic).
7   *jolly*: fine, excellent.
18 *parcel gilt*: partly gilded (with pun on 'guilt'). *dead men's pay*: pay due to dead soldiers; dishonest officers kept the names of dead men on their rolls for their own profit.
22 *blue-coats*: servants.
27 *superstitious puritan*: over-scrupulous purist.
28 *yet ceremonial man*: nevertheless a lover of ceremony.

Dost search, and like a needy broker, prize   30
The silk and gold he wears, and to that rate
So high, or low, dost raise thy formal hat;
That wilt consort none, until thou have known
What lands he hath in hope, or of his own,
As though all thy companions should make thee   35
Jointures, and marry thy dear company.
Why shouldst thou (that dost not only approve,
But in rank itchy lust, desire and love
The nakedness and bareness to enjoy,
Of thy plump muddy whore, or prostitute boy)   40
Hate virtue, though she be naked and bare?
At birth and death our bodies naked are;
And till our souls be unapparellèd
Of bodies, they from bliss are banishèd.
Man's first blest state was naked; when by sin   45
He lost that, yet he was clothed but in beast's skin;
And in this coarse attire, which I now wear,
With God, and with the muses, I confer.
    But since thou, like a contrite penitent,
Charitably warned of thy sins, dost repent   50
These vanities and giddinesses, lo,
I shut my chamber door, and come, let's go!
But sooner may a cheap whore, who hath been
Worn by as many several men in sin
As are black feathers, or musk-colour hose,   55

30   *prize*: apprize.
32   *hat* (1635): 'hate' (1633).
36   *Jointures*: estates held jointly by husband and wife.
38   *rank*: licentious.
39   *bareness* (MSS.): 'barrenness' (1633).
40   *muddy*: foul.
47   *this coarse attire*: i.e. that of the scholar.
50   *warned* (1635): 'warmed' (1633).
55   *black . . . hose*: These were much in fashion. *musk-colour*: reddish brown.

Name her child's right true father, 'mongst all those;
Sooner may one guess who shall bear away
The Infant of London, heir to an India;
And sooner may a gulling weather spy
60 By drawing forth heaven's scheme tell certainly
What fashioned hats, or ruffs, or suits next year
Our subtle-witted antic youths will wear,
Than thou, when thou depart'st from me, can show
Whither, why, when, or with whom thou wouldst go.
65 But how shall I be pardoned my offence,
That thus have sinned against my conscience?
    Now we are in the street; he first of all,
Improvidently proud, creeps to the wall,
And so imprisoned and hemmed in by me,
70 Sells for a little state his liberty;
Yet though he cannot skip forth now to greet
Every fine silken painted fool we meet,
He them to him with amorous smiles allures,
And grins, smacks, shrugs, and such an itch endures
75 As 'prentices, or schoolboys, which do know
Of some gay sport abroad, yet dare not go.
And as fiddlers stop lowest at highest sound,
So to the most brave stoops he nigh'st the ground.

58 *Infant*: properly a prince(-ss) of Spain; here the richest
    heir(-ess) in London, who is, consequently, the most
    sought after in marriage.
59 *weather spy*: weather prophet, astrologer.
60 *heaven's scheme*: a diagram showing positions of the
    heavenly bodies; a horoscope. *scheme* (1635): 'scenes' (1633).
62 *subtle-witted* (MSS.): 'subtle wittied' (1633). *antic*: fantastic.
68 *to the wall*: i.e. to the most favoured side of the pavement.
70 *state*: dignity. *his* (1635): 'high' (1633).
73 *them* (1635): 'then' (1633).
77 *lowest*: i.e. furthest from the neck and nearest the bottom
    of the violin.
78 *brave*: splendid, grand. *stoops* (1635): 'stooped' (1633).

But to a grave man he doth move no more
Than the wise politic horse would heretofore,   80
Or thou, O elephant, or ape, wilt do
When any names the King of Spain to you.
Now leaps he upright, jogs me, and cries, 'Do you see
Yonder well-favoured youth?' 'Which?' 'Oh, 'tis he
That dances so divinely.' 'Oh,' said I,   85
'Stand still, must you dance here for company?'
He drooped, we went, till one which did excel
Th' Indians in drinking his tobacco well
Met us; they talked; I whispered, 'Let us go,
'T may be you smell him not, truly I do.'   90
He hears not me, but on the other side
A many-coloured peacock having spied,
Leaves him and me; I for my lost sheep stay;
He follows, overtakes, goes on the way,
Saying, 'Him, whom I last left, all repute   95
For his device in handsoming a suit,
To judge of lace, pink, panes, print, cut, and pleat,
Of all the court to have the best conceit.'
'Our dull comedians want him: let him go;
But oh, God strengthen thee, why stoop'st thou so?'   100
'Why? he hath travelled.' 'Long?' 'No, but to me'
(Which understand none) 'he doth seem to be

79–82 The performing horse, elephant, and ape were well-
    known curiosities in the early 1590s. They were trained
    to respond to, or ignore, audience's requests, and to
    express loyalty to Elizabeth and disapproval of the King
    of Spain.
81–2 Reproduced from 1635 ed. (omitted 1633).
88 *drinking*: inhaling.
95 *all* (1635): 's'all' (1633). *repute*: consider.
96 *device*: resourcefulness. *handsoming*: embellishing.
97 *pink*: decorative eyelet. *panes*: ornamental strips, slashes.
    print: crimping of pleats, as in a ruff. *cut*: a slash.
98 *conceit*: judgement.
99 *Our dull comedians want him*: i.e. they need him for their
    repertoire.

Perfect French, and Italian.' I replied,
'So is the pox.' He answered not, but spied
105 More men of sort, of parts, and qualities.
At last his love he in a window spies,
And like light dew exhaled, he flings from me,
Violently ravished, to his lechery.
Many were there, he could command no more;
110 He quarrelled, fought, bled; and turned out of door,
Directly came to me hanging the head,
And constantly a while must keep his bed.

Poems, 1633

Satire III

Kind pity chokes my spleen; brave scorn forbids
Those tears to issue which swell my eyelids;
I must not laugh, nor weep sins, and be wise;
Can railing then cure these worn maladies?
5 Is not our mistress, fair religion,
As worthy of all our soul's devotion,
As virtue was in the first blinded age?
Are not heaven's joys as valiant to assuage
Lusts, as earth's honour was to them? Alas,
10 As we do them in means, shall they surpass
Us in the end? And shall thy father's spirit
Meet blind philosophers in heaven, whose merit
Of strict life may be imputed faith, and hear

107 *like light dew exhaled*: i.e. he is drawn to his lady as dew is
drawn up to the sun.
108 *lechery* (1635): 'liberty' (1633).
111 *hanging the head*: The phrase has sexual reference.
SATIRE III: Probably written 1594–5.
1 *spleen*: bitter mockery. The spleen was considered the
seat of both mirth and melancholy.
3 *weep*: lament.
7 *first blinded age*: i.e. pagan times.
9 *them*: i.e. pagans, who devoted themselves to the virtue of
earthly fame.
12 *blind*: i.e. pagan.

Thee, whom he taught so easy ways and near
To follow, damned? Oh, if thou dar'st, fear this;   15
This fear great courage and high valour is.
Dar'st thou aid mutinous Dutch, and dar'st thou lay
Thee in ships, wooden sepulchres, a prey
To leaders' rage, to storms, to shot, to dearth?
Dar'st thou dive seas, and dungeons of the earth?   20
Hast thou courageous fire to thaw the ice
Of frozen North discoveries? and thrice
Colder than salamanders, like divine
Children in th' oven, fires of Spain, and the Line,
Whose countries limbecks to our bodies be,   25
Canst thou for gain bear? and must every he
Which cries not, 'Goddess!' to thy mistress, draw,
Or eat thy poisonous words? Courage of straw!
O desperate coward, wilt thou seem bold, and
To thy foes and his, who made thee to stand   30
Sentinel in his world's garrison, thus yield,
And for forbidden wars leave th' appointed field?
Know thy foes: the foul Devil, whom thou
Strivest to please, for hate, not love, would allow
Thee fain his whole realm, to be quit; and as   35

17 *mutinous Dutch*: The Low Countries, in revolt against
    Spain, were aided by English troops in the 1580s and
    1590s.
23 *salamanders*: fabulous creatures whose bodies were suffi-
    ciently cold to enable them to withstand fire.
23–4 *divine Children in th' oven*: i.e. Shadrach, Meshach, and Abed-
    nego, who were thrown by Nebuchadnezzar into a
    furnace and survived unharmed (Dan. 3.19–28).
24 *Spain*: i.e. the Spanish Inquisition. *the Line*: the equator.
25 *limbecks*: stills.
27 *draw*: i.e. fight a duel.
30, 31 *his*: i.e. God's.
32 *forbidden wars*: i.e. wars for earthly honour.
33 *foes*: viz. the Devil, the world, and the flesh. *foes: the foul
    Devil* (MSS.): 'foe, the foul Devil h' is' (1633).
34–5 *would . . . quit*: i.e. would willingly give you his entire
    kingdom to be free of the debts he owes you for your
    service.

The world's all parts wither away and pass,
So the world's self, thy other loved foe, is
In her decrepit wane, and thou loving this,
Dost love a withered and worn strumpet; last,
40   Flesh, itself's death, and joys, which flesh can taste,
Thou lovest; and thy fair goodly soul, which doth
Give this flesh power to taste joy, thou dost loathe.
   Seek true religion. Oh, where? *Mirreus*,
Thinking her unhoused here and fled from us,
45   Seeks her at Rome; there, because he doth know
That she was there a thousand years ago;
He loves her rags so, as we here obey
The statecloth where the prince sat yesterday.
Crantz to such brave loves will not be enthralled,
50   But loves her only, who at Geneva is called
Religion, plain, simple, sullen, young,
Contemptuous, yet unhandsome; as among
Lecherous humours, there is one that judges
No wenches wholesome but coarse country drudges.
55   *Graius* stays still at home here, and because
Some preachers, vile ambitious bawds, and laws,
Still new like fashions, bid him think that she
Which dwells with us is only perfect, he
Embraceth her whom his godfathers will

---

40   *itself's* (MSS.): 'itself' (1633).
43–69 Various religious persuasions are exemplified in *Mirreus* (Roman Catholic), *Crantz* (Calvinist), *Graius* (Anglican), *Phrygius* (who rejects all beliefs), and *Gracchus* (an eclectic).
44   *here*: i.e. in England. *here* (1635): 'her' (1633).
47   *her* (MSS.): 'the' (1633). *rags*: remnants. *obey*: bow to.
48   *statecloth*: canopy over the throne.
49   *brave*: showy.
51   *sullen*: sombre.
53   *Lecherous humours*: lechers' fancies.
56–7 *laws, Still new*: Many laws were passed in Elizabeth's reign with the aim of establishing the English Church.
57   *bid* (MSS.): 'bids' (1633).
58   *only*: alone.

Tender to him, being tender; as wards still   60
Take such wives as their guardians offer, or
Pay values. Careless *Phrygius* doth abhor
All, because all cannot be good; as one,
Knowing some women whores, dares marry none.
Gracchus loves all as one, and thinks that so   65
As women do in divers countries go
In divers habits, yet are still one kind,
So doth, so is religion; and this blind-
ness too much light breeds. But unmovèd thou
Of force must one, and forced but one allow,   70
And the right; ask thy father which is she,
Let him ask his; though truth and falsehood be
Near twins, yet truth a little elder is;
Be busy to seek her; believe me this,
He's not of none, nor worst, that seeks the best.   75
To adore, or scorn an image, or protest,
May all be bad; doubt wisely; in strange way
To stand inquiring right is not to stray;
To sleep, or run wrong is. On a huge hill,
Cragg'd and steep, truth stands, and he that will   80
Reach her, about must and about must go,
And what the hill's suddenness resists, win so;
Yet strive so, that before age, death's twilight,

---

60   *Tender . . . tender*: offer to him as an infant.
62   *Pay values*: pay fines, i.e. those imposed on a ward who
      refused an arranged marriage (here analogous with fines
      imposed on one who did not attend parish church).
68–9 *this . . . breeds*: i.e. too much light breeds this blindness.
70   *Of force*: of necessity.
71–2 *ask . . . his*: The assumption is that one can find true re-
      ligion by recalling the earliest and purest state of the
      church. Cf. Deut. 32.7.
75   *none*: i.e. no religion.
76   *protest*: i.e. as a Protestant.
77   *way*: road.
82   And in this way overcome the resistance which the hill's
      steepness offers to his ascent.

Thy soul rest, for none can work in that night.
85 To will implies delay, therefore now do:
Hard deeds, the body's pains; hard knowledge too
The mind's endeavours reach, and mysteries
Are like the sun, dazzling, yet plain to all eyes.
Keep the truth which thou hast found; men do not
  stand
90 In so ill case that God hath with his hand
Signed kings blank charters to kill whom they hate;
Nor are they vicars, but hangmen, to fate.
Fool and wretch, wilt thou let thy soul be tied
To man's laws, by which she shall not be tried
95 At the last day? Will it then boot thee
To say a Philip, or a Gregory,
A Harry, or a Martin taught thee this?
Is not this excuse for mere contraries,
Equally strong? cannot both sides say so?
That thou mayest rightly obey power, her bounds
100   know;
Those past, her nature and name is changed; to be
Then humble to her is idolatry.
As streams are, power is; those blest flowers that dwell
At the rough stream's calm head thrive and do well,
105 But having left their roots, and themselves given
To the stream's tyrannous rage, alas, are driven
Through mills and rocks and woods, and at last, almost
Consumed in going, in the sea are lost:
So perish souls which more choose men's unjust
110 Power from God claimed, than God himself to trust.

Poems, 1633

92 Nor are they the vicegerents, but the instruments, of
   fate.
96-7 *Philip . . . Gregory . . . Harry . . . Martin*: Philip II of Spain;
   Pope Gregory XIII (or XIV); Henry VIII; Martin Luther.
98 *mere*: complete.

THOMAS LODGE

A Fig for Momus

To Master E. Dig[by]
Satire I

Digby, whence comes it that the world begins
To wink at follies and to soothe up sins?
Can other reason be alleged than this,
The world soothes sin because it sinful is?
The man that lives by bribes and usury   5
Winks, like a fox, at loathsome lechery;
Craft gives ambition leave to lay his plot,
And cross his friend because he sounds him not;
All men are willing with the world to halt,
But no man takes delight to know his fault.   10
He is a gallant fit to serve my lord
Which claws and soothes him up at every word;
That cries, when his lame poesy he hears,
''Tis rare, my lord, 'twill pass the nicest ears.'
This makes *Anphidius* welcome to good cheer,   15
And spend his master forty pounds a year,
And keep his plaice-mouthed wife in welts and guards,
For flattery can never want rewards.
And therefore *Humphrey* holds this paradox:

A FIG FOR MOMUS: i.e. In defiance of the carping critic
    (Momus was god of fault-finding and ridicule).
SATIRE 1: *E. Dig[by]*: probably Everard Digby, Master of
    Ceremonies at Lincoln's Inn, 1572–3.
2   *soothe up*: gloss over.
8   *sounds*: fathoms.
9   *halt*: play false.
12   *claws*: flatters.
14   *pass*: be approved by.
16   *his master*: i.e. of his master's money.
17   *plaice-mouthed*: i.e. narrow-mouthed; half-witted. *welts
    and guards*: frills and trimmings.

20 'Tis better be a fool than be a fox;
For folly is rewarded and respected,
Where subtlety is hated and rejected;
Self-will doth frown when honest zeal reproves,
To hear good counsel error never loves.

25 Tell pursy *Rollus*, lusking in his bed,
That humours by excessive ease are bred,
That sloth corrupts, and chokes the vital sprites,
And kills the memory, and hurts the lights:
He will not stick, after a cup of sack,

30 To flout his counsellor behind his back.
For with a world of mischiefs and offence,
Unbridled will rebels against the sense,
And thinketh it no little prejudice
To be reproved, though by good advice;

35 For wicked men repine their sins to hear,
And folly flings, if counsel touch him near.
Tell *Sextus*' wife, whose shoes are underlaid,
Her gait is girlish, and her foot is splayed:
She'll rail with open mouth, as Martial doth;

40 But if you praise her, though you speak not sooth,
You shall be welcome both to bed and board,
And use her self, her husband, and his sword.
Tell blear-eyed *Linus* that his sight is clear,
He'll pawn himself to buy thee bread and beer;

45 But touch me *Quintus* with his stinking breath,
The dastard will defy thee to the death.
Thus, though men's great deformities be known,

---

25 *pursy*: fat. *lusking*: lazing.
26 *humours*: i.e. physical and mental disorders brought about
   by an imbalance in the four 'humours' or bodily fluids.
28 *lights*: lungs.
33 *prejudice*: injury.
36 *flings*: dances about wildly.
37 *underlaid*: raised up with false soles (as was the fashion).
39 *Martial*: the Roman epigrammatist (c. A.D. 40–104).
45 *touch*: twit. *me*: ethical dative.

They grieve to hear and take them for their own.
Find me a niggard that doth want the shift
To call his cursèd avarice good thrift;   50
A rake-hell, sworn to prodigality,
That dares not term it liberality;
A lecher that hath lost both flesh and fame,
That holds not lechery a pleasant game.
And why? because they cloak their shame by this,   55
And will not see the horror what it is;
And cunning sin, being clad in virtue's shape,
Flies much reproof, and many scorns doth 'scape.
Last day I chanced, in crossing of the street,
With *Diffilus*, the innkeeper, to meet;   60
He wore a silken nightcap on his head,
And looked as if he had been lately dead.
I asked him how he fared: 'Not well,' quoth he,
'An ague this two months hath troubled me.'
I let him pass, and laughed to hear his 'scuse;   65
For I knew well he had the pox by *Luce*,
And wore his nightcap ribboned at the ears,
Because of late he sweat away his hairs;
But had a stranger chanced to spy him then,
He might have deemed him for a civil man.   70
Thus with the world the world dissembles still,
And to their own confusions follow ill,
Holding it true felicity to fly,
Not from the sin, but from the seeing eye.
Then in this world who winks at each estate   75
Hath found the means to make him fortunate:
To colour hate with kindness, to defraud
In private those in public we applaud;
To keep this rule, kaw me and I kaw thee,

49 *shift*: expedient.
70 *civil*: sober, decent.
75 *winks at each estate*: connives with men of each degree.
79 *kaw*: flatter (the phrase is proverbial).

80 To play the saints, whereas we devils be.
    Whate'er men do, let them not reprehend,
    For cunning knaves will cunning knaves defend.
    Truth is pursued by hate, then is he wise
    That to the world his worldly wit applies;
85 What, is he wise? aye, as Amphestus strong,
    That burnt his face because his beard was long.

A Fig for Momus, 1595

JOSEPH HALL

Virgidemiarum
Book II, Satire iii

    Who doubts the laws fell down from heaven's height,
    Like to some gliding star in winter's night?
    Themis, the scribe of God, did long agone
    Engrave them deep in during marble stone,
5   And cast them down on this unruly clay,
    That men might know to rule and to obey.
    But now their characters depravèd been,
    By them that would make gain of others' sin;
    And now hath wrong so masterèd the right
10 That they live best that on wrong's offal light;
    So loathly fly, that lives on gallèd wound,
    And scabby festers inwardly unsound,
    Feeds fatter with that pois'nous carrion
    Than they that haunt the healthy limbs alone.
15 Woe to the weal where many lawyers be!

85–6 Amphestus, who suffered because of his long beard (pre-
        sumably his wisdom), has not been identified.
VIRGIDEMIARUM: 'Of harvests of rods' (i.e. the whipping
        rods of the satirist).
BOOK II, SATIRE III:
3   *Themis*: goddess of law and justice.
11 *gallèd*: chafed.
15 *weal*: state.

For there is sure much store of malady.
'Twas truly said, and truly was foreseen,
The fat kine are devourèd of the lean.
Genus and Species long since barefoot went,
Upon their ten toes in wild wanderment, 20
Whiles father Bartol on his footcloth rode,
Upon high pavement gaily silver-strowed.
Each home-bred science percheth in the chair,
Whiles sacred arts grovel on the groundsel bare.
Since peddling barbarisms gan be in request, 25
Nor classic tongues, nor learning, found no rest.
The crouching client, with low-bended knee,
And many 'Worships', and fair flattery,
Tells on his tale as smoothly as him list,
But still the lawyer's eye squints on his fist; 30
If that seem linèd with a larger fee,
Doubt not the suit, the law is plain for thee;
Tho must he buy his vainer hope with price,
Disclout his crowns, and thank him for advice.
So have I seen in a tempestuous stour 35
Some briar-bush showing shelter from the shower
Unto the hopeful sheep, that fain would hide
His fleecy coat from that same angry tide;

17–18 Referring to Pharaoh's dream, Gen. 41.1–4.
19 *Genus and Species*: nicknames for scholars, derived from terms in Logic.
20 *in wild wanderment*: wandering desolate.
21 *Bartol*: Bartolus of Sassoferrato, Professor of Law at the University of Perugia 1342/3–1357. *footcloth*: rich cloth spread across a horse's back to the ground, as a mark of dignity.
22 *Upon high pavement*: i.e. in the middle of the street, where men of rank rode.
23 *home-bred*: earth-born.
24 *groundsel*: ground.
25 *peddling*: contemptible.
33 *Tho*: then.
34 *Disclout*: unwrap from a handkerchief. *thank him*: i.e. with the crowns.
35 *stour*: tumult.

The ruthless briar, regardless of his plight,
40 Lays hold upon the fleece he should acquit,
And takes advantage of the careless prey,
That thought she in securer shelter lay.
The day is fair, the sheep would fare to feed:
The tyrant briar holds fast his shelter's meed,
45 And claims it for the fee of his defence,
So robs the sheep, in favour's fair pretence.

Book II, Satire vi

A gentle squire would gladly entertain
Into his house some trencher-chaplain,
Some willing man that might instruct his sons,
And that would stand to good conditions.
5 First, that he lie upon the truckle-bed,
Whiles his young master lieth o'er his head.
Secondly, that he do on no default
Ever presume to sit above the salt.
Third, that he never change his trencher twice.
10 Fourth, that he use all comely courtesies,
Sit bare at meals, and one half rise and wait.
Last, that he never his young master beat
But he must ask his mother to define
How many jerks she would his breech should line.
15 All these observed, he could contented be
To give five marks and winter livery.

44 *shelter's meed*: reward for having given shelter.
BOOK II, SATIRE VI:
2 *trencher-chaplain*: domestic chaplain.
5 *truckle-bed*: small bed on wheels, fitting under ordinary bed; in universities it was used by the tutor's pupil.
8 *above the salt*: i.e. at the higher, more favoured part of the table.
9 *trencher*: plate.
11 *bare*: bareheaded. *wait*: serve.
14 *jerks*: strokes.
16 *marks*: a mark = 66p.

Book III, Satire vi

When *Gullion* died (who knows not *Gullion*?)
And his dry soul arrived at Acheron,
He fair besought the ferryman of hell
That he might drink to dead Pantagruel.
Charon was afraid lest thirsty *Gullion*   5
Would have drunk dry the river Acheron,
Yet last consented for a little hire;
And down he dips his chops deep in the mire,
And drinks, and drinks, and swallows in the stream,
Until the shallow shores all naked seem.   10
Yet still he drinks, nor can the boatman's cries,
Nor crabbèd oars, nor prayers make him rise;
So long he drinks, till the black caravel
Stands still, fast gravelled on the mud of hell.
There stand they still, nor can go nor retire,   15
Though greedy ghosts quick passage did require;
Yet stand they still, as though they lay at rode,
Till *Gullion* his bladder would unload.
They stand, and wait, and pray for that good hour,
Which when it came, they sailèd to the shore.   20
But never since dareth the ferryman
Once entertain the ghost of *Gullion*.
Drink on, dry soul, and pledge Sir *Gullion*;
Drink to all healths, but drink not to thine own.

    •   •   •   •   •   •   •

Virgidemiarum, 1597

BOOK III, SATIRE VI: The poem is apparently unfinished.
  4 *Pantagruel*: the last of the giants, in Rabelais' *Gargantua and Pantagruel* (1532–64); his name means 'the all-thirsty one'.
13 *caravel*: ship.
17 *at rode*: at anchor.

JOHN MARSTON

The Scourge of Villainy

Satire VII
A Cynic Satire

'A man, a man, a kingdom for a man!'
'Why, how now, currish mad Athenian?
Thou Cynic dog, seest not streets do swarm
With troops of men?' 'No, no, for Circe's charm
5   Hath turned them all to swine. I never shall
Think those same Samian saws authentical,
But rather, I dare swear, the souls of swine
Do live in men; for that same radiant shine,
That lustre wherewith nature's nature decked
10   Our intellectual part, that gloss, is soiled
With staining spots of vile impiety
And muddy dirt of sensuality.
These are no men but apparitions,
Ignes fatui, glow-worms, fictions,
15   Meteors, rats of Nilus, fantasies,
Colosses, pictures, shades, resemblances.

                              'Ho, Linceus!
Seest thou yon gallant in the sumptuous clothes,
How brisk, how spruce, how gorgeously he shows?
20   Note his French herring-bones, but note no more,
Unless thou spy his fair appendant whore

THE SCOURGE OF VILLAINY, SATIRE VII: The satire is in the
    form of a dialogue between Diogenes (the Athenian
    Cynic philosopher) and Linceus (a passer-by).
1   Cf. *Richard III* V.iv.7. It was said that Diogenes searched
    Athens for men but claimed he found only scoundrels.
6   *Samian saws*: teachings of Pythagoras of Samos, that the
    souls of men transmigrated into animals.
14   *Ignes fatui*: will-o'-the-wisps.
20   *French herring-bones*: French cloth with herring-bone pat-
    tern; syphilis (the 'French disease') which attacked the
    bones may be implied.

That lackeys him. Mark nothing but his clothes,
His new-stamped complement, his cannon oaths;
Mark those, for nought but such lewd viciousness
E'er gracèd him, save Sodom beastliness.   25
Is this a man? Nay, an incarnate devil,
That struts in vice and glorieth in evil.
    'A man, a man!' 'Peace, Cynic, yon is one,
A complete soul of all perfection.'
'What, mean'st thou him that walks all open-breasted, 30
Drawn through the ear with ribbons, plumy-crested?
He that doth snort in fat-fed luxury,
And gapes for some grinding monopoly?
He that in effeminate invention,
In beastly source of all pollution,   35
In riot, lust, and fleshly seeming-sweetness,
Sleeps sound, secure under the shade of greatness?
Mean'st thou that senseless, sensual epicure,
That sink of filth, that guzzle most impure?
What, he? Linceus, on my word thus presume,   40
He's nought but clothes and scenting sweet perfume.
His very soul, assure thee, Linceus,
Is not so big as is an atomus.
Nay, he is spriteless; sense or soul hath none,
Since last Medusa turned him to a stone.   45
    'A man, a man! Lo, yonder I espy
The shade of Nestor in sad gravity;
Since old *Silenus* brake his ass's back,
He now is forced his paunch and guts to pack
In a fair tumbrel.' 'Why, sour satirist,   50

23 *complement*: ceremoniousness.
30 *open-breasted*: a sign of effeminacy.
33 *gapes*: craves.
39 *guzzle*: gutter.
47 *Nestor*: old wise general in the Trojan War. *sad*: solemn.
48 *Silenus*: named after the Greek demi-god, Bacchus's com-
    panion, who was so fat he broke the back of the ass he rode.
50 *tumbrel*: dung-cart (i.e. his coach).

Canst thou unman him? Here I dare insist
And soothly say he is a perfect soul,
Eats nectar, drinks ambrosia, sans control.
An inundation of felicity
55 Fats him with honour and huge treasury.'
'Canst thou not, Linceus, cast thy searching eye
And spy his imminent catastrophe?
He's but a sponge, and shortly needs must leese
His wrong-got juice, when greatness' fist shall squeeze
60 His liquor out. Would not some shallow head,
That is with seeming shadows only fed,
Swear yon same damask-coat, yon guarded man,
Were some grave sober Cato Utican?
When let him but in judgement's sight uncase,
65 He's nought but budge, old guards, brown fox-fur face.
He hath no soul the which the Stagirite
Termed rational; for beastly appetite,
Base dunghill thoughts, and sensual action
Hath made him lose that fair creation;
70 And now no man, since Circe's magic charm
Hath turned him to a maggot, that doth swarm
In tainted flesh, whose foul corruption
Is his fair food, whose generation
Another's ruin. Oh, Canaan's dread curse,
75 To live in people's sins! nay, far more worse,
To muck rank hate. But sirrah, Linceus,

58 *leese*: release.
62–76 Details here are traditionally associated with the figure of the Usurer.
62 *guarded*: elaborately trimmed.
63 *Cato Utican*: Cato of Utica (95–46 B.C.), orator and soldier, the classical embodiment of civic and moral rectitude.
64 *uncase*: strip off.
65 *budge*: inferior fur from lamb's wool. *guards*: trimmings. *face*: facing.
66 *the Stagirite*: i.e. Aristotle of Stagira.
74 *Canaan's dread curse*: i.e. the curse of usurers and usury.
76 *muck*: manure, fertilize.

Seest thou that troop that now affronteth us?
They are nought but eels, that never will appear
Till that tempestuous winds or thunder tear
Their slimy beds. But prithee, stay awhile;　　　　80
Look, yon comes John-a-noke and John-a-stile.
They are nought but slow-paced dilatory pleas,
Demure demurrers, still striving to appease
Hot zealous love. The language that they speak
Is the pure barbarous blacksaunt of the Gete;　　　85
Their only skill rests in collusions,
Abatements, stopples, inhibitions.
Heavy-paced jades, dull-pated jobbernowls!
Quick in delays, checking with vain controls
Fair justice' course; vile necessary evils,　　　　90
Smooth seem-saints, yet damned incarnate devils!
　'Far be it from my sharp satiric muse
Those grave and reverend legists to abuse
That aid Astraea, that do further right;
But these Megaeras that inflame despite,　　　　95
That broach deep rancour, that do study still
To ruin right, that they their paunch may fill
With Irus' blood; these Furies I do mean,
These hedgehogs, that disturb Astraea's scene.

81　*John-a-noke and John-a-stile*: fictitious names for parties in
　　lawcases; here applied to lawyers themselves.
83　*demurrers*: pleadings which temporarily halt a lawsuit
　　until certain issues have been settled.
85　*blacksaunt*: discordant noise (from 'black sanctus', a bur-
　　lesque hymn). *Gete*: i.e. savage. The Getae were the bar-
　　barians living near the Black Sea, among whom Ovid
　　was forced to live in exile.
86–7 *in collusions . . . inhibitions*: i.e. in legal jargon. The terms are
　　technical ones for certain offences and legal procedures.
88　*jobbernowls*: blockheads.
94　*Astraea*: goddess of equity.
95　*Megaeras*: i.e. Furies, dreaded deities of retribution (of
　　whom Megaera was one).
98　*Irus*: a beggar in the *Odyssey*; here, a poor man.
99　*hedgehogs*: callously inconsiderate people.

100 'A man, a man!' 'Peace, Cynic, yon's a man;
Behold yon sprightly dread Mavortian;
With him I stop thy currish barking chops.'
'What, mean'st thou him that in his swaggering slops
Wallows unbracèd all along the street?

105 He that salutes each gallant he doth meet
With "Farewell, sweet captain; kind heart, adieu!"
He that last night tumbling, thou didst view,
From out the Great Man's Head, and thinking still
He had been sentinel of warlike Brill,

110 Cries out, "Qui va là? zounds, qui?" and out doth draw
His transformed poniard to a syringe straw,
And stabs the drawer. What, that ringo root?
Mean'st thou that wasted leg, puff-bombast boot?
What, he that's drawn and quarterèd with lace?

115 That Westphalian gammon, clove-stuck face?
Why, he is nought but huge blaspheming oaths,
Swart snout, big looks, misshapen Switzers' clothes.
Weak meagre lust hath now consumèd quite
And wasted clean away his martial sprite;

120 Enfeebling riot, all vices' confluence,
Hath eaten out that sacred influence
Which made him man.
That divine part is soaked away in sin,

---

101 *Mavortian*: 'Mars-like man'.
103 *slops*: baggy breeches.
108 *the Great Man's Head*: a tavern (probably one of many named The Saracen's Head).
109 *Brill*: garrison in Flanders manned by British troops.
111 His poniard scabbard contains a syringe used for sexual purposes.
112 *drawer*: tapster. *ringo root*: eryngo, root of the sea holly, used as an aphrodisiac.
113 *puff-bombast*: stuffed.
115 *Westphalian gammon*: Westphalia produced high quality ham. *clove-stuck face*: His face, disfigured by the pox, resembles an orange stuck with cloves, used (ironically) to ward off infection.
117 *misshapen Switzers' clothes*: large breeches of the Swiss.

In sensual lust; and midnight bezzling,
Rank inundation of luxuriousness   125
Have tainted him with such gross beastliness
That now the seat of that celestial essence
Is all possessed with Naples' pestilence.
Fat peace and dissolute impiety
Have lullèd him in such security   130
That now, let whirlwinds and confusion tear
The centre of our state, let giants rear
Hill upon hill, let Western Termagant
Shake heaven's vault: he with his occupant
Are clinged so close, like dew-worms in the morn,   135
That he'll not stir till out his guts are torn
With eating filth. *Tubrio*, snort on, snort on!
Till thou art waked with sad confusion.

   'Now rail no more at my sharp Cynic sound,
Thou brutish world that, in all vileness drowned,   140
Hast lost thy soul; for nought but shades I see;
Resemblances of men inhabit thee.

   'Yon tissue-slop, yon holy-crossèd pane
Is but a water spaniel that will fain
And kiss the water whilst it pleasures him,   145
But being once arrivèd at the brim,
He shakes it off.

   'Yon in the cap'ring cloak, a mimic ape
That only strives to seem another's shape.

   'Yon's Aesop's ass; yon sad civility   150
Is but an ox that with base drudgery

---

124 *bezzling*: drunken revelry.
128 *Naples' pestilence*: i.e. syphilis.
133 *Termagant*: turbulent god of the Saracens.
134 *occupant*: whore.
137 *eating filth*: i.e. the filthy disease which eats him up.
143 *tissue-slop*: baggy breeches. *holy-crossèd pane*: doublet orna-
     mented with criss-crossed laces.
144 *fain*: be glad. 'fawn' (1599).
150 *Aesop's ass*: i.e. ass in a lion's skin, from Aesop's fable.

Ears up the land, whilst some gilt ass doth chaw
The golden wheat, he well apaid with straw.
   'Yon's but a muck-hill overspread with snow,
155 Which with that veil doth even as fairly show
As the green meads, whose native outward fair
Breathes sweet perfumes into the neighbour air.
   'Yon effeminate sanguine Ganymede
Is but a beaver, hunted for the bed.'
160   'Peace, Cynic, see what yonder doth approach.'
'A cart? a tumbrel?' 'No, a badgèd coach.'
'What's in 't? some man?' 'No, nor yet womankind,
But a celestial angel fair refined.'
'The devil as soon! Her mask so hinders me
165 I cannot see her beauty's deity.
Now that is off, she is so vizarded,
So steeped in lemons' juice, so surphulèd,
I cannot see her face. Under one hood
Two faces, but I never understood
170 Or saw one face under two hoods till now!
'Tis the right semblance of old Janus' brow.
Her mask, her vizard, her loose-hanging gown
For her loose-lying body, her bright spangled crown,
Her long slit sleeve, stiff busk, puff-farthingale
175 Is all that makes her thus angelical.
Alas, her soul struts round about her neck,

152 *Ears up*: ploughs. *chaw*: chew.
153 *apaid*: contented.
158 *sanguine Ganymede*: amorous catamite.
159 The beaver was hunted to make bed-covers; the 'Gany-
mede' is likewise hunted to cover a bed.
161 *badgèd*: emblazoned.
166 *vizarded*: masked (with cosmetics).
167 *surphulèd*: painted with make-up.
171 *Janus*: god of ways and openings, who had two faces.
174 *busk*: corset. *puff-farthingale*: frame extending the dress out
from the hips.
176–8 *soul . . . seat of sense . . . intellectual*: referring to the three
parts of the soul: appetitive, sensitive, and intellectual.
176 *struts round about her neck*: i.e. is her ruff.

Her seat of sense is her rebato set,
Her intellectual is a feignèd niceness:
Nothing but clothes and simpering preciseness.
   'Out on these puppets, painted images,   180
Haberdashers' shops, torchlight maskeries,
Perfuming pans, Dutch ancients, glow-worms bright,
That soil our souls and damp our reason's light!
Away, away, hence, coachman! go enshrine
Thy new-glazed puppet in Port Esquiline.   185
Blush, *Martia*, fear not or look pale—all's one:
Margara keeps thy set complexion.
   'Sure, I ne'er think those axioms to be true,
That souls of men from that great Soul ensue
And of his essence do participate   190
As 'twere by pipes, when so degenerate,
So adverse, is our nature's motion
To his immaculate condition,
That such foul filth from such fair purity,
Such sensual acts from such a Deity,   195
Can ne'er proceed. But if that dream were so,
Then sure the slime that from our souls do flow
Have stopped those pipes by which it was conveyed,
And now no human creatures, once disrayed
Of that fair gem.   200
Beasts' sense, plants' growth, like being, as a stone;
But out, alas, our cognizance is gone.'

The Scourge of Villainy, 1598

177 *rebato*: frame supporting the ruff.
182 *Dutch ancients*: i.e. ensigns of wantonness.
185 *new-glazed*: newly varnished. *Port Esquiline*: i.e. the dung-
     hill near the Esquiline Gate of Rome.
187 *Margara*: a cosmetic.
199 *now no human creatures*: i.e. men are no longer *human* beings.
     disrayed: despoiled.
200 *that fair gem*: i.e. reason.
201 I.e. men have senses (like beasts), can grow (like plants),
     and can exist (like a stone).
202 *cognizance*: understanding (the attribute peculiar to man-
     kind).

EVERARD GUILPIN

Skialetheia

Satire IV

What a scald humour is this jealous care,
Which turns a man to a familiar!
See how *Trebatio* yonder haunts his wife,
And dares not lose sight of her for his life.
5   And now there's one speaks to her, mark his grace,
See how he bastes himself in his own grease.
Note what a squint askew he casts, as he
Already saw his head's horned-armoury.
Foul-weather jealousy to a forward spring
10   Makes weeds grow rank, but spoils a better thing;
Sows tares, 'gainst harvest, in the fields of love,
And doggèd humour Dog-days-like doth prove,
Scorching love's glorious world with glowing tongue;
A serpent by which love to death is stung;
15   A fire to waste his pleasant summer bowers,
Ruin his mansions, and deface his towers.
    Yonder goes *Caelius* playing fast and loose
With his wife's arm, but not for love, God knows;
Suspicion is the cause, she well doth know;
20   Can she then love him that doth wrong her so?
If she refuse to walk with him he'll frown;
Forwearied both, they rest; he on her gown
Sits—for his ease, he saith—afraid in heart

SKIALETHEIA: The word means 'A shadow of truth'.
SATIRE IV:
1 *scald*: contemptible.
2 *familiar*: attendant spirit.
8 *head's horned-armoury*: cuckold's horns.
9 *to*: in.
12 *doggèd*: ill-tempered. *Dog-days-like*: i.e. hot and pestilential.
23 *he saith*: 'she saith' (1598).

Lest suddenly she should give him the start.
Thus doth he make her prisoner to his fear,   25
And himself thrall to self-consuming care.
  A male-kind sparrow once mistook his nest,
And fled for harbour to fair *Livia*'s breast;
Her husband caught him with a jealous rage,
Swearing to keep him prisoner in a cage.   30
Then a poor fly, dreading no netty snare,
Was caught in curlèd meshes of her hair,
Humming a sad note for 's imprisonment:
When the mad beast with ruder hands doth rent
That golden fleece for haste to take the fly,   35
And straightways at a window gins to pry,
Busy, sharp-sighted blind-man-hob, to know
Whether 'twere male or female taken so.
  Mark how *Severus* frigs from room to room
To see and not to see his martyrdom.   40
Peevish disease! which doth all food distaste
But what kills health, and that's a pleasing feast,—
Like weavers' shuttles which run to and fro,
Rav'ling their own guts with their running so.
  He which infects these with this lunacy   45
Is an odd figent jack called Jealousy;
His head is like a windmill's trunk, so big,
Wherein ten thousand thoughts run whirligig,
Play at barley-break, and dance the Irish hay,
Civil and peaceful like the Centaurs' fray.   50

27   *male-kind sparrow*: cock-sparrow (associated with lechery).
37   *blind-man-hob*: the blind-folded man in the game of Hob-man's Blind (Blind-man's-buff).
39   *frigs*: fidgets.
44   *Rav'ling*: entangling.
46   *figent jack*: restless knave.
49   *barley-break*: a country game. *hay*: a country dance.
50   *Centaurs' fray*: fierce battle which occurred when the drunken Centaurs disrupted the Lapithae wedding-feast (Ovid, *Met.* XII. 210–535).

His body is so fallen away and lean
That scarce it can his logger head sustain.
He hath as many hundred thousand eyes
As Argus had, like stars placed in the skies,—
55 Though to no purpose, for blind love can see,
Having no eyes, farther than Jealousy.
Gulf-breasted is he, silent and profound,
Cat-footed for sly pace, and without sound;
Porpentine-backèd, for he lies on thorns;
60 Is it not pity such a beast wants horns?
Is it not pity such a beast should so
Possess men's thoughts, and tympanize with woe
Their big-swoll'n hearts? For let *Severus* hear
A cuckoo sing in June, he sweats for fear;
65 And coming home, he whirries through the house;
Each hole that makes an inmate of a mouse
Is ransacked by him for the cuckold-maker;
He beats his wife, and 'mongst his maids doth swagger
T' extort confession from them who hath been
70 Familiar with his wife, wreaking his teen
Upon her ruffs and jewels, burning, tearing,
Flinging and hurling, scolding, staring, swearing.
He's as discreet, civil a gentleman
As Harry Peasecod, or a Bedlam man,
75 A drunken captain, or a ramping whore,
Or swaggering blue-coat at an alehouse door.
    What an infection's this, which thus doth fire
Men's most discreetest tempers, and doth tire

52 *logger*: large, stupid.
59 *Porpentine*: porcupine.
62 *tympanize*: puff up.
65 *whirries*: dashes.
70 *teen*: vexation.
74 *Harry Peasecod*: possibly a name for a country bumpkin
    who lives riotously in the city.
75 *ramping*: raging.
76 *blue-coat*: servant.

Their souls with fury, and doth make them thirst
To carouse bowls of poison till they burst! 80
Oh, this it is to be too wise in sin,
Too well experienced and skilled therein;
For false suspicion of another is
A sure condemning of our own amiss.
Unless a man have into practice brought 85
The theoric art of love which Ovid wrote,
Unless his own lewd life have taught him more
Than Aretine's adventurous wand'ring whore,
Unless he have an ancient soldier been,
Brags of the marks, and shows the scars of sin, 90
How could he be so gorged with loving-hate
As to think women so insatiate?
How could he know their strategems and shifts,
Their politic delays and wily drifts?
No, no, 'tis true, he hath been naught himself, 95
And lewdness fathereth this wayward elf.
Then take this for a maxim general rule:
No jealous man but is or knave or fool.

Skialetheia, 1598

86 I.e. Ovid's *Ars Amatoria.*
88 *Aretine's adventurous wand'ring whore: La Puttana Errante* ('The
     Wandering Whore'), *c.* 1538, was a bawdy poem attributed
     to Pietro Aretino (1492–1556); in fact it was written by
     Lorenzo Veniero.
95 *naught:* wicked.
96 *elf:* creature.

PASTORALS

THE SHEPHERD COLIN CLOUT, PIPING HIS
ELEGY ON THE DEATH OF DIDO, IS CROWNED
WITH A LAUREL WREATH
From Spenser, *The Shepheardes Calender,* 1579,
November.

Although the matter they take in hand seemeth commonly in appearance rude and homely, as the usual talk of simple clowns, yet do they indeed utter in the same much pleasant and profitable delight. For under these persons, as it were in a cloak of simplicity, they would either set forth the praises of their friends without the note of flattery, or inveigh grievously against abuses without any token of bitterness.

Webbe, A Discourse of English Poetry, 1586

As for the pastoral . . . , though many times they savour of wantonness and love and toying, and now and then breaking the rules of poetry go into plain scurrility, yet even the worst of them may be not ill applied, and are, I must confess, too delightful.

Harington, A Preface, or Rather a Brief
Apology of Poetry, 1591

If we present a pastoral, we show the harmless love of shepherds diversely moralized, distinguishing between the craft of the city and the innocence of the sheep-cote.

Thomas Heywood, An Apology for Actors, 1612

The subject of pastorals, as the language of it, ought to be poor, silly, and of the coarsest woof in appearance. Nevertheless, the most high and most noble matters of the world may be shadowed in them, and for certain sometimes are. . . .

The tabor striking up, if thou hast in thee any country-quicksilver, thou hadst rather be at the sport than hear thereof. Farewell.

Drayton, 'To the Reader of his Pastorals', 1619

GEORGE TURBERVILE

[*The Difference Between Town and Country*]
from *The Eclogues of the Poet B. Mantuan, Carmelitan,
Turned into English Verse*

The shepherd Fulica narrates a tale composed by Amyntas,
a 'townish man'.

What time the world began,
And things as yet were newly framed,
  then God did link a man
With woman ay to live,
  and married them yfere.   5
He willed the man to get the babes,
  the woman babes to bear,
And taught them how they should
  their children eke beget.
At first they plied their business well,   10
  and did their task yset,—
Would so they had done still,
  and let the fruit alone,
And never tasted of that tree
  the apple grew upon!   15
The woman woxe a dame,
  both boy and wench she bore,
And yearly so by like increase
  with men the earth did store.
When fifteen years were past,   20

THE DIFFERENCE BETWEEN TOWN AND COUNTRY: Baptista
  Spagnuoli of Mantua (Mantuan) (1448–1515) was a Car-
  melite Friar who in 1513 became General of the Carmelite
  Order. He was a prolific writer of verse and prose. His ten
  Latin eclogues, first printed in 1498, were highly influential
  in the Renaissance.
5 *yfere*: together.
16 *woxe a dame*: grew to be a mother.

God came again that way,
And there he found the woman whilst
   she gan her babes array.
Him she descried afar,
25   as she at threshold sat.
(This while was Adam gone afield,
   this woman's wedded mate:
He careless fed his flock,
   as then was no mistrust
30 Of falsehood 'twixt the man and wife;
   but when that growing lust
Made many marriage knots,
   then false they gan to play:
They knocked the goat about the pate
35   and reft his horns away
To graft on husband's head;
   then jealous seed begun
To take his root in husband's breast:
   he doubted of his son;
40 For men that false a bourd
   themselves are wont to play,
Mistrust their wives will go about
   their ancient debts to pay.)
Herewith the mother blushed,
45   and bear herself in hand
So many babes would overmuch
   against his liking stand,
And make her be suspect
   of too much wanton lust;
50 She ran and hid me some in hay,
   and some in chaff she thrust.
In came the mighty God,

36 I.e. as the sign of a cuckold.
40 *bourd*: game.
45 *bear herself in hand*: led herself to believe.
50 *me*: ethical dative.

and having blessed the place,
Said, 'Woman, fetch me all thy babes
   that I may see their face.'   55
The mother brought the bigg'st,
   and let the lesser lie;
God liked them well, as men are wont
   (as daily proof doth try)
Of fowls and scenting hounds   60
   to like the eldest best.
First to the senior of his sons
   thus spake the God, and blessed:
'Take thou this kingly mace,
   supply a kesar's room.'   65
Unto the second brother, arms,
   and made him Mars his groom:
'Be thou a duke,' quoth he,
   'and daunt thy foes in fight.'
And then at last he showed out rods   70
   and axe to open sight,
With twigs of tender vine,
   and noble Roman dart,
And offices gan deal about,
   to every babe a part.   75
Wherewith the mother, glad
   to see her sons extolled,
Ran in and fetched out all her brood,
   and said, 'Thou, God, behold!
These are my belly fruit,   80
   these in my womb I bear
As well as those: vouchsafe to let
   these have some part of share.'

65   *kesar's*: emperor's.
68   *duke*: general.
70–1 *rods and axe*: i.e. the *fasces*, symbols of consulship and other
    high office in Rome.
72   *twigs of tender vine*: i.e. the *vites*, staffs of Roman centurions.
73   *dart*: spear.

Their bristled pates were white
   with chaff, the straw it hung
85 About their arms, and spider webs
   that to the wattles clung.
Those liked him nought at all,
   not one he fancied well,
90 But frowning said, 'Avaunt, you elves,
   of mow and mould you smell.
Take you the goring goad,
   and country punching prick;
Take you the spitting spade in hand,
95   and garden setting stick;
To you the coulter 'longs,
   the yoke and other trash;
You shall be ploughmen, carters you,
   with whip to give the lash;
100 You shall be shepherds you,
   haycutters, delve the soil;
You shall be seamen, cowherds eke,
   turmoiled with endless toil.
But yet, among you all,
105   we do appoint that some
Shall leave the clownish country life
   and to the town shall come:
As pudding-makers, cooks,
   the butchers, pie-wives eke,
110 And other such-like sluttish arts
   of whom I do not speak;
That wonted are to sweat

87 *wattles*: saplings used as building materials.
90 *elves*: wretched creatures.
91 *mow*: dust.
93 *punching prick*: goad.
94 *spitting*: digging.
95 *setting stick*: stick for making holes when planting.
102 *cowherds*: printed as 'cowards'—the two words were
   thought to be related etymologically.

210

and at the coals to burn,
Like drudges, wasting all their days
   to serve their master's turn.'   115
This done, the mighty God
   departed for the skies.
Thus 'twixt the town and country did
   the difference first arise;
Thus were the clowns ymade, as good   120
   Amyntas doth devise.

The Eclogues of the Poet B. Mantuan
(1567), VI [154–274]

SIR PHILIP SIDNEY

From *The Countess of Pembroke's Arcadia*, 1593

My sheep are thoughts, which I both guide and serve;
Their pasture is fair hills of fruitless love;
On barren sweets they feed, and feeding starve;
I wail their lot, but will not other prove.
My sheephook is wanhope, which all upholds;   5
My weeds, desire, cut out in endless folds.
   What wool my sheep shall bear, whiles thus they live,
   In you it is, you must the judgement give.

Strephon.   Ye goatherd gods, that love the grassy
     mountains,
   Ye nymphs that haunt the springs in pleasant
     valleys,

117 *for*: 'from' (1567).
MY SHEEP ARE THOUGHTS: This and the following poems
   from Sidney's *Arcadia* were probably written 1577–80.
  5 *wanhope*: despair.
YE GOATHERD GODS: The shepherds Strephon and Klaius, in
   love with the shepherdess Urania, mourn her departure

Ye satyrs joyed with free and quiet forests,
Vouchsafe your silent ears to plaining music,
5   Which to my woes gives still an early morning,
And draws the dolour on till weary evening.

Klaius.   O Mercury, foregoer to the evening,
    O heavenly huntress of the savage mountains,
    O lovely star, entitled of the morning,
10   While that my voice doth fill these woeful valleys,
    Vouchsafe your silent ears to plaining music,
    Which oft hath echo tired in secret forests.

Strephon.   I that was once free-burgess of the forests,
    Where shade from sun, and sports I sought at
        evening,
15   I that was once esteemed for pleasant music,
    Am banished now among the monstrous mountains
    Of huge despair, and foul affliction's valleys;
    Am grown a shriek-owl to myself each morning.

Klaius.   I that was once delighted every morning,
20   Hunting the wild inhabiters of forests,
    I that was once the music of these valleys,
    So darkened am, that all my day is evening;
    Heart-broken so, that molehills seem high
        mountains;
    And fill the vales with cries instead of music.

from Arcadia. The poem is a double sestina. A sestina
consists of six six-line stanzas (a double sestina has twelve
stanzas) and a final envoy of three lines. In every stanza the
lines end with the same six words (unrhymed), arranged
in a certain sequence: the end-words of one stanza are
the same as those of the preceding stanza in the order
615243. After six stanzas every variation in the sequence
has appeared. The six end-words are also repeated in the
envoy; in this case they are in their initial order 123456.
4 *plaining*: lamenting.
5 *gives* (1590): 'give' (1593).

Strephon.   Long since, alas, my deadly swannish music   25
  Hath made itself a crier of the morning,
  And hath with wailing strength climbed highest
    mountains;
  Long since my thoughts more desert be than forests;
  Long since I see my joys come to their evening,
  And state thrown down to over-trodden valleys.   30

Klaius.   Long since the happy dwellers of these valleys
  Have prayed me leave my strange exclaiming
    music,
  Which troubles their day's work, and joys of
    evening;
  Long since I hate the night, more hate the
    morning;
  Long since my thoughts chase me like beasts in
    forests,
               35
  And make me wish myself laid under mountains.

Strephon.   Meseems I see the high and stately mountains
  Transform themselves to low dejected valleys;
  Meseems I hear, in these ill-changèd forests,
  The nightingales do learn of owls their music;   40
  Meseems I feel the comfort of the morning
  Turned to the mortal serene of an evening.

Klaius.   Meseems I see a filthy cloudy evening
  As soon as sun begins to climb the mountains;
  Meseems I feel a noisome scent, the morning,   45
  When I do smell the flowers of these valleys;
  Meseems I hear, when I do hear sweet music,
  The dreadful cries of murdered men in forests.

---

25   *deadly swannish music*: music like the swan sings before
  death.
42   *mortal serene*: evening dew, held to bring death.

Strephon.   I wish to fire the trees of all these forests;
50   I give the sun a last farewell each evening;
          I curse the fiddling finders-out of music;
          With envy I do hate the lofty mountains,
          And with despite despise the humble valleys;
          I do detest night, evening, day, and morning.

55 *Klaius.*   Curse to myself my prayer is, the morning;
          My fire is more than can be made with forests;
          My state more base than are the basest valleys;
          I wish no evenings more to see, each evening;
          Shamèd, I hate myself in sight of mountains,
60   And stop mine ears, lest I grow mad with music.

Strephon.   For she whose parts maintained a perfect music,
          Whose beauty shined more than the blushing
                morning,
          Who much did pass in state the stately mountains,
          In straightness passed the cedars of the forests,
65   Hath cast me, wretch, into eternal evening,
          By taking her two suns from these dark valleys.

Klaius.   For she to whom compared the alps are valleys,
          She whose least word brings from the spheres
                their music,
          At whose approach the sun rose in the evening,
          Who, where she went, bare in her forehead
70   morning,
          Is gone, is gone, from these our spoilèd forests,
          Turning to deserts our best pastured mountains.

Strephon   These mountains witness shall, so shall these
& Klaius.   valleys,
                These forests eke, made wretched by our music,
                Our morning hymn is this, and song at
75   evening.

    66   *her two suns*: i.e. her eyes.

O sweet woods, the delight of solitariness!
Oh, how much I do like your solitariness!
Where man's mind hath a freed consideration
Of goodness to receive lovely direction;
Where senses do behold th' order of heav'nly host,　　5
And wise thoughts do behold what the Creator is.
Contemplation here holdeth his only seat,
Bounded with no limits, borne with a wing of hope,
Climbs even unto the stars; nature is under it.
Nought disturbs thy quiet, all to thy service yields;　　10
Each sight draws on a thought, thought mother of science;
Sweet birds kindly do grant harmony unto thee;
Fair trees' shade is enough fortification,
Nor danger to thyself, if be not in thyself.

O sweet woods, the delight of solitariness!　　15
Oh, how much I do like your solitariness!
Here nor treason is hid, veilèd in innocence,
Nor envy's snaky eye finds any harbour here,
Nor flatterers' venomous insinuations,
Nor cunning humorists' puddled opinions,　　20
Nor courteous ruin of profferèd usury,
Nor time prattled away, cradle of ignorance,
Nor causeless duty, nor cumber of arrogance,
Nor trifling title of vanity dazzleth us,
Nor golden manacles stand for a paradise;　　25
Here wrong's name is unheard, slander a monster is.
Keep thy sprite from abuse, here no abuse doth haunt.
What man grafts in a tree dissimulation?

O SWEET WOODS: An experiment in the use of the classical
　　Asclepiad metre, whose scansion (— — — ∪ ∪ — — ∪
　　∪ — ∪　∪) precedes the poem in some MSS. For com-
　　ment on quantitative verse see note to Campion, 'Come,
　　let us sound' (p. 121).
14　if be: i.e. if it be.
20　cunning: 'coming' (1593). humorists: men of disordered tem-
　　perament. puddled: confused.
23　cumber: affliction.

O sweet woods, the delight of solitariness!
30   Oh, how well I do like your solitariness!
Yet, dear soil, if a soul closed in a mansion
As sweet as violets, fair as a lily is,
Straight as cedar, a voice stains the canary bird's,
Whose shade safety doth hold, danger avoideth her;
35   Such wisdom that in her lives speculation;
Such goodness that in her simplicity triumphs;
Where envy's snaky eye winketh or else dieth;
Slander wants a pretext, flattery gone beyond;
Oh, if such a one have bent to a lonely life,
40   Her steps glad we receive, glad we receive her eyes,
And think not she doth hurt our solitariness,
For such company decks such solitariness.

[*The Song of Philisides*]
from 'As I my little flock on Ister bank'

Such manner time there was (what time, I n'ot)
When all this earth, this dam or mould of ours,
Was only woned with such as beasts begot;
Unknown as then were they that builded towers;

32   *a lily*: 'lily' (1593).
34   *safety*: 'safely' (1593).
35   *speculation*: contemplation.
THE SONG OF ⸻HILISIDES: The song, in the form of a beast
    fable, is a political allegory of how monarchy develops
    into tyranny and the ruthless exploitation of the com-
    mon people, if the power of the aristocracy is weakened.
    It was taught to the shepherd Philisides (Sidney) by 'old
    Languet' (Hubert Languet, Sidney's adviser and friend,
    who had been with him in Vienna, 'on Ister bank', in 1573
    and 1574). The song is a compliment to Languet's wisdom
    as a statesman.
1   *n'ot*: know not.
3   *woned*: inhabited.

The cattle wild or tame, in nature's bowers   5
  Might freely roam or rest, as seemèd them;
  Man was not man, their dwellings in to hem.

The beasts had sure some beastly policy,
For nothing can endure where order n'is;
For once the lion by the lamb did lie;   10
The fearful hind the leopard did kiss;
Hurtless was tiger's paw and serpent's hiss.
  This think I well, the beasts with courage clad,
  Like senators, a harmless empire had.

At which, whether the others did repine,   15
(For envy harb'reth most in feeblest hearts)
Or that they all to changing did incline,
(As even in beasts their dams leave, changing parts)
The multitude to Jove a suit imparts,
  With neighing, blaying, braying, and barking,   20
  Roaring, and howling, for to have a king.

A king, in language theirs they said they would,
(For then their language was a perfect speech);
The birds likewise with chirps and pewing could,
Cackling and chattering, that of Jove beseech.   25
Only the owl still warned them not to seech
  So hastily that which they would repent;
  But saw they would, and he to deserts went.

 6 *as seemèd them*: as they pleased.
 8 *policy*: order of government.
13 *beasts with courage clad*: i.e. nobler animals.
20 *blaying*: bleating.
26 *seech*: seek.

217

Jove wisely said (for wisdom wisely says):
30 'O beasts, take heed what you of me desire;
Rulers will think all things made them to please,
And soon forget the swink due to their hire.
But since you will, part of my heavenly fire
    I will you lend; the rest yourselves must give,
35   That it both seen and felt may with you live.'

Full glad they were, and took the naked sprite,
Which straight the earth yclothèd in his clay;
The lion, heart; the ounce gave active might;
The horse, good shape; the sparrow, lust to play;
40 Nightingale, voice, enticing songs to say;
    Elephant gave a perfect memory;
    And parrot, ready tongue that to apply.

The fox gave craft; the dog gave flattery;
Ass, patience; the mole, a working thought;
45 Eagle, high look; wolf, secret cruelty;
Monkey, sweet breath; the cow her fair eyes brought;
The ermine, whitest skin, spotted with nought;
    The sheep, mild-seeming face; climbing, the bear;
    The stag did give the harm-eschewing fear.

50 The hare, her sleights; the cat, his melancholy;
Ant, industry; the coney, skill to build;
Cranes, order; storks, to be appearing holy;
Chameleon, ease to change; duck, ease to yield;
Crocodile, tears, which might be falsely spilled;
55   Ape great thing gave, though he did mowing stand:
    The instrument of instruments, the hand.

32 *swink*: labour.
38 *ounce*: lynx.
51 *coney*: rabbit.
55 *mowing*: grimacing.

Each other beast likewise his present brings;
And, but they drad their prince they oft should want,
They all consented were to give him wings.
And ay more awe towards him for to plant,   60
To their own work this privilege they grant:
   That from thenceforth to all eternity
   No beast should freely speak, but only he.

Thus man was made, thus man their lord became;
Who at the first, wanting or hiding pride,   65
He did to beasts' best use his cunning frame,
With water drink, herbs meat, and naked hide,
And fellow-like let his dominion slide;
   Not in his sayings saying 'I', but 'we',
   As if he meant his lordship common be.   70

But when his seat so rooted he had found,
That they now skilled not how from him to wend,
Then gan in guiltless earth full many a wound,
Iron to seek, which 'gainst itself should bend,
To tear the bowels that good corn should send;   75
   But yet the common dam none did bemoan,
   Because, though hurt, they never heard her groan.

Then gan he factions in the beasts to breed,
Where, helping weaker sort, the nobler beasts,
As tigers, leopards, bears, and lions' seed,   80
Disdained with this, in deserts sought their rests,
Where famine ravine taught their hungry chests;
   That craftily he forced them to do ill,
   Which being done, he afterwards would kill.

58   *but they drad*: had they not feared. *oft*: 'ought' (1593).
78   *he*: 'the' (1593).
81   *Disdained*: angered. *this*: i.e. man 'helping weaker sort'
     (l. 79).

85 For murders done (which never erst was seen)
    By those great beasts, as for the weaker's good,
    He chose themselves his guarders for to been
    'Gainst those of might, of whom in fear they stood,
    As horse and dog, not great, but gentle blood.
90   Blithe were the commons, cattle of the field,
        Tho when they saw their foen of greatness killed.

    But they or spent or made of slender might,
    Then quickly did the meaner cattle find
    The great beams gone, the house on shoulders light;
95 For by and by the horse fair bits did bind;
    The dog was in a collar taught his kind;
        As for the gentle birds, like case might rue,
        When falcon they, and goshawk, saw in mew.

    Worst fell to smallest birds and meanest herd,
100 Whom, now his own, full like his own he used;
    Yet first but wool or feathers off he teared,
    And when they were well used to be abused,
    For hungry throat their flesh with teeth he bruised;
        At length for glutton taste he did them kill;
105   At last, for sport their silly lives did spill.

87 *themselves*: i.e. the weaker beasts.
91 *Tho*: then.
92 *they*: i.e. the 'great beasts'.
94 I.e. the strong pillars of the government (the aristocracy)
    being gone, the political structure cannot be supported
    by the weak (the common people) and threatens to
    collapse.
96 *kind*: natural place.
98 *mew*: cage.
103 *throat*: 'teeth' (1593).

220

But yet, O man, rage not beyond thy need;
Deem it no glory to swell in tyranny.
Thou art of blood: joy not to see things bleed;
Thou fearest death: think they are loath to die;
A plaint of guiltless hurt doth pierce the sky.   110
  And you, poor beasts, in patience bide your hell,
  Or know your strengths, and then you shall do well.

'As I my little flock on Ister bank' [43–154]

EDMUND SPENSER

[*Elegy on Dido*]
from *The Shepheardes Calender*

Colin Clout is asked to pipe an elegy on the death of Dido,
'some mayden of greate bloud'.

Up then *Melpomene* thou mournefulst Muse of nyne,
Such cause of mourning never hadst afore:
Up grieslie ghostes and up my rufull ryme,
Matter of myrth now shalt thou have no more.
For dead shee is, that myrth thee made of yore.   5
  Dido my deare alas is dead,
  Dead and lyeth wrapt in lead:
    O heavie herse,
Let streaming teares be pourèd out in store:
    O carefull verse.   10

---

112 *know your strengths*: i.e. recognize the aristocracy as your
    protectors.
ELEGY ON DIDO: The poem is loosely imitative of Marot's
    elegy, *De Madame Loyse de Savoye*, 1531. The identity of Dido,
    kept secret by Spenser, has never been discovered.
1 *Melpomene*: the muse of tragedy.
10 *carefull*: sorrowful.

Shepheards, that by your flocks on Kentish downes abyde,
Waile ye this wofull waste of natures warke:
Waile we the wight, whose presence was our pryde:
Waile we the wight, whose absence is our carke.
15 The sonne of all the world is dimme and darke:
    The earth now lacks her wonted light,
    And all we dwell in deadly night,
        O heavie herse.
Breake we our pypes, that shrild as lowde as Larke,
20   O carefull verse.

Why doe we longer live, (ah why live we so long)
Whose better dayes death hath shut up in woe?
The fayrest floure our gyrlond all emong,
Is faded quite and into dust ygoe.
25 Sing now ye shepheards daughters, sing no moe
    The songs that *Colin* made in her prayse,
    But into weeping turne your wanton layes,
        O heavie herse,
Now is time to dye. Nay time was long ygoe,
30   O carefull verse.

Whence is it, that the flouret of the field doth fade,
And lyeth buryed long in Winters bale:
Yet soone as spring his mantle doth display,
It floureth fresh, as it should never fayle?
35 But thing on earth that is of most availe,
    As vertues braunch and beauties budde,
    Reliven not for any good.
        O heavie herse,
The braunch once dead, the budde eke needes must quaile,
40   O carefull verse.

12 *waste*: destruction. *warke*: work.
14 *carke*: sorrow.
24 *ygoe*: gone.
32 *bale*: malignant influence.
35 *availe*: value.

She while she was, (that was, a woful word to sayne)
For beauties prayse and plesaunce had no pere:
So well she couth the shepherds entertayne,
With cakes and cracknells and such country chere.
Ne would she scorne the simple shepheards swaine,   45
  For she would cal hem often heme
    And give hem curds and clouted Creame.
      O heavie herse,
Als *Colin cloute* she would not once disdayne.
      O carefull verse.   50

But nowe sike happy cheere is turnd to heavie chaunce,
Such pleasaunce now displast by dolors dint:
All Musick sleepes, where death doth leade the daunce,
And shepherds wonted solace is extinct.
The blew in black, the greene in gray is tinct,   55
  The gaudie girlonds deck her grave,
    The faded flowres her corse embrave.
      O heavie herse,
Morne nowe my Muse, now morne with teares besprint.
      O carefull verse.   60

O thou greate shepheard *Lobbin*, how great is thy griefe,
Where bene the nosegayes that she dight for thee:
The coloured chaplets wrought with a chiefe,
The knotted rushrings, and gilte Rosemaree?
For shee deeméd nothing too deere for thee.   65

44 *cracknells*: biscuits.
46 *heme*: home.
47 *clouted*: clotted.
57 *embrave*: adorn.
59 *besprint*: besprinkled.
61 *Lobbin*: Dido's lover.
62 *dight*: made.
63 *chiefe*: head, top.

Ah they bene all yclad in clay,
One bitter blast blewe all away.
　　　O heavie herse,
Thereof nought remaynes but the memoree.
70　　　O carefull verse.

Ay me that dreerie death should strike so mortall
　　　stroke,
That can undoe Dame natures kindly course:
The faded lockes fall from the loftie oke,
The flouds do gaspe, for dryèd is theyr sourse,
75 And flouds of teares flowe in theyr stead perforse.
　　　The mantled medowes mourne,
　　　Theyr sondry colours tourne.
　　　　O heavie herse,
The heavens doe melt in teares without remorse.
80　　　O carefull verse.

The feeble flocks in field refuse their former foode,
And hang theyr heads, as they would learne to weepe:
The beastes in forest wayle as they were woode,
Except the Wolves, that chase the wandring sheepe:
85 Now she is gon that safely did hem keepe;
　　　The Turtle on the barèd braunch,
　　　Laments the wound, that death did launch.
　　　　O heavie herse,
And *Philomele* her song with teares doth steepe.
90　　　O carefull verse.

72　*kindly*: natural.
76–7 *mourne, . . . tourne* (1581): 'morune, . . . torune' (1579). *tourne*:
　　turn.
79　*remorse*: stinting.
83　*woode*: frantic.
89　*Philomele*: the nightingale.

224

The water Nymphs, that wont with her to sing and
     daunce,
And for her girlond Olive braunches beare,
Now balefull boughes of Cypres doen advaunce:
The Muses, that were wont greene bayes to weare,
Now bringen bitter Eldre braunches seare,   95
   The fatall sisters eke repent,
   Her vitall threde so soone was spent.
      O heavie herse,
Morne now my Muse, now morne with heavie cheare.
      O carefull verse.   100

O trustlesse state of earthly things, and slipper hope
Of mortal men, that swincke and sweate for nought,
And shooting wide, doe misse the markèd scope:
Now have I learnd (a lesson derely bought)
That nys on earth assuraunce to be sought: 105
   For what might be in earthlie mould,
   That did her buried body hould,
      O heavie herse,
Yet saw I on the beare when it was brought.
      O carefull verse.   110

But maugre death, and dreaded sisters deadly spight,
And gates of hel, and fyrie furies forse:
She hath the bonds broke of eternall night,
Her soule unbodied of the burdenous corpse.
Why then weepes Lobbin so without remorse?   115

   96   *fatall sisters*: the three Fates, who spin and cut the thread
       of life.
 101   *slipper*: slippery.
 102   *swincke*: toil.
 103   *scope*: target.
 105   *nys*: there is not.
 111   *maugre*: despite.

O Lobb, thy losse no longer lament,
Dido nis dead, but into heaven hent.
    O happye herse,
Cease now my Muse, now cease thy sorrowes sourse,
120   O joyfull verse.

Why wayle we then? why weary we the Gods with
      playnts,
As if some evill were to her betight?
She raignes a goddesse now emong the saintes,
That whilome was the saynt of shepheards light:
125 And is enstallèd nowe in heavens hight.
    I see thee blessèd soule, I see,
    Walke in *Elisian* fieldes so free.
      O happy herse,
Might I once come to thee (O that I might)
130   O joyfull verse.

Unwise and wretched men to weete whats good or ill,
We deeme of Death as doome of ill desert:
But knewe we, fooles, what it us bringes until,
Dye would we dayly, once it to expert.
135 No daunger there the shepheard can astert:
    Fayre fieldes and pleasaunt layes there bene,
    The fieldes ay fresh, the grasse ay greene:
      O happy herse,
Make hast ye shepheards, thether to revert,
140   O joyfull verse.

117 *hent*: taken.
122 *betight*: befallen.
124 That once was the shining saint of shepherds.
131 *weete*: know.
133 *until*: to.
134 *expert*: experience.
135 *astert*: befall.
136 *layes*: leas.

Dido is gone afore (whose turne shall be the next?)
There lives shee with the blessèd Gods in blisse,
There drincks she *Nectar* with *Ambrosia* mixt,
And joyes enjoyes, that mortall men doe misse.
The honor now of highest gods she is,   145
   That whilome was poore shepheards pryde,
   While here on earth she did abyde.
      O happy herse,
Ceasse now my song, my woe now wasted is.
      O joyfull verse.   150

The Shepheardes Calender (1579), *November* [53–202]

[*The Dance of the Graces*]
from *The Faerie Queene*

Sir Calidore, on his quest of the Blatant Beast, encounters some shepherds. Tempted by the attractions of the pastoral world and by the beauty of the shepherdess Pastorella, he forsakes his quest and adopts the shepherd's life himself.

One day as he did raunge the fields abroad,
   Whilest his faire *Pastorella* was elsewhere,
   He chaunst to come, far from all peoples troad,
   Unto a place, whose pleasaunce did appere
   To passe all others, on the earth which were: 5
   For all that ever was by natures skill
   Devized to worke delight, was gathered there,
   And there by her were pourèd forth at fill,
As if this to adorne, she all the rest did pill.

THE DANCE OF THE GRACES:
  3 *troad*: path.
  9 *pill*: plunder.

10 It was an hill plaste in an open plaine,
     That round about was bordered with a wood
     Of matchlesse hight, that seem'd th' earth to disdaine,
     In which all trees of honour stately stood,
     And did all winter as in sommer bud,
15   Spredding pavilions for the birds to bowre,
     Which in their lower braunches sung aloud;
     And in their tops the soring hauke did towre,
Sitting like King of fowles in majesty and powre.

     And at the foote thereof, a gentle flud
20   His silver waves did softly tumble downe,
     Unmard with ragged mosse or filthy mud,
     Ne mote wylde beastes, ne mote the ruder clowne
     Thereto approch, ne filth mote therein drowne:
     But Nymphes and Faeries by the bancks did sit,
25   In the woods shade, which did the waters crowne,
     Keeping all noysome things away from it,
And to the waters fall tuning their accents fit.

     And on the top thereof a spacious plaine
     Did spred it selfe, to serve to all delight,
30   Either to daunce, when they to daunce would faine,
     Or else to course about their bases light;
     Ne ought there wanted, which for pleasure might
     Desirèd be, or thence to banish bale:
     So pleasauntly the hill with equall hight,
35   Did seeme to overlooke the lowly vale;
Therefore it rightly cleepèd was mount *Acidale.*

22 *clowne*: rustic.
31 *course about their bases*: i.e. play the game of prisoner's base.
33 *bale*: grief.
36 *cleepèd*: named. *Acidale*: fount in Boeotia in which Venus
    and the Graces bathed. The name is from the Greek
    'free from care'.

228

They say that *Venus*, when she did dispose
   Her selfe to pleasaunce, usèd to resort
   Unto this place, and therein to repose
   And rest her selfe, as in a gladsome port,   40
   Or with the Graces there to play and sport;
   That even her owne Cytheron, though in it
   She usèd most to keepe her royall court,
   And in her soveraine Majesty to sit,
She in regard hereof refusde and thought unfit.   45

Unto this place when as the Elfin Knight
   Approcht, him seemèd that the merry sound
   Of a shrill pipe he playing heard on hight,
   And many feete fast thumping th' hollow ground,
   That through the woods their Eccho did rebound.   50
   He nigher drew, to weete what mote it be;
   There he a troupe of Ladies dauncing found
   Full merrily, and making gladfull glee,
And in the midst a Shepheard piping he did see.

He durst not enter into th' open greene,   55
   For dread of them unwares to be descryde,
   For breaking of their daunce, if he were seene;
   But in the covert of the wood did byde,
   Beholding all, yet of them unespyde.
   There he did see, that pleasèd much his sight,   60
   That even he him selfe his eyes envyde,
   An hundred naked maidens lilly white,
All raungèd in a ring, and dauncing in delight.

40 *port*: fashion.
42 *Cytheron*: perhaps an error for Cythera, an island sacred to
    Venus, who was born from the sea near its shores.
48 *on hight*: loudly.
51 *weete*: discover.

All they without were raungèd in a ring,
65   And dauncèd round; but in the midst of them
Three other Ladies did both daunce and sing,
The whilest the rest them round about did hemme,
And like a girlond did in compasse stemme:
And in the middest of those same three, was placed
70   Another Damzell, as a precious gemme,
Amidst a ring most richly well enchaced,
That with her goodly presence all the rest much graced.

Looke how the Crowne, which *Ariadne* wore
Upon her yvory forehead that same day,
75   That *Theseus* her unto his bridale bore,
When the bold *Centaures* made that bloudy fray,
With the fierce *Lapithes*, which did them dismay;
Being now placèd in the firmament,
Through the bright heaven doth her beams display,
80   And is unto the starres an ornament,
Which round about her move in order excellent.

Such was the beauty of this goodly band,
Whose sundry parts were here too long to tell:
But she that in the midst of them did stand,
85   Seem'd all the rest in beauty to excell,
Crownd with a rosie girlond, that right well

---

68 *stemme*: encircle.
71 *enchaced*: set.
73–8 Spenser changes the legends: Ariadne (*ariagne*, 'most
    pure') was borne from Crete as Theseus' consort after he
    had slain the Minotaur, but her crown was stellified by
    Bacchus, who married her after Theseus had deserted
    her on Naxos (Ovid, *Met.* VIII. 169–82). The fierce battle of
    the Lapithae and Centaurs in fact occurred at the wed-
    ding of Pirithous and Hippodamia, at which Theseus was
    present (*Met.* XII. 210–535). The banishment of the drunk-
    en Centaurs from the feast was regarded as the triumph
    of civilization and 'civility' over barbarism.

Did her beseeme. And ever, as the crew
About her daunst, sweet flowres, that far did smell,
And fragrant odours they uppon her threw;
But most of all, those three did her with gifts endew.　　90

Those were the Graces, daughters of delight,
　　Handmaides of *Venus*, which are wont to haunt
　　Uppon this hill, and daunce there day and night:
　　Those three to men all gifts of grace do graunt,
　　And all, that *Venus* in her selfe doth vaunt,　　95
　　Is borrowèd of them. But that faire one,
　　That in the midst was placèd paravaunt,
　　Was she to whom that shepheard pypt alone,
That made him pipe so merrily, as never none.

She was to weete that jolly Shepheards lasse,　　100
　　Which pipèd there unto that merry rout,
　　That jolly shepheard, which there pipèd, was
　　Poore *Colin Clout* (who knowes not *Colin Clout*?)
　　He pypt apace, whilest they him daunst about.
　　Pype jolly shepheard, pype thou now apace　　105
　　Unto thy love, that made thee low to lout:
　　Thy love is present there with thee in place,
Thy love is there advaunst to be another Grace.

87　*crew*: band.
97　*paravaunt*: above all others.
100　*to weete*: to wit. *that jolly Shepheards lasse*: The 'faire one' to
　　whom Colin pipes cannot be identified exclusively with
　　either Rosalind (Colin's beloved in other poems) or with
　　Elizabeth Boyle (Spenser's own bride). As a humble
　　'countrey lasse', endowed with all the divine gifts of the
　　Graces, she remains a mysterious figure (ll. 182–9), repre-
　　senting in a general way both the inspiration for, and the
　　object of, the poet-lover's devotion.
101　*rout*: group.
103　*Colin Clout*: Spenser's pastoral pseudonym.
106　*lout*: bow.

Much wondred *Calidore* at this straunge sight,
110   Whose like before his eye had never seene,
     And standing long astonishèd in spright,
     And rapt with pleasaunce, wist not what to weene;
     Whether it were the traine of beauties Queene,
     Or Nymphes, or Faeries, or enchaunted show,
115   With which his eyes mote have deluded beene.
     Therefore resolving, what it was, to know,
Out of the wood he rose, and toward them did go.

But soone as he appearèd to their vew,
     They vanisht all away out of his sight,
120   And cleane were gone, which way he never knew;
     All save the shepheard, who for fell despight
     Of that displeasure, broke his bag-pipe quight,
     And made great mone for that unhappy turne.
     But *Calidore*, though no lesse sory wight,
125   For that mishap, yet seeing him to mourne,
Drew neare, that he the truth of all by him mote learne.

And first him greeting, thus unto him spake,
     'Haile jolly shepheard, which thy joyous dayes
     Here leadest in this goodly merry make,
130   Frequented of these gentle Nymphes alwayes,
     Which to thee flocke, to heare thy lovely layes;
     Tell me, what mote these dainty Damzels be,
     Which here with thee doe make their pleasant playes?
     Right happy thou, that mayst them freely see:
135 But why when I them saw, fled they away from me?'

'Not I so happy,' answerd then that swaine,
     'As thou unhappy, which them thence didst chace,
     Whom by no meanes thou canst recall againe,
     For being gone, none can them bring in place,

> 121 *despight*: anger.
> 123 *unhappy*: luckless.

But whom they of them selves list so to grace.'   140
'Right sory I,' saide then Sir *Calidore*,
'That my ill fortune did them hence displace.
But since things passèd none may now restore,
Tell me, what were they all, whose lacke thee grieves
  so sore.'

Tho gan that shepheard thus for to dilate;   145
 'Then wote thou shepheard, whatsoever thou bee,
 That all those Ladies, which thou sawest late,
 Are *Venus* Damzels, all within her fee,
 But differing in honour and degree:
 They all are Graces, which on her depend,   150
 Besides a thousand more, which ready bee
 Her to adorne, when so she forth doth wend:
But those three in the midst, doe chiefe on her attend.

'They are the daughters of sky-ruling Jove,
 By him begot of faire *Eurynome*,   155
 The Oceans daughter, in this pleasant grove,
 As he this way comming from feastfull glee,
 Of *Thetis* wedding with *Aeacidee*,
 In sommers shade him selfe here rested weary.
 The first of them hight mylde *Euphrosyne*,   160
 Next faire *Aglaia*, last *Thalia* merry:
Sweete Goddesses all three which me in mirth do
  cherry.

145 *Tho*: then. *dilate*: expound.
148 *fee*: service.
150 *depend*: accompany as attendants.
154–6 Ultimately from Hesiod, *Theogony* 907–11.
157–8 *feastfull . . . Aeacidee*: the wedding of Thetis and Peleus
  (son of Aeacus), at which the goddess Eris flung the apple
  of discord among the guests. It is Spenser's own idea that
  the Graces were conceived immediately after the feast.
160–1 *Euphrosyne*: 'Joy'. *Aglaia*: 'The Radiant'. *Thalia*: 'The
  Flowering'.
162 *cherry*: cheer.

'These three on men all gracious gifts bestow,
　　Which decke the body or adorne the mynde,
165　To make them lovely or well favoured show,
　　As comely carriage, entertainement kynde,
　　Sweete semblaunt, friendly offices that bynde,
　　And all the complements of curtesie:
　　They teach us, how to each degree and kynde
170　We should our selves demeane, to low, to hie;
To friends, to foes, which skill men call Civility.

'Therefore they alwaies smoothly seeme to smile,
　　That we likewise should mylde and gentle be,
　　And also naked are, that without guile
175　Or false dissemblaunce all them plaine may see,
　　Simple and true from covert malice free:
　　And eeke them selves so in their daunce they bore,
　　That two of them still froward seem'd to bee,
　　But one still towards shew'd her selfe afore;
That good should from us goe, then come in greater
180　　store.

'Such were those Goddesses, which ye did see;
　　But that fourth Mayd, which there amidst them traced,
　　Who can aread, what creature mote she bee,
　　Whether a creature, or a goddesse graced
185　With heavenly gifts from heven first enraced?
　　But what so sure she was, she worthy was,
　　To be the fourth with those three other placed:
　　Yet was she certes but a countrey lasse,
Yet she all other countrey lasses farre did passe.

167　*semblaunt*: countenance.
168　*complements*: ceremonies.
178　*froward*: 'fromward', turned away. *froward* (1611): 'forward'
　　(1596).
183　*aread*: divine.
185　*enraced*: implanted.

234

'So farre as doth the daughter of the day,   190
  All other lesser lights in light excell,
  So farre doth she in beautyfull array,
  Above all other lasses beare the bell,
  Ne lesse in vertue that beseemes her well,
  Doth she exceede the rest of all her race,   195
  For which the Graces that here wont to dwell,
  Have for more honor brought her to this place,
And gracèd her so much to be another Grace.

'Another Grace she well deserves to be,
  In whom so many Graces gathered are,   200
  Excelling much the meane of her degree;
  Divine resemblaunce, beauty soveraine rare,
  Firme Chastity, that spight ne blemish dare;
  All which she with such courtesie doth grace,
  That all her peres cannot with her compare,   205
  But quite are dimmèd, when she is in place.
She made me often pipe and now to pipe apace.

'Sunne of the world, great glory of the sky,
  That all the earth doest lighten with thy rayes,
  Great *Gloriana*, greatest Majesty,   210
  Pardon thy shepheard, mongst so many layes,
  As he hath sung of thee in all his dayes,
  To make one minime of thy poore handmayd,
  And underneath thy feete to place her prayse,
  That when thy glory shall be farre displayd   215
To future age of her this mention may be made.'

---

190 *the daughter of the day*: i.e. Venus, the evening star.
193 *beare the bell*: carry off the prize.
203 *dare*: injure.
210 *Gloriana*: i.e. Queen Elizabeth.
213 *minime*: musical note.

When thus that shepherd ended had his speach,
    Sayd *Calidore*; 'Now sure it yrketh mee,
    That to thy blisse I made this luckelesse breach,
220   As now the author of thy bale to be,
    Thus to bereave thy loves deare sight from thee:
    But gentle Shepheard pardon thou my shame,
    Who rashly sought that, which I mote not see.'
    Thus did the courteous Knight excuse his blame,
225 And to recomfort him, all comely meanes did frame.

In such discourses they together spent
    Long time, as fit occasion forth them led;
    With which the Knight him selfe did much content,
    And with delight his greedy fancy fed,
230   Both of his words, which he with reason red;
    And also of the place, whose pleasures rare
    With such regard his sences ravishèd,
    That thence, he had no will away to fare,
But wisht, that with that shepheard he mote dwelling
    share.

The Faerie Queene (1596), Bk. **VI**,
Canto x [Sts. 5–30]

FULKE GREVILLE

Away with these self-loving lads,
Whom Cupid's arrow never glads;
Away, poor souls, that sigh and weep
In love of those that lie asleep:
5   For Cupid is a meadow-god,
     And forceth none to kiss the rod.

230 *red*: spoke.
AWAY WITH THESE SELF-LOVING LADS: First published in
    England's Helicon, 1600, but probably written about twenty
    years earlier. Set to music by J. Dowland, *The First Book of
    Songs or Airs*, 1597.

Sweet Cupid's shafts, like destiny,
Do causeless good or ill decree;
Desert is born out of his bow,
Reward upon his wing doth go;   10
  What fools are they that have not known
  That Love likes no laws but his own!

My songs they be of Cynthia's praise;
I wear her rings on holy-days;
In every tree I write her name,   15
And every day I read the same;
  Where honour Cupid's rival is,
  There miracles are seen of his.

If Cynthia crave her ring of me,
I blot her name out of the tree;   20
If doubt do darken things held dear,
Then well fare nothing once a year;
  For many run, but one must win,
  Fools only hedge the cuckoo in.

The worth that worthiness should move   25
Is love, that is the bow of Love;
And love as well thee foster can,
As can the mighty nobleman.
  Sweet saint, 'tis true you worthy be,
  Yet without love, nought worth to me.   30

Caelica, 1633

18   *his*: i.e. Cupid's.
24 I.e. only fools try to confine the cuckoo between walls
    (in the hope of enjoying eternal spring), since it will
    simply fly over the top.
26–7 In *England's Helicon* the lines read:
        'Is love, which is the due of love;
        And love as well the shepherd can, . . .'
27   *thee foster*: 'the foster' (Dowland). *foster*: forester.

JOHN LYLY

Song

Pan's Syrinx was a girl indeed,
Though now she's turned into a reed;
From that dear reed Pan's pipe does come,
A pipe that strikes Apollo dumb.
5 Nor flute, nor lute, nor gittern can
So chant it, as the pipe of Pan;
Cross-gartered swains, and dairy girls,
With faces smug and round as pearls,
When Pan's shrill pipe begins to play,
10 With dancing wear out night and day.
The bagpipe's drone his hum lays by,
When Pan sounds up his minstrelsy;
His minstrelsy! O base! This quill,
Which at my mouth with wind I fill,
15 Puts me in mind, though her I miss,
That still my Syrinx' lips I kiss.

Midas (1632), IV.i

SONG: PAN'S SYRINX: This lyric from the play *Midas* may not
be by Lyly. The play, without the song, was first pub-
lished in 1592 (written *c.* 1589). The song is sung by Pan
attempting to outdo Apollo in a music contest. Midas,
who foolishly judges Pan's to be the better composition,
is later punished by Apollo; ironically, however, con-
temporary opinion agrees with Midas. The incident is
based on Ovid, *Met.* XI. 146–79.

1–3 See *Met.* I. 689–712.
8 *smug*: fresh.

ROBERT GREENE

Doron's Description of Samela

Like to Diana in her summer weed,
Girt with a crimson robe of brightest dye,
      Goes fair Samela.
Whiter than be the flocks that straggling feed,
When washed by Arethusa faint they lie,   5
      Is fair Samela.
As fair Aurora in her morning-grey,
Decked with the ruddy glister of her love,
      Is fair Samela.
Like lovely Thetis on a calmèd day,   10
Whenas her brightness Neptune's fancy move,
      Shines fair Samela.
Her tresses gold, her eyes like glassy streams,
Her teeth are pearl, the breasts are ivory
      Of fair Samela;   15
Her cheeks, like rose and lily, yield forth gleams,
Her brows bright arches framed of ebony.
      Thus fair Samela
Passeth fair Venus in her bravest hue,
And Juno in the show of majesty   20
      (For she is Samela),
Pallas in wit: all three, if you well view,
For beauty, wit, and matchless dignity,
      Yield to Samela.

Menaphon, 1589

DORON'S DESCRIPTION OF SAMELA:
  5 *Arethusa*: a river in Sicily. *Arethusa faint*: some eds. emend
    to 'Arethusa's fount'.

Doron's Eclogue Joined with Carmela's

Sit down, Carmela; here are cobs for kings,
Sloes black as jet, or like my Christmas shoes,
Sweet cider, which my leathern bottle brings;
Sit down, Carmela, let me kiss thy toes.

Carmela

5   Ah, Doron! ah, my heart! thou art as white
As is my mother's calf or brinded cow;
Thine eyes are like the slow-worms in the night,
Thine hairs resemble thickest of the snow.

The lines within thy face are deep and clear,
10   Like to the furrows of my father's wain;
Thy sweat upon thy face doth oft appear
Like to my mother's fat and kitchen-gain.

Ah, leave my toe and kiss my lips, my love:
My lips and thine, for I have given it thee;
15   Within thy cap 'tis thou shalt wear my glove;
At football sport thou shalt my champion be.

Doron

Carmela dear, even as the golden ball
That Venus got, such are thy goodly eyes;
When cherries' juice is jumbled therewithal,
20   Thy breath is like the steam of apple pies.

DORON'S ECLOGUE:
1   *cobs*: 'cubs' (1589). Cobs are a kind of nut.
7   *slow-worms*: she means 'glow-worms'; slow-worms are blind and at night are invisible.
12 *kitchen-gain*: dripping.
17-18 *the golden ball That Venus got*: i.e. the 'apple of discord', awarded to Venus by Paris, who judged her fairer than Juno or Pallas.

Thy lips resemble two cowcumbers fair,
Thy teeth like to the tusks of fattest swine,
Thy speech is like the thunder in the air;
Would God thy toes, thy lips, and all were mine!

Carmela

Doron, what thing doth move this wishing grief?   25

Doron

'Tis Love, Carmela, ah, 'tis cruel Love!
That like a slave and caitiff villain thief,
Hath cut my throat of joy for thy behove.

Carmela

Where was he born?

Doron

    In faith, I know not where,
But I have had much talking of his dart.   30
Ay me, poor man, with many a trampling tear
I feel him wound the forehearse of my heart.

What, do I love? O no, I do but talk;
What, shall I die for love? O no, not so;
What, am I dead? O no, my tongue doth walk;   35
Come, kiss, Carmela, and confound my woe.

Carmela

Even with this kiss, as once my father did,
I seal the sweet indentures of delight;
Before I break my vow the gods forbid,
No, not by day, nor yet by darksome night.   40

28   *behove*: promise.
32   *forehearse*: coined word, probably from the French *herse*
     ('portcullis'). There is a pun on 'hearse'.

Doron

Even with this garland made of hollyhocks
I cross thy brows from every shepherd's kiss.
Heigh-ho, how glad am I to touch thy locks!
My frolic heart even now a free man is.

Carmela

45   I thank you, Doron, and will think on you;
I love you, Doron, and will wink on you;
I seal your charter patent with my thumbs:
Come, kiss and part, for fear my mother comes.

Menaphon, 1589

NICHOLAS BRETON

The Ploughman's Song

In the merry month of May,
In a morn by break of day,
Forth I walkèd by the wood-side,
Whereas May was in his pride.
5   There I spièd, all alone,
Phyllida and Corydon.
Much ado there was, God wot,
He would love and she would not.
She said, never man was true;
10   He said, none was false to you.

THE PLOUGHMAN'S SONG: Sung by 'three excellent musicians... disguised in ancient country attire', under Queen Elizabeth's window during her stay at Elvetham, Hampshire, in 1591. A musical setting appeared in M. East, *Madrigals*, 1604, and in Henry Youll, *Canzonets*, 1608.

He said he had loved her long;
She said, love should have no wrong.
Corydon would kiss her then;
She said maids must kiss no men
Till they did for good and all.   15
Then she made the shepherd call
All the heavens to witness truth:
Never loved a truer youth.
Thus with many a pretty oath,
Yea and nay, and faith and troth,   20
Such as silly shepherds use
When they will not love abuse,
Love, which had been long deluded,
Was with kisses sweet concluded.
And Phyllida with garlands gay   25
Was made the Lady of the May.

Anon., *The Honourable Entertainment* . . .
at Elvetham, 1591

A Report Song in a Dream
Between a Shepherd and his Nymph

Shall we go dance the hay?   The hay?
Never pipe could ever play
   better shepherds' roundelay.

Shall we go sing the song?   The song?
Never love did ever wrong;   5
   fair maids, hold hands all along.

Shall we go learn to woo?   To woo?
Never thought came ever to,
   better deed could better do.

10   Shall we go learn to kiss?   To kiss?
       Never heart could ever miss
          comfort, where true meaning is.

       Thus at base they run,   They run,
       When the sport was scarce begun;—
15   but I waked, and all was done.

England's Helicon, 1600

[*Aglaia Walks Abroad*]
from *The Passionate Shepherd*

       Come abroad, you blessèd muses,
       Ye that Pallas chiefly chooses
       When she would commend a creature
       In the honour of love's nature;
5   For the sweet Aglaia fair,
       All to sweeten all the air,
       Is abroad this blessèd day;
       Haste ye, therefore, come away,
       And to kill love's maladies,
10   Meet her with your melodies.
       Flora hath been all about,
       And hath brought her wardrobe out,
       With her fairest sweetest flowers,
       All to trim up all your bowers.
15   Bid the shepherds and their swains
       See the beauty of their plains;

A REPORT SONG:
13   *base*: i.e. the game of prisoner's base.

And command them, with their flocks,
To do reverence on the rocks,
Where they may so happy be
As her shadow but to see.   20
Bid the birds in every bush
Not a bird to be at hush,
But to sit, chirrup, and sing
To the beauty of the spring.
Call the sylvan nymphs together,   25
Bid them bring their musics hither;
Trees their barky silence break,
Crack, yet though they cannot speak.
Bid the purest whitest swan
Of her feathers make her fan;   30
Let the hound the hare go chase,
Lambs and rabbits run at base;
Flies be dancing in the sun,
While the silkworms' webs are spun.
Hang a fish on every hook,   35
As she goes along the brook.
So with all your sweetest powers
Entertain her in your bowers,
Where her ear may joy to hear
How ye make your sweetest choir;   40
And in all your sweetest vein,
Still, Aglaia! strike the strain.
But when she her walk doth turn,
Then begin as fast to mourn:
All your flowers and garlands wither,   45
Put up all your pipes together;
Never strike a pleasing strain
Till she come abroad again.

The Passionate Shepherd (1604),
Past. II [ll. 35–82]

SAMUEL DANIEL

An Ode

Now each creature joys the other,
   Passing happy days and hours;
One bird reports unto another,
   In the fall of silver showers,
5   Whilst the earth, our common mother,
   Hath her bosom decked with flowers.

Whilst the greatest torch of heaven
   With bright rays warms Flora's lap,
Making nights and days both even,
10   Cheering plants with fresher sap;
My field, of flowers quite bereaven,
   Wants refresh of better hap.

Echo, daughter of the air,
   Babbling guest of rocks and hills,
15   Knows the name of my fierce fair,
   And sounds the accents of my ills;
Each thing pities my despair,
   Whilst that she her lover kills;

Whilst that she, oh, cruel maid!
20   Doth me and my love despise;
My life's flourish is decayed,
   That depended on her eyes.
But her will must be obeyed,
   And well he ends for love who dies.

Delia, 1601

AN ODE: First published 1592. Set to music by J. Farmer, *The First Set of English Madrigals,* 1599, and G. Handford, *Airs,* 1609.

A Pastoral

O happy golden age!
  Not for that rivers ran
  With streams of milk, and honey dropped from
    trees;
  Not that the earth did gage
  Unto the husbandman   5
  Her voluntary fruits, free without fees;
  Not for no cold did freeze,
  Nor any cloud beguile
  Th' eternal flow'ring spring,
  Wherein lived everything,   10
  And whereon th' heavens perpetually did smile;
  Not for no ship had brought,
  From foreign shores, or wars or wares ill sought.
But only for that name—
  That idle name of wind,   15
  That idol of deceit, that empty sound—
  Called Honour, which became
  The tyrant of the mind,
  And so torments our nature without ground,
  Was not yet vainly found,   20
  Nor yet sad griefs imparts
  Amidst the sweet delights
  Of joyful, amorous wights;
  Nor were his hard laws known to free-born hearts;
  But golden laws like these,   25
  Which nature wrote: 'That's lawful which doth
    please.'

A PASTORAL: Translated from Tasso, *Aminta* (1581), Chorus
after Act I. Like most Renaissance descriptions of the
Golden Age, it is based ultimately on Hesiod, *Works and
Days* 109–20, Vergil, Ecl. IV, and Ovid, *Met.* I. 89–112; how-
ever, the theme of freedom from honour's tyranny is
absent from the classical sources.
4 *gage*: pledge.

Then amongst flowers and springs,
    Making delightful sport,
    Sat lovers without conflict, without flame;
30   And nymphs and shepherds sings,
    Mixing in wanton sort
    Whisp'rings with songs, then kisses with the same,
    Which from affection came.
    The naked virgin then
35   Her roses fresh reveals,
    Which now her veil conceals,
    The tender apples in her bosom seen;
    And oft in rivers clear
    The lovers with their loves consorting were.
40 Honour, thou first didst close
    The spring of all delight,
    Denying water to the amorous thirst;
    Thou taught'st fair eyes to lose
    The glory of their light,
45   Restrained from men, and on themselves reversed.
    Thou in a lawn didst first
    Those golden hairs incase,
    Late spread unto the wind;
    Thou mad'st loose grace unkind;
50   Gav'st bridle to their words, art to their pace.
    O Honour, it is thou
    That mak'st that stealth, which love doth free
      allow;
  It is thy work that brings
    Our griefs and torments thus.
55   But thou, fierce lord of nature and of love,
    The qualifier of kings,
    What dost thou here with us,
    That are below thy power, shut from above?
    Go, and from us remove;
60   Trouble the mighty's sleep;
    Let us neglected, base,

Live still without thy grace,
And th' use of th' ancient happy ages keep.
Let's love; this life of ours
Can make no truce with time that all devours.   65

   Let's love; the sun doth set and rise again,
   But whenas our short light
Comes once to set, it makes eternal night.

Works, 1601

MICHAEL DRAYTON

[*Rowland's Ode to Beta*]
from *Idea: The Shepherd's Garland*

O thou fair silver Thames, O clearest crystal flood!
Beta alone the phoenix is of all thy watery brood;
    The queen of virgins only she,
    And thou the queen of floods shalt be;
Let all thy nymphs be joyful then to see this happy day;   5
Thy Beta now alone shall be the subject of my lay.

With dainty and delightsome strains of sweetest virelays,
Come, lovely shepherds, sit we down and chant our
    Beta's praise;
    And let us sing so rare a verse,
    Our Beta's praises to rehearse,   10
That little birds shall silent be, to hear poor shepherds
    sing,
And rivers backward bend their course and flow unto
    the spring.

ROWLAND'S ODE TO BETA: Rowland is Drayton's pastoral
   pseudonym. Beta is Queen Elizabeth. The ode is in-
   debted to Spenser's 'laye of fayre Eliza', in *The Shepheardes*
   Calender, Aprill.
  7 *virelays:* songs.

Range all thy swans, fair Thames, together on a rank,
And place them duly one by one upon thy stately bank;
15   Then set together all agood,
              Recording to the silver flood,
And crave the tuneful nightingale to help you with
              her lay,
The ouzel and the throstlecock, chief music of our May.

Oh, see what troops of nymphs been sporting on the
              strands!
And they been blessèd nymphs of peace with olives in
20   their hands.
              How merrily the muses sing,
              That all the flow'ry meadows ring!
And Beta sits upon the bank in purple and in pall,
And she the queen of muses is, and wears the coronal.

25 Trim up her golden tresses with Apollo's sacred tree:
O happy sight unto all those that love and honour thee!
              The blessèd angels have prepared
              A glorious crown for thy reward,
Not such a golden crown as haughty Caesar wears,
30 But such a glittering starry crown as Ariadne bears.

Make her a goodly chapelet of azured columbine,
And wreathe about her coronet with sweetest eglantine;
              Bedeck our Beta all with lilies,
              And the dainty daffodillies,
With roses damask, white, and red, and fairest flower-
35   de-lice,
With cowslips of Jerusalem, and cloves of paradise.

18   *ouzel*: blackbird. *throstlecock*: male thrush.
23   *pall*: a rich robe.
25   *Apollo's sacred tree*: i.e. the laurel.
30   Ariadne's crown was stellified as the Corona Borealis
     (Ovid, *Fasti* III. 507–16).

O thou fair torch of heaven, the day's most dearest light,
And thou bright-shining Cynthia, the glory of the night;
    You stars, the eyes of heaven,
    And thou, the gliding levin,   40
And thou, O gorgeous Iris, with all strange colours
    dyed:
When she streams forth her rays, then dashed is all
    your pride.

See how the day stands still, admiring of her face!
And time, lo, stretcheth forth her arms thy Beta to
    embrace;
    The sirens sing sweet lays,   45
    The tritons sound her praise.
Go pass on, Thames, and hie thee fast unto the ocean
    sea,
And let thy billows there proclaim thy Beta's holy-day;

And water thou the blessèd root of that green olive
    tree,
With whose sweet shadow all thy banks with peace
    preservèd be,   50
    Laurel for poets and conquerors,
    And myrtle for love's paramours,
That fame may be thy fruit, the boughs preserved by
    peace;
And let the mournful cypress die, now storms and
    tempests cease.

40   *levin*: lightning.
48   *Beta's holy-day*: perhaps referring to the national celebra-
    tion of Accession Day, 17 November. The festival com-
    memorated the coming of Elizabeth, the Virgin Queen,
    and England's release from Papal tyranny under Mary
    (see ll. 67–72).

We'll straw the shore with pearl where Beta walks
55   alone,
And we will pave her princely bower with richest
        Indian stone,
      Perfume the air and make it sweet,
      For such a goddess it is meet;
For if her eyes for purity contend with Titan's light,
No marvel then although they so do dazzle human
60   sight.

Sound out your trumpets then from London's stately
        towers,
To beat the stormy winds aback and calm the raging
        showers;
      Set too the cornet and the flute,
      The orpharion and the lute,
65 And tune the tabor and the pipe to the sweet violons,
And move the thunder in the air with loudest clarions.

Beta, long may thine altars smoke with yearly sacrifice,
And long thy sacred temples may their sabbaths
        solemnize,
      Thy shepherds watch by day and night,
70   Thy maids attend the holy light,
And thy large empire stretch her arms from East unto
        the West;
And thou under thy feet mayst tread that foul seven-
        headed beast.

Idea: The Shepherd's Garland (1593),
Ecl. III [ll. 49–120]

64 *orpharion*: a stringed instrument.
65 *tabor*: a small drum.
66 *clarions*: trumpets.
72 *foul seven-headed beast*: i.e. the Church of Rome. In *England's
Helicon*, 1600, the line was changed to read 'And Albion
on the Apennines advance her conquering crest.'

[*The Shepherd's Daffodil*]
from *Pastorals*

Batte.   Gorbo, as thou cam'st this way
   By yonder little hill,
   Or as thou through the fields didst stray,
   Saw'st thou my Daffodil?

   She's in a frock of Lincoln green,   5
   Which colour likes her sight,
   And never hath her beauty seen
   But through a veil of white;

   Than roses richer to behold,
   That trim up lovers' bowers,   10
   The pansy and the marigold,
   Though Phoebus' paramours.

Gorbo.   Thou well describ'st the daffodil;
   It is not full an hour
   Since by the spring near yonder hill   15
   I saw that lovely flower.

Batte.   Yet my fair flower thou didst not meet,
   Nor news of her didst bring,
   And yet my Daffodil's more sweet
   Than that by yonder spring.   20

Gorbo.   I saw a shepherd that doth keep
   In yonder field of lilies,
   Was making, as he fed his sheep,
   A wreath of daffodillies.

THE SHEPHERD'S DAFFODIL: First published, under this
   title, in *England's Helicon*, 1600.
 6   *likes*: befits.

25   *Batte.*   Yet, Gorbo, thou delud'st me still,
        My flower thou didst not see;
        For know, my pretty Daffodil
        Is worn of none but me.

        To show itself but near her seat
30   No lily is so bold,
        Except to shade her from the heat,
        Or keep her from the cold.

    Gorbo.   Through yonder vale as I did pass,
        Descending from the hill,
35   I met a smirking bonny lass;
        They call her Daffodil;

        Whose presence, as along she went,
        The pretty flowers did greet,
        As though their heads they downward bent
40   With homage to her feet.

        And all the shepherds that were nigh,
        From top of every hill,
        Unto the valleys loud did cry,
        'There goes sweet Daffodil.'

45   *Batte.*   Aye, gentle shepherd, now with joy
        Thou all my flocks dost fill,
        That's she alone, kind shepherd's boy;
        Let us to Daffodil.

Pastorals (1619), Ecl. IX [ll. 85–132]

35 *smirking*: smiling.

WILLIAM SHAKESPEARE

Song

[Spring]

When daisies pied, and violets blue,
   And lady-smocks all silver-white,
And cuckoo-buds of yellow hue
   Do paint the meadows with delight,
The cuckoo then on every tree   5
Mocks married men, for thus sings he:
      Cuckoo;
Cuckoo, cuckoo! Oh, word of fear,
Unpleasing to a married ear!

When shepherds pipe on oaten straws,   10
   And merry larks are ploughmen's clocks,
When turtles tread, and rooks, and daws,
   And maidens bleach their summer smocks,
The cuckoo then on every tree
Mocks married men, for thus sings he: 15
      Cuckoo;
Cuckoo, cuckoo! Oh, word of fear,
Unpleasing to a married ear!

Winter

When icicles hang by the wall,
   And Dick the shepherd blows his nail,   20
And Tom bears logs into the hall,
   And milk comes frozen home in pail,

SONG: WHEN DAISIES PIED: Written c. 1594. The song occurs
   at the end of the play as a 'dialogue . . . compiled in
   praise of the Owl and the Cuckoo'.
2–3 printed in the order 3–2 in 1623.
12 *turtles tread*: turtledoves mate.
20 *blows his nail*: i.e. whiles away the time by blowing on his
   fingers.

When blood is nipped, and ways be foul,
Then nightly sings the staring owl:
Tu-whit, tu-who,—a merry note,
While greasy Joan doth keel the pot.

When all aloud the wind doth blow,
    And coughing drowns the parson's saw,
And birds sit brooding in the snow,
    And Marion's nose looks red and raw;
When roasted crabs hiss in the bowl,
Then nightly sings the staring owl:
Tu-whit, to-who,—a merry note,
While greasy Joan doth keel the pot.

Love's Labour's Lost (1632), V [ii]

Song

Amiens.   Under the greenwood tree
Who loves to lie with me,
And turn his merry note
Unto the sweet bird's throat,
Come hither, come hither, come hither.
Here shall he see
No enemy
But winter and rough weather.

26   *keel the pot*: cool the pot (to prevent it boiling over).
28   *saw*: adage.
31   *crabs*: crab-apples.
SONG: UNDER THE GREENWOOD TREE: Written *c.* 1599. This
   song and the following are sung by attendants of the
   banished Duke in the forest of Arden.

All.   Who doth ambition shun,
        And loves to live i' th' sun,   10
        Seeking the food he eats,
        And pleased with what he gets,
      Come hither, come hither, come hither.
        Here shall he see
        No enemy   15
      But winter and rough weather.

Jaques.   If it do come to pass
        That any man turn ass,
        Leaving his wealth and ease
        A stubborn will to please,   20
      Ducdame, ducdame, ducdame.
        Here shall he see
        Gross fools as he,
      An if he will come to me.

As You Like It (1623), II.v

Song

      Blow, blow, thou winter wind,
      Thou art not so unkind
        As man's ingratitude;
      Thy tooth is not so keen
      Because thou art not seen,   5
        Although thy breath be rude.
Heigh-ho! sing heigh-ho, unto the green holly;
Most friendship is feigning, most loving mere folly.
        Then, heigh-ho, the holly!
        This life is most jolly.   10

17–24 A mocking response by the cynical Jaques. He explains
his variation on the refrain (l. 21) as 'a Greek invocation
to call fools into a circle.'
SONG: BLOW, BLOW, THOU WINTER WIND:
9 *Then*: 'The' (1623).

Freeze, freeze, thou bitter sky,
That dost not bite so nigh
　　As benefits forgot;
Though thou the waters warp,
15　　Thy sting is not so sharp
　　As friend remembered not.
Heigh-ho! sing heigh-ho, unto the green holly;
Most friendship is feigning, most loving mere folly.
　　Then, heigh-ho, the holly!
20　　This life is most jolly.

As You Like It (1623), II.vii

ANONYMOUS

Come away, come, sweet love!
The golden morning breaks;
All the earth, all the air
Of love and pleasure speaks.
5　　Teach thine arms then to embrace,
And sweet rosy lips to kiss,
And mix our souls in mutual bliss.
Eyes were made for beauty's grace,
Viewing, rueing love's long pain,
10　　Procured by beauty's rude disdain.

Come away, come, sweet love!
The golden morning wastes,
While the sun from his sphere
His fiery arrows casts,

14　*warp*: wrinkle by freezing.
COME AWAY, COME:
　9　*love's long pain* (reading in *England's Helicon*, 1600): 'love-long
　　pains' (1597).

Making all the shadows fly,   15
Playing, staying in the grove
To entertain the stealth of love.
Thither, sweet love, let us hie,
Flying, dying in desire,
Winged with sweet hopes and heavenly fire.   20

Come away, come, sweet love!
Do not in vain adorn
Beauty's grace, that should rise
Like to the naked morn.
Lilies on the river's side   25
And fair Cyprian flowers new blown
Desire no beauties but their own.
Ornament is nurse of pride;
Pleasure, measure, love's delight.
Haste then, sweet love, our wishèd flight.   30

J. Dowland, *The First Book of Songs
or Airs*, 1597

THOMAS LODGE

Old Damon's Pastoral

From fortune's frowns and change removed,
    Wend, silly flocks, in blessèd feeding;
None of Damon more beloved,
    Feed, gentle lambs, while I sit reading.

26 *Cyprian flowers*: anemones (associated with Venus, whose
home was Cyprus); or simply 'lovers' flowers'.

5   Careless worldlings, outrage quelleth
      All the pride and pomp of city:
But true peace with shepherds dwelleth,
      Shepherds who delight in pity.
Whether grace of heaven betideth
10   On our humble minds such pleasure,
Perfect peace with swains abideth,
      Love and faith is shepherds' treasure.
On the lower plains the thunder
      Little thrives and nought prevaileth,
15   Yet in cities breedeth wonder,
      And the highest hills assaileth.

Envy of a foreign tyrant
      Threat'neth kings, not shepherds humble;
Age makes silly swains delirant,
20   Thirst of rule gars great men stumble.
What to other seemeth sorry,
      Abject state, and humble biding,
Is our joy and country glory;
      Highest states have worse betiding.
25   Golden cups do harbour poison,
      And the greatest pomp, dissembling;
Court of seasoned words hath foison,
      Treason haunts in most assembling.

Homely breasts do harbour quiet,
30   Little fear, and mickle solace;
States suspect their bed and diet,
      Fear and craft do haunt the palace.
Little would I, little want I,
      Where the mind and store agreeth;

OLD DAMON'S PASTORAL:
19   *delirant*: crazed.
20   *gars*: makes.
27   *foison*: abundance.
31   *States*: princes.

Smallest comfort is not scanty,   35
   Least he longs that little seeth.
Time hath been that I have longed,
   (Foolish I, to like of folly)
To converse where honour thronged,
   To my pleasures linkèd wholly.   40

Now I see, and seeing sorrow,
   That the day, consumed, returns not;
Who dare trust upon tomorrow,
   When nor time nor life sojourns not?

England's Helicon, 1600

THOMAS CAMPION

I care not for these ladies
That must be wooed and prayed;
Give me kind Amaryllis,
The wanton country maid.
Nature art disdaineth,   5
Her beauty is her own;
   Her when we court and kiss,
   She cries, 'Forsooth, let go!'
   But when we come where comfort is,
   She never will say no.   10

If I love Amaryllis,
She gives me fruit and flowers;
But if we love these ladies,
We must give golden showers.

I CARE NOT FOR THESE LADIES: The music is a jig, a lively
   country dance measure. For setting, see *Works of Thomas
   Campion,* ed. W. R. Davis, 1969, p. 23.
14 *golden showers*: i.e. great wealth. The reference is to the se-
   duction of Danae by Jove in the form of a shower of gold;
   the tale was interpreted as the power of riches to win love.

15   Give them gold that sell love,
    Give me the nut-brown lass,
      Who when we court and kiss,
      She cries, 'Forsooth, let go!'
      But when we come where comfort is,
20   She never will say no.

    These ladies must have pillows,
    And beds by strangers wrought;
    Give me a bower of willows,
    Of moss and leaves unbought,
25   And fresh Amaryllis,
    With milk and honey fed;
      Who when we court and kiss,
      She cries, 'Forsooth, let go!'
      But when we come where comfort is,
30   She never will say no.

A Book of Airs, 1601

SIR WALTER RALEGH

The Passionate Man's Pilgrimage
supposed to be written by one at the point of death

Give me my scallop-shell of quiet,
My staff of faith to walk upon,
My scrip of joy, immortal diet,

THE PASSIONATE MAN'S PILGRIMAGE: Probably written in
    the Tower in 1603, after Ralegh had suffered a grossly
    unjust trial and had been condemned to death. (He was
    reprieved on the day fixed for his execution.)
1   *scallop-shell*: pilgrim's badge. A shell from the Galician
    shore was worn by those who had visited the shrine of
    St James at Compostella.
3   *scrip*: small bag.

My bottle of salvation,
My gown of glory, hope's true gage: 5
And thus I'll take my pilgrimage.

Blood must be my body's balmer:
No other balm will there be given,
Whilst my soul, like a white palmer,
Travels to the land of heaven,   10
Over the silver mountains,
Where spring the nectar fountains;
And there I'll kiss
The bowl of bliss,
And drink my eternal fill   15
On every milken hill.
My soul will be a-dry before,
But after it will ne'er thirst more.
And by the happy blissful way
More peaceful pilgrims I shall see,   20
That have shook off their gowns of clay
And go apparelled fresh like me.
I'll bring them first
To slake their thirst,
And then to taste those nectar suckets,   25
At the clear wells
Where sweetness dwells,
Drawn up by saints in crystal buckets.

And when our bottles and all we
Are filled with immortality,   30
Then the holy paths we'll travel,
Strewed with rubies thick as gravel,
Ceilings of diamonds, sapphire floors,
High walls of coral, and pearl bowers.

5 *gage*: pledge.
9 *palmer*: pilgrim.
25 *suckets*: sweetmeats.

35 From thence to heaven's bribeless hall,
Where no corrupted voices brawl,
No conscience molten into gold,
Nor forged accusers bought and sold,
No cause deferred, nor vain-spent journey,
40 For there Christ is the King's Attorney,
Who pleads for all without degrees,
And he hath angels, but no fees.
When the grand twelve million jury
Of our sins and sinful fury
45 'Gainst our souls black verdicts give,
Christ pleads his death, and then we live.
Be thou my speaker, taintless pleader,
Unblotted lawyer, true proceeder;
Thou movest salvation even for alms,
50 Not with a bribèd lawyer's palms.

And this is my eternal plea
To him that made heaven, earth, and sea,
Seeing my flesh must die so soon,
And want a head to dine next noon:
55 Just at the stroke when my veins start and spread,
Set on my soul an everlasting head;
Then am I ready, like a palmer fit,
To tread those blest paths which before I writ.

A. Scoloker, *Daiphantus*, 1604

40 The King's Attorney at Ralegh's trial was Sir Edward
Coke, whose bullying invective was largely responsible
for his conviction.
41 *without degrees*: regardless of rank.
42 *angels*: a pun on angel, the gold coin.
49 *for alms*: i.e. as an act of charity.

POEMS OF THE PASSIONATE SHEPHERD AND HIS NYMPH

CHRISTOPHER MARLOWE

The Passionate Shepherd to his Love

Come live with me and be my love,
And we will all the pleasures prove
That valleys, groves, hills, and fields,
Woods, or steepy mountain yields.

And we will sit upon the rocks,   5
Seeing the shepherds feed their flocks
By shallow rivers to whose falls
Melodious birds sing madrigals.

And I will make thee beds of roses
And a thousand fragrant posies,   10
A cap of flowers, and a kirtle
Embroidered all with leaves of myrtle;

THE PASSIONATE SHEPHERD: Written *c.* 1588; first published
(in shorter form) in *The Passionate Pilgrim*, 1599. It was made
into a broadsheet ballad (ent. 1603), with Ralegh's *Reply*
set to the same tune. For the setting by W. Corkine (1612),
to which Marlowe's, Ralegh's, and Donne's poems may
all have been sung, see Donne, *Elegies and The Songs and
Sonnets*, ed. Helen Gardner, Oxford, 1965, p. 239.
8   *sing (Passionate Pilgrim)*: 'sings' (1600).
10   *posies*: 'poesies' (1600).
11   *kirtle*: skirt.

A gown made of the finest wool
Which from our pretty lambs we pull;
15 Fair linèd slippers for the cold,
With buckles of the purest gold;

A belt of straw and ivy buds,
With coral clasps and amber studs:
And if these pleasures may thee move,
20 Come live with me and be my love.

The shepherds' swains shall dance and sing
For thy delight each May morning:
If these delights thy mind may move,
Then live with me and be my love.

England's Helicon, 1600

SIR WALTER RALEGH

The Nymph's Reply to the Shepherd

If all the world and love were young,
And truth in every shepherd's tongue,
These pretty pleasures might me move
To live with thee and be thy love.

5 Time drives the flocks from field to fold,
When rivers rage and rocks grow cold,
And Philomel becometh dumb;
The rest complains of cares to come.

The flowers do fade, and wanton fields
10 To wayward winter reckoning yields;
A honey tongue, a heart of gall,
Is fancy's spring, but sorrow's fall.

THE NYMPH'S REPLY:
12 *fall*: autumn.

Thy gowns, thy shoes, thy beds of roses,
Thy cap, thy kirtle, and thy posies
Soon break, soon wither, soon forgotten,—   15
In folly ripe, in reason rotten.

Thy belt of straw and ivy buds,
Thy coral clasps, and amber studs,
All these in me no means can move
To come to thee and be thy love.   20

But could youth last and love still breed,
Had joys no date nor age no need,
Then these delights my mind might move
To live with thee and be thy love.

England's Helicon, 1600

JOHN DONNE

The Bait

Come live with me and be my love,
And we will some new pleasures prove,
Of golden sands, and crystal brooks,
With silken lines, and silver hooks.

There will the river whispering run,   5
Warmed by thy eyes, more than the sun.
And there the enamoured fish will stay,
Begging themselves they may betray.

14   *posies*: 'poesies' (1600).
THE BAIT: Probably written before 1600, to an already existing
      tune. Title is from *Poems*, 1635.

267

When thou wilt swim in that live bath,
10 Each fish, which every channel hath,
Will amorously to thee swim,
Gladder to catch thee than thou him.

If thou to be so seen be'st loath,
By sun or moon, thou dark'nest both;
15 And if myself have leave to see,
I need not their light, having thee.

Let others freeze with angling reeds,
And cut their legs with shells and weeds,
Or treacherously poor fish beset
20 With strangling snare, or windowy net.

Let coarse bold hands from slimy nest
The bedded fish in banks out-wrest,
Or curious traitors, sleave-silk flies,
Bewitch poor fishes' wand'ring eyes.

25 For thee, thou need'st no such deceit,
For thou thyself art thine own bait;
That fish that is not catched thereby,
Alas, is wiser far than I.

Poems, 1633

18   *with* (1635): 'which' (1633).
23   *curious*: exquisite. *sleave-silk* (1635): 'sleave-sick' (1633).
Sleave-silk is unravelled silk.

OVIDIAN ROMANCES

VENUS WITH THE DYING ADONIS
From A. Alciati, *Omnia . . . Emblemata*, Antwerp, 1577
(Folger Shakespeare Library)

Tranio.   While we do admire
This virtue and this moral discipline,
Let's be no Stoics nor no stocks, I pray,
Or so devote to Aristotle's checks
As Ovid be an outcast quite abjured. . . .
No profit grows where is no pleasure ta'en.
                    Shakespeare, *The Taming of the Shrew* I.i

The laws of love are full of pure divinity,
Beauty, it is attractive and divine;
This caused Cynthia, that had vowed virginity,
Her hornèd compass to the earth decline,
    To give long-sleeping Latmian swain a kiss:
    Her fairness did deserve no less than this.
                    Thomas Heywood, *Oenone and Paris* (1594), St. 115

. . . so the sweet witty soul of Ovid lives in mellifluous and
honey-tongued Shakespeare; witness his *Venus and Adonis*, . . .
                    Meres, *Palladis Tamia*, 1598

Harebrain.   . . . wanton pamphlets, as *Hero and
Leander, Venus and Adonis*; oh, two luscious mary-bone pies for
a young married wife!
                    Middleton, *A Mad World, my Masters* (1608), I.ii

CHRISTOPHER MARLOWE

Hero and Leander

On Hellespont, guilty of true love's blood,
In view and opposite, two cities stood,
Sea-borderers, disjoined by Neptune's might;
The one Abydos, the other Sestos hight.
At Sestos Hero dwelt; Hero the fair,   5
Whom young Apollo courted for her hair,
And offered as a dower his burning throne,
Where she should sit for men to gaze upon.
The outside of her garments were of lawn,
The lining purple silk, with gilt stars drawn;   10
Her wide sleeves green, and bordered with a grove
Where Venus in her naked glory strove
To please the careless and disdainful eyes
Of proud Adonis, that before her lies.
Her kirtle blue, whereon was many a stain,   15
Made with the blood of wretched lovers slain.
Upon her head she ware a myrtle wreath,
From whence her veil reached to the ground beneath.
Her veil was artificial flowers and leaves,
Whose workmanship both man and beast deceives.   20
Many would praise the sweet smell as she passed,
When 'twas the odour which her breath forth cast;
And there for honey, bees have sought in vain,
And, beat from thence, have lighted there again.
About her neck hung chains of pebble-stone,   25

HERO AND LEANDER: Marlowe's poem was left unfinished at
  his death in 1593. It was first published in 1598. It appeared
  again in the same year, with George Chapman's con-
  tinuation: Chapman divided Marlowe's lines (at l. 484)
  into two 'sestiads' and extended the story by adding four
  more of his own. Marlowe's poem is printed here in its
  original form, from the first edition.
3 *Sea-borderers* (1629): 'Sea-borders' (1598).
4 *hight*: named.
15 *kirtle*: skirt.

271

Which, lightened by her neck, like diamonds shone.
She ware no gloves, for neither sun nor wind
Would burn or parch her hands, but to her mind,
Or warm or cool them, for they took delight
30   To play upon those hands, they were so white.
Buskins of shells all silvered usèd she,
And branched with blushing coral to the knee,
Where sparrows perched, of hollow pearl and gold,
Such as the world would wonder to behold;
35   Those with sweet water oft her handmaid fills,
Which, as she went, would chirrup through the bills.
Some say, for her the fairest Cupid pined,
And looking in her face, was strooken blind.
But this is true: so like was one the other,
40   As he imagined Hero was his mother;
And oftentimes into her bosom flew,
About her naked neck his bare arms threw,
And laid his childish head upon her breast,
And with still panting rocked, there took his rest.
45   So lovely fair was Hero, Venus' nun,
As nature wept, thinking she was undone,
Because she took more from her than she left,
And of such wondrous beauty her bereft;
Therefore, in sign her treasure suffered wrack,
50   Since Hero's time hath half the world been black.
Amorous Leander, beautiful and young,
(Whose tragedy divine Musaeus sung)
Dwelt at Abydos; since him dwelt there none
For whom succeeding times make greater moan.
55   His dangling tresses that were never shorn,
Had they been cut and unto Colchis borne,

44   *still*: constant.
52   *Musaeus*: Greek grammarian of the fifth century A.D., who wrote a poem on Hero and Leander. He is here confused with the semi-legendary Orphic poet of ancient Greece.
56   *Colchis*: land to which the Argonauts sailed in quest of the Golden Fleece.

Would have allured the vent'rous youth of Greece
To hazard more than for the Golden Fleece.
Fair Cynthia wished his arms might be her sphere;
Grief makes her pale, because she moves not there.   60
His body was as straight as Circe's wand;
Jove might have sipped out nectar from his hand.
Even as delicious meat is to the taste,
So was his neck in touching, and surpassed
The white of Pelops' shoulder. I could tell ye   65
How smooth his breast was, and how white his belly,
And whose immortal fingers did imprint
That heavenly path, with many a curious dint,
That runs along his back; but my rude pen
Can hardly blazon forth the loves of men,   70
Much less of powerful gods; let it suffice
That my slack muse sings of Leander's eyes,
Those orient cheeks and lips, exceeding his
That leapt into the water for a kiss
Of his own shadow, and despising many,   75
Died ere he could enjoy the love of any.
Had wild Hippolytus Leander seen,
Enamoured of his beauty had he been;
His presence made the rudest peasant melt,
That in the vast uplandish country dwelt;   80
The barbarous Thracian soldier, moved with nought,
Was moved with him, and for his favour sought.
Some swore he was a maid in man's attire,
For in his looks were all that men desire:
A pleasant smiling cheek, a speaking eye,   85
A brow for love to banquet royally;

65 *Pelops' shoulder*: Pelops was cut up and offered by his father
    as food for the gods; he was later restored to life, and his
    shoulder—all that had been eaten—was replaced by one
    of ivory.
68 *curious*: exquisite.
73 *his*: i.e. Narcissus'.
77–8 Hippolytus staunchly preferred hunting to love.

And such as knew he was a man, would say,
'Leander, thou art made for amorous play;
Why art thou not in love, and loved of all?
90   Though thou be fair, yet be not thine own thrall.'
    The men of wealthy Sestos every year,
For his sake whom their goddess held so dear,
Rose-cheeked Adonis, kept a solemn feast;
Thither resorted many a wand'ring guest
95   To meet their loves; such as had none at all,
Came lovers home from this great festival.
For every street, like to a firmament,
Glistered with breathing stars, who, where they went,
Frighted the melancholy earth, which deemed
100   Eternal heaven to burn, for so it seeemed
As if another Phaeton had got
The guidance of the sun's rich chariot.
But, far above the loveliest, Hero shined,
And stole away th' enchanted gazer's mind;
105   For like sea-nymphs' inveigling harmony,
So was her beauty to the standers-by.
Nor that night-wand'ring, pale, and wat'ry star
(When yawning dragons draw her thirling car
From Latmos' mount up to the gloomy sky,
110   Where, crowned with blazing light and majesty,
She proudly sits) more overrules the flood,
Than she the hearts of those that near her stood.
Even as when gaudy nymphs pursue the chase,
Wretched Ixion's shaggy-footed race,
115   Incensed with savage heat, gallop amain
From steep pine-bearing mountains to the plain,

101–2 Phaeton was allowed by his father Phoebus to drive the
     chariot of the sun. When he lost control of the horses
     the earth was threatened with conflagration.
107 *night-wand'ring . . . star*: i.e. the moon.
108 *thirling*: whirling.
109 *Latmos' mount*: home of Endymion, beloved of the moon.
114 I.e. the Centaurs, fathered by Ixion.

So ran the people forth to gaze upon her,
And all that viewed her were enamoured on her.
And as in fury of a dreadful fight,
Their fellows being slain or put to flight,   120
Poor soldiers stand with fear of death dead-strooken,
So at her presence all, surprised and tooken,
Await the sentence of her scornful eyes;
He whom she favours lives, the other dies.
There might you see one sigh, another rage,   125
And some, their violent passions to assuage,
Compile sharp satires; but alas, too late,
For faithful love will never turn to hate.
And many, seeing great princes were denied,
Pined as they went, and thinking on her, died.   130
On this feast day, oh, cursèd day and hour!
Went Hero thorough Sestos, from her tower
To Venus' temple, where unhappily,
As after chanced, they did each other spy.
So fair a church as this had Venus none;   135
The walls were of discoloured jasper stone,
Wherein was Proteus carvèd, and o'erhead
A lively vine of green sea-agate spread,
Where by one hand light-headed Bacchus hung,
And with the other wine from grapes out-wrung.   140
Of crystal shining fair the pavement was;
The town of Sestos called it Venus' glass.
There might you see the gods in sundry shapes,
Committing heady riots, incest, rapes;
For know that underneath this radiant floor   145
Was Danae's statue in a brazen tower;
Jove slyly stealing from his sister's bed

---

136 *discoloured*: particoloured.
146 Danae, imprisoned in a brazen tower, was seduced by
Jove, who entered in a shower of gold.
147 *his sister's*: i.e. his wife Juno's.

To dally with Idalian Ganymed;
And for his love Europa bellowing loud,
150   And tumbling with the rainbow in a cloud;
Blood-quaffing Mars heaving the iron net
Which limping Vulcan and his Cyclops set;
Love kindling fire to burn such towns as Troy;
Silvanus weeping for the lovely boy
155   That now is turned into a cypress tree,
Under whose shade the wood-gods love to be.
And in the midst a silver altar stood;
There Hero sacrificing turtles' blood,
Vailed to the ground, vailing her eyelids close,
160   And modestly they opened as she rose;
Thence flew love's arrow with the golden head,
And thus Leander was enamourèd.
Stone-still he stood, and evermore he gazed,
Till with the fire that from his count'nance blazed,
165   Relenting Hero's gentle heart was strook;
Such force and virtue hath an amorous look.
    It lies not in our power to love, or hate,
For will in us is overruled by fate.
When two are stripped, long ere the course begin,
170   We wish that one should lose, the other win;
And one especially do we affect
Of two gold ingots, like in each respect.
The reason no man knows; let it suffice,

148 *Idalian*: i.e. of Mount Ida, where Ganymede was a shep-
herd-boy before he became the gods' cup-bearer.
149 Jove wooed Europa in the shape of a bull.
150 *the rainbow*: i.e. Iris.
151 *iron net*: i.e. that in which Mars was entrapped with Venus,
Vulcan's wife.
154 *the lovely boy*: i.e. Cyparissus, who was transformed into a
cypress tree while mourning the death of a stag he had
killed.
158 *turtles*: turtledoves.
159 *Vailed*: bowed in reverence. *vailing*: lowering.
166 *virtue*: power.

What we behold is censured by our eyes.
Where both deliberate, the love is slight;   175
Who ever loved, that loved not at first sight?
   He kneeled, but unto her devoutly prayed;
Chaste Hero to herself thus softly said:
'Were I the saint he worships, I would hear him;'
And as she spake those words, came somewhat near
     him.   180
He started up; she blushed as one ashamed;
Wherewith Leander much more was inflamed.
He touched her hand; in touching it she trembled;
Love deeply grounded hardly is dissembled.
These lovers parlèd by the touch of hands;   185
True love is mute, and oft amazèd stands.
Thus while dumb signs their yielding hearts entangled,
The air with sparks of living fire was spangled;
And night, deep drenched in misty Acheron,
Heaved up her head, and half the world upon   190
Breathed darkness forth (dark night is Cupid's day).
And now begins Leander to display
Love's holy fire with words, with sighs, and tears,
Which like sweet music entered Hero's ears;
And yet at every word she turned aside,   195
And always cut him off as he replied.
At last, like to a bold sharp sophister,
With cheerful hope thus he accosted her:
   'Fair creature, let me speak without offence;
I would my rude words had the influence   200
To lead thy thoughts as thy fair looks do mine,
Then shouldst thou be his prisoner who is thine.
Be not unkind and fair; misshapen stuff
Are of behaviour boisterous and rough.
Oh, shun me not, but hear me ere you go,   205
God knows, I cannot force love, as you do.

174 *censured*: judged.
206 *force*: resist.

My words shall be as spotless as my youth,
Full of simplicity and naked truth.
This sacrifice, whose sweet perfume descending
210   From Venus' altar to your footsteps bending,
Doth testify that you exceed her far,
To whom you offer, and whose nun you are.
Why should you worship her? her you surpass
As much as sparkling diamonds flaring glass.
215   A diamond set in lead his worth retains;
A heavenly nymph, beloved of human swains,
Receives no blemish, but ofttimes more grace;
Which makes me hope, although I am but base,
Base in respect of thee, divine and pure,
220   Dutiful service may thy love procure;
And I in duty will excel all other,
As thou in beauty dost exceed Love's mother.
Nor heaven, nor thou, were made to gaze upon;
As heaven preserves all things, so save thou one.
225   A stately builded ship, well rigged and tall,
The ocean maketh more majestical;
Why vowest thou then to live in Sestos here,
Who on love's seas more glorious wouldst appear?
Like untuned golden strings all women are,
230   Which long time lie untouched, will harshly jar.
Vessels of brass, oft handled, brightly shine;
What difference betwixt the richest mine
And basest mould, but use? for both, not used,
Are of like worth. Then treasure is abused,
235   When misers keep it; being put to loan,
In time it will return us two for one.
Rich robes themselves and others do adorn;
Neither themselves nor others, if not worn.
Who builds a palace, and rams up the gate,
240   Shall see it ruinous and desolate.

214 *flaring*: glaring, showy.

278

Ah, simple Hero, learn thyself to cherish!
Lone women, like to empty houses, perish.
Less sins the poor rich man that starves himself
In heaping up a mass of drossy pelf,
Than such as you; his golden earth remains,   245
Which after his decease some other gains;
But this fair gem, sweet in the loss alone,
When you fleet hence, can be bequeathed to none;
Or if it could, down from th' enamelled sky
All heaven would come to claim this legacy,   250
And with intestine broils the world destroy,
And quite confound nature's sweet harmony.
Well therefore by the gods decreed it is
We human creatures should enjoy that bliss.
One is no number; maids are nothing, then,   255
Without the sweet society of men.
Wilt thou live single still? one shalt thou be,
Though never-singling Hymen couple thee.
Wild savages, that drink of running springs,
Think water far excels all earthly things,   260
But they that daily taste neat wine, despise it;
Virginity, albeit some highly prize it,
Compared with marriage, had you tried them both,
Differs as much as wine and water doth.
Base bullion for the stamp's sake we allow;   265
Even so for men's impression do we you;
By which alone, our reverend fathers say,
Women receive perfection every way.
This idol which you term virginity
Is neither essence subject to the eye,   270
No, nor to any one exterior sense,
Nor hath it any place of residence,
Nor is 't of earth or mould celestial,
Or capable of any form at all.

251 *intestine broils*: civil wars.
265 *for the stamp's sake*: i.e. for coinage.

275 Of that which hath no being, do not boast;
    Things that are not at all, are never lost.
    Men foolishly do call it virtuous;
    What virtue is it, that is born with us?
    Much less can honour be ascribed thereto;
280 Honour is purchased by the deeds we do.
    Believe me, Hero, honour is not won
    Until some honourable deed be done.
    Seek you, for chastity, immortal fame,
    And know that some have wronged Diana's name?
285 Whose name is it, if she be false or not,
    So she be fair, but some vile tongues will blot?
    But you are fair, ay me, so wondrous fair,
    So young, so gentle, and so debonair,
    As Greece will think, if thus you live alone,
290 Some one or other keeps you as his own.
    Then, Hero, hate me not, nor from me fly,
    To follow swiftly blasting infamy.
    Perhaps thy sacred priesthood makes thee loath;
    Tell me, to whom mad'st thou that heedless oath?'
295   'To Venus,' answered she; and as she spake,
    Forth from those two tralucent cisterns brake
    A stream of liquid pearl, which down her face
    Made milk-white paths, whereon the gods might trace
    To Jove's high court. He thus replied: 'The rites
300 In which love's beauteous empress most delights
    Are banquets, Doric music, midnight revel,
    Plays, masques, and all that stern age counteth evil.
    Thee as a holy idiot doth she scorn,
    For thou, in vowing chastity, hast sworn
305 To rob her name and honour, and thereby
    Commit'st a sin far worse than perjury,
    Even sacrilege against her deity,
    Through regular and formal purity.

    301 *Doric music*: Music in the Dorian mode was simple and
       solemn; it is not clear why 'stern age' should condemn it.

To expiate which sin, kiss and shake hands;
Such sacrifice as this Venus demands.'   310
   Thereat she smiled, and did deny him so
As, put thereby, yet might he hope for mo;
Which makes him quickly reinforce his speech,
And her in humble manner thus beseech:
   'Though neither gods nor men may thee deserve,   315
Yet for her sake whom you have vowed to serve,
Abandon fruitless cold virginity,
The gentle queen of love's sole enemy.
Then shall you most resemble Venus' nun,
When Venus' sweet rites are performed and done.   320
Flint-breasted Pallas joys in single life,
But Pallas and your mistress are at strife.
Love, Hero, then, and be not tyrannous,
But heal the heart that thou hast wounded thus;
Nor stain thy youthful years with avarice;   325
Fair fools delight to be accounted nice.
The richest corn dies if it be not reaped;
Beauty alone is lost, too warily kept.'
These arguments he used, and many more,
Wherewith she yielded, that was won before.   330
Hero's looks yielded, but her words made war;
Women are won when they begin to jar.
Thus having swallowed Cupid's golden hook,
The more she strived, the deeper was she strook;
Yet, evilly feigning anger, strove she still,   335
And would be thought to grant against her will.
So having paused awhile, at last she said:
'Who taught thee rhetoric to deceive a maid?
Ay me! such words as these should I abhor,
And yet I like them for the orator.'   340
   With that Leander stooped to have embraced her,
But from his spreading arms away she cast her,

326 *nice*: coy.
332 *jar*: dispute.

281

And thus bespake him: 'Gentle youth, forbear
To touch the sacred garments which I wear.
345 Upon a rock, and underneath a hill,
Far from the town, where all is whist and still,
Save that the sea playing on yellow sand
Sends forth a rattling murmur to the land,
Whose sound allures the golden Morpheus
350 In silence of the night to visit us,
My turret stands; and there, God knows, I play
With Venus' swans and sparrows all the day.
A dwarfish beldame bears me company,
That hops about the chamber where I lie,
355 And spends the night, that might be better spent,
In vain discourse and apish merriment.
Come thither.' As she spake this, her tongue tripped,
For unawares 'Come thither' from her slipped;
And suddenly her former colour changed,
360 And here and there her eyes through anger ranged.
And like a planet moving several ways
At one self instant, she, poor soul, assays,
Loving, not to love at all, and every part
Strove to resist the motions of her heart;
365 And hands so pure, so innocent, nay such
As might have made heaven stoop to have a touch,
Did she uphold to Venus, and again
Vowed spotless chastity, but all in vain.
Cupid beats down her prayers with his wings;
370 Her vows above the empty air he flings;
All deep enraged, his sinewy bow he bent,
And shot a shaft that burning from him went;
Wherewith she, strooken, looked so dolefully,
As made Love sigh to see his tyranny.

361–2 *a planet . . . instant*: In the Ptolemaic universe each planet
moved in its own sphere while its motion was influenced
by other spheres.

And as she wept, her tears to pearl he turned, 375
And wound them on his arm, and for her mourned.
Then towards the palace of the Destinies,
Laden with languishment and grief, he flies,
And to those stern nymphs humbly made request,
Both might enjoy each other, and be blest. 380
But with a ghastly dreadful countenance,
Threat'ning a thousand deaths at every glance,
They answered Love, nor would vouchsafe so much
As one poor word, their hate to him was such.
Hearken awhile, and I will tell you why: 385
Heaven's wingèd herald, Jove-born Mercury,
The selfsame day that he asleep had laid
Enchanted Argus, spied a country maid,
Whose careless hair, instead of pearl t' adorn it,
Glistered with dew, as one that seemed to scorn it; 390
Her breath as fragrant as the morning rose,
Her mind pure, and her tongue untaught to gloze;
Yet proud she was, for lofty pride that dwells
In towered courts is oft in shepherds' cells,
And too too well the fair vermilion knew, 395
And silver tincture of her cheeks, that drew
The love of every swain. On her this god
Enamoured was, and with his snaky rod
Did charm her nimble feet, and made her stay,
The while upon a hillock down he lay, 400
And sweetly on his pipe began to play,
And with smooth speech her fancy to assay;
Till in his twining arms he locked her fast,
And then he wooed with kisses, and at last,
As shepherds do, her on the ground he laid, 405
And tumbling in the grass, he often strayed
Beyond the bounds of shame, in being bold
To eye those parts which no eye should behold.

392 *gloze*: use deceptive speech.
398 *snaky rod*: caduceus.

And like an insolent commanding lover,
410 Boasting his parentage, would needs discover
The way to new Elysium; but she,
Whose only dower was her chastity,
Having striv'n in vain, was now about to cry,
And crave the help of shepherds that were nigh.
415 Herewith he stayed his fury, and began
To give her leave to rise; away she ran;
After went Mercury, who used such cunning,
As she, to hear his tale, left off her running;
Maids are not won by brutish force and might,
420 But speeches full of pleasure and delight;
And knowing Hermes courted her, was glad
That she such loveliness and beauty had
As could provoke his liking, yet was mute,
And neither would deny nor grant his suit.
425 Still vowed he love; she, wanting no excuse
To feed him with delays, as women use,
Or thirsting after immortality,
(All women are ambitious naturally)
Imposed upon her lover such a task
430 As he ought not perform, nor yet she ask.
A draught of flowing nectar she requested,
Wherewith the king of gods and men is feasted.
He, ready to accomplish what she willed,
Stole some from Hebe (Hebe Jove's cup filled)
435 And gave it to his simple rustic love;
Which being known (as what is hid from Jove?)
He inly stormed, and waxed more furious
Than for the fire filched by Prometheus,
And thrusts him down from heaven; he wand'ring here
440 In mournful terms, with sad and heavy cheer,
Complained to Cupid. Cupid, for his sake,
To be revenged on Jove did undertake;
And those on whom heaven, earth, and hell relies,
I mean the adamantine Destinies,

He wounds with love, and forced them equally   445
To dote upon deceitful Mercury.
They offered him the deadly fatal knife
That shears the slender threads of human life;
At his fair feathered feet the engines laid
Which th' earth from ugly Chaos' den upweighed;   450
These he regarded not, but did entreat
That Jove, usurper of his father's seat,
Might presently be banished into hell,
And agèd Saturn in Olympus dwell.
They granted what he craved, and once again   455
Saturn and Ops began their golden reign.
Murder, rape, war, lust, and treachery
Were with Jove closed in Stygian empery.
But long this blessèd time continued not;
As soon as he his wishèd purpose got,   460
He, reckless of his promise, did despise
The love of th' everlasting Destinies;
They seeing it, both Love and him abhorred,
And Jupiter unto his place restored.
And but that Learning, in despite of Fate,   465
Will mount aloft, and enter heaven gate,
And to the seat of Jove itself advance,
Hermes had slept in hell with Ignorance;
Yet as a punishment they added this,
That he and Poverty should always kiss.   470
And to this day is every scholar poor;
Gross gold from them runs headlong to the boor.
Likewise, the angry Sisters, thus deluded,
To venge themselves on Hermes, have concluded
That Midas' brood shall sit in Honour's chair,   475
To which the Muses' sons are only heir;

452 *his father's*: i.e. Saturn's.
456 *Ops*: Saturn's wife, goddess of fertility.
465-8 Hermes (Mercury) was god of learning.
475 *Midas' brood*: i.e. people like King Midas, prototype of
    stupidity and greed.

And fruitful wits that inaspiring are,
Shall, discontent, run into regions far;
And few great lords in virtuous deeds shall joy,
480 But be surprised with every garish toy;
And still enrich the lofty servile clown,
Who with encroaching guile keeps learning down.
Then muse not Cupid's suit no better sped,
Seeing in their loves the Fates were injurèd.
485　　By this, sad Hero, with love unacquainted,
Viewing Leander's face, fell down and fainted.
He kissed her, and breathed life into her lips,
Wherewith, as one displeased, away she trips.
Yet as she went, full often looked behind,
490 And many poor excuses did she find
To linger by the way, and once she stayed,
And would have turned again, but was afraid,
In off'ring parley, to be counted light.
So on she goes, and in her idle flight,
495 Her painted fan of curlèd plumes let fall,
Thinking to train Leander therewithal.
He, being a novice, knew not what she meant,
But stayed, and after her a letter sent,
Which joyful Hero answered in such sort
500 As he had hope to scale the beauteous fort
Wherein the liberal Graces locked their wealth,
And therefore to her tower he got by stealth.
Wide open stood the door, he need not climb;
And she herself, before the 'pointed time,
505 Had spread the board, with roses strowed the room,
And oft looked out, and mused he did not come.
At last he came; oh, who can tell the greeting
These greedy lovers had at their first meeting?
He asked, she gave, and nothing was denied;

477　*inaspiring*: 'in aspiring' (1598).
496　*train*: allure.

286

Both to each other quickly were affied. 510
Look how their hands, so were their hearts united,
And what he did she willingly requited.
Sweet are the kisses, the embracements sweet,
When like desires and affections meet;
For from the earth to heaven is Cupid raised, 515
Where fancy is in equal balance peised.
Yet she this rashness suddenly repented,
And turned aside, and to herself lamented,
As if her name and honour had been wronged
By being possessed of him for whom she longed; 520
Aye, and she wished, albeit not from her heart,
That he would leave her turret and depart.
The mirthful god of amorous pleasure smiled
To see how he this captive nymph beguiled;
For hitherto he did but fan the fire, 525
And kept it down that it might mount the higher.
Now waxed she jealous lest his love abated,
Fearing her own thoughts made her to be hated.
Therefore unto him hastily she goes,
And like light Salmacis, her body throws 530
Upon his bosom, where with yielding eyes
She offers up herself, a sacrifice
To slake his anger if he were displeased.
Oh, what god would not therewith be appeased?
Like Aesop's cock, this jewel he enjoyed, 535
And as a brother with his sister toyed,
Supposing nothing else was to be done,
Now he her favour and goodwill had won.

---

510 *affied*: betrothed.
516 *peised*: weighed.
530 *Salmacis*: water-nymph who loved Hermaphroditus;
   when she embraced him, praying the gods to unite them,
   the two were made into one bisexual form.
535 The cock in Aesop's fable rejected a jewel he found be-
   cause it was not a grain of corn.

But know you not that creatures wanting sense
540 By nature have a mutual appetence,
And wanting organs to advance a step,
Moved by love's force, unto each other lep?
Much more in subjects having intellect,
Some hidden influence breeds like effect.
545 Albeit Leander, rude in love and raw,
Long dallying with Hero, nothing saw
That might delight him more, yet he suspected
Some amorous rites or other were neglected.
Therefore unto his body hers he clung;
550 She, fearing on the rushes to be flung,
Strived with redoubled strength; the more she strived,
The more a gentle pleasing heat revived,
Which taught him all that elder lovers know;
And now the same gan so to scorch and glow,
555 As in plain terms, yet cunningly, he craved it;
Love always makes those eloquent that have it.
She, with a kind of granting, put him by it,
And ever as he thought himself most nigh it,
Like to the tree of Tantalus she fled,
560 And seeming lavish, saved her maidenhead.
Ne'er king more sought to keep his diadem,
Than Hero this inestimable gem.
Above our life we love a steadfast friend,
Yet when a token of great worth we send,
565 We often kiss it, often look thereon,
And stay the messenger that would be gone;
No marvel then though Hero would not yield
So soon to part from that she dearly held;
Jewels being lost are found again, this never;
570 'Tis lost but once, and once lost, lost forever.

540 *appetence*: longing.
559 *tree of Tantalus*: tree laden with fruit which continually
escaped the reach of the hungry Tantalus in hell.

Now had the morn espied her lover's steeds;
Whereat she starts, puts on her purple weeds,
And red for anger that he stayed so long,
All headlong throws herself the clouds among.
And now Leander, fearing to be missed,   575
Embraced her suddenly, took leave, and kissed.
Long was he taking leave, and loath to go,
And kissed again, as lovers use to do.
Sad Hero wrung him by the hand, and wept,
Saying, 'Let your vows and promises be kept.'   580
Then, standing at the door, she turned about,
As loath to see Leander going out.
And now the sun that through th' horizon peeps,
As pitying these lovers, downward creeps;
So that in silence of the cloudy night,   585
Though it was morning, did he take his flight.
But what the secret trusty night concealed,
Leander's amorous habit soon revealed;
With Cupid's myrtle was his bonnet crowned,
About his arms the purple riband wound   590
Wherewith she wreathed her largely-spreading hair;
Nor could the youth abstain, but he must wear
The sacred ring wherewith she was endowed,
When first religious chastity she vowed;
Which made his love through Sestos to be known,   595
And thence unto Abydos sooner blown
Than he could sail; for incorporeal Fame,
Whose weight consists in nothing but her name,
Is swifter than the wind, whose tardy plumes
Are reeking water and dull earthly fumes.   600
Home when he came, he seemed not to be there,
But like exilèd air thrust from his sphere,

597 *Fame*: i.e. Rumour.
600 *reeking*: vaporous.
602 *thrust from his sphere*: i.e. displaced from its proper 'sphere'
in the Ptolemaic system.

Set in a foreign place; and straight from thence,
Alcides-like, by mighty violence
605   He would have chased away the swelling main
That him from her unjustly did detain.
Like as the sun in a diameter
Fires and inflames objects removèd far,
And heateth kindly, shining lat'rally;
610   So beauty sweetly quickens when 'tis nigh,
But being separated and removed,
Burns where it cherished, murders where it loved.
Therefore even as an index to a book,
So to his mind was young Leander's look.
615   Oh, none but gods have power their love to hide;
Affection by the count'nance is descried.
The light of hidden fire itself discovers,
And love that is concealed betrays poor lovers.
His secret flame apparently was seen;
620   Leander's father knew where he had been,
And for the same mildly rebuked his son,
Thinking to quench the sparkles new begun.
But love, resisted once, grows passionate,
And nothing more than counsel lovers hate.
625   For as a hot proud horse highly disdains
To have his head controlled, but breaks the reins,
Spits forth the ringled bit, and with his hooves
Checks the submissive ground, so he that loves,
The more he is restrained, the worse he fares.
630   What is it now but mad Leander dares?
'O Hero, Hero!' thus he cried full oft;
And then he got him to a rock aloft,
Where having spied her tower, long stared he on 't,
And prayed the narrow toiling Hellespont

> 604 *Alcides*: Hercules.
> 607 *in a diameter*: i.e. with direct rays.
> 609 *lat'rally*: obliquely.
> 619 *apparently*: clearly.
> 628 *Checks*: strikes.

To part in twain, that he might come and go;   635
But still the rising billows answered 'No.'
With that he stripped him to the iv'ry skin,
And crying, 'Love, I come,' leaped lively in.
Whereat the sapphire-visaged god grew proud,
And made his cap'ring Triton sound aloud,   640
Imagining that Ganymede, displeased,
Had left the heavens; therefore on him he seized.
Leander strived; the waves about him wound,
And pulled him to the bottom, where the ground
Was strewed with pearl, and in low coral groves   645
Sweet singing mermaids sported with their loves
On heaps of heavy gold, and took great pleasure
To spurn in careless sort the shipwreck treasure.
For here the stately azure palace stood,
Where kingly Neptune and his train abode.   650
The lusty god embraced him, called him 'love,'
And swore he never should return to Jove.
But when he knew it was not Ganymed,
For under water he was almost dead,
He heaved him up, and looking on his face,   655
Beat down the bold waves with his triple mace,
Which mounted up, intending to have kissed him,
And fell in drops like tears, because they missed him.
Leander, being up, began to swim,
And looking back, saw Neptune follow him;   660
Whereat aghast, the poor soul gan to cry,
'Oh, let me visit Hero ere I die!'
The god put Helle's bracelet on his arm,
And swore the sea should never do him harm.
He clapped his plump cheeks, with his tresses played,   665
And smiling wantonly, his love bewrayed.

663 *Helle*: daughter of Athamas and Nephele who, while
    fleeing in her mother's air-borne chariot, fell into the
    Hellespont, which was named after her.
666 *bewrayed*: revealed.

He watched his arms, and as they opened wide,
At every stroke betwixt them would he slide,
And steal a kiss, and then run out and dance,
670   And as he turned, cast many a lustful glance,
And throw him gaudy toys to please his eye,
And dive into the water, and there pry
Upon his breast, his thighs, and every limb,
And up again, and close beside him swim,
675   And talk of love. Leander made reply,
'You are deceived, I am no woman, I.'
Thereat smiled Neptune, and then told a tale,
How that a shepherd, sitting in a vale,
Played with a boy so fair and kind,
680   As for his love both earth and heaven pined;
That of the cooling river durst not drink
Lest water-nymphs should pull him from the brink;
And when he sported in the fragrant lawns,
Goat-footed satyrs and up-staring fauns
685   Would steal him thence. Ere half this tale was done,
'Ay me,' Leander cried, 'th' enamoured sun,
That now should shine on Thetis' glassy bower,
Descends upon my radiant Hero's tower.
Oh, that these tardy arms of mine were wings!'
690   And as he spake, upon the waves he springs.
Neptune was angry that he gave no ear,
And in his heart revenging malice bare;
He flung at him his mace, but as it went
He called it in, for love made him repent.
695   The mace, returning back, his own hand hit,
As meaning to be venged for darting it.
When this fresh bleeding wound Leander viewed,
His colour went and came, as if he rued
The grief which Neptune felt. In gentle breasts
700   Relenting thoughts, remorse, and pity rests;

671 *throw*: 'threw' (1598).
687 *Thetis' glassy bower*: i.e. the sea.

And who have hard hearts and obdurate minds
But vicious, harebrained, and illit'rate hinds?
The god, seeing him with pity to be moved,
Thereon concluded that he was beloved.
(Love is too full of faith, too credulous,   705
With folly and false hope deluding us.)
Wherefore, Leander's fancy to surprise,
To the rich ocean for gifts he flies.
'Tis wisdom to give much; a gift prevails
When deep persuading oratory fails.   710
    By this, Leander, being near the land,
Cast down his weary feet and felt the sand.
Breathless albeit he were, he rested not
Till to the solitary tower he got,
And knocked, and called, at which celestial noise   715
The longing heart of Hero much more joys
Than nymphs and shepherds when the timbrel rings,
Or crooked dolphin when the sailor sings.
She stayed not for her robes, but straight arose,
And drunk with gladness, to the door she goes;   720
Where, seeing a naked man, she screeched for fear,
(Such sights as this to tender maids are rare)
And ran into the dark herself to hide.
Rich jewels in the dark are soonest spied;
Unto her was he led, or rather drawn,   725
By those white limbs which sparkled through the lawn.
The nearer that he came, the more she fled,
And seeking refuge, slipped into her bed.
Whereon Leander sitting, thus began,
Through numbing cold all feeble, faint, and wan: 730
    'If not for love, yet, love, for pity sake,
Me in thy bed and maiden bosom take;

717 *timbrel*: tambourine.
718 *the sailor*: i.e. Arion, the Greek musician, who was rescued
       from drowning by dolphins who were charmed by his
       music.

At least vouchsafe these arms some little room,
Who, hoping to embrace thee, cheerly swum;
735   This head was beat with many a churlish billow,
And therefore let it rest upon thy pillow.'
Herewith affrighted Hero shrunk away,
And in her lukewarm place Leander lay,
Whose lively heat, like fire from heaven fet,
740   Would animate gross clay, and higher set
The drooping thoughts of base declining souls,
Than dreary Mars carousing nectar bowls.
His hands he cast upon her like a snare;
She, overcome with shame and sallow fear,
745   Like chaste Diana, when Actaeon spied her,
Being suddenly betrayed, dived down to hide her;
And as her silver body downward went,
With both her hands she made the bed a tent,
And in her own mind thought herself secure,
750   O'ercast with dim and darksome coverture.
And now she lets him whisper in her ear,
Flatter, entreat, promise, protest, and swear;
Yet ever as he greedily assayed
To touch those dainties, she the harpy played,
755   And every limb did, as a soldier stout,
Defend the fort and keep the foeman out;
For though the rising iv'ry mount he scaled,
Which is with azure circling lines impaled,
Much like a globe (a globe may I term this,
760   By which love sails to regions full of bliss)
Yet there with Sisyphus he toiled in vain,
Till gentle parley did the truce obtain.
Wherein Leander on her quivering breast,
Breathless spoke something, and sighed out the rest;

742 *dreary*: bloody.
758 *impaled*: decoratively surrounded.
763–84 printed in the order 775–84, 763–74 in 1598.

Which so prevailed, as he with small ado   765
Enclosed her in his arms, and kissed her too.
And every kiss to her was as a charm,
And to Leander as a fresh alarm;
So that the truce was broke, and she, alas,
Poor silly maiden, at his mercy was.   770
Love is not full of pity, as men say,
But deaf and cruel where he means to prey.
Even as a bird, which in our hands we wring,
Forth plungeth, and oft flutters with her wing,
She trembling strove; this strife of hers, like that   775
Which made the world, another world begat
Of unknown joy. Treason was in her thought,
And cunningly to yield herself she sought.
Seeming not won, yet won she was at length;
In such wars women use but half their strength.   780
Leander now, like Theban Hercules,
Entered the orchard of th' Hesperides,
Whose fruit none rightly can describe but he
That pulls or shakes it from the golden tree.
And now she wished this night were never done,   785
And sighed to think upon th' approaching sun;
For much it grieved her that the bright daylight
Should know the pleasure of this blessèd night,
And them like Mars and Erycine displayed,
Both in each other's arms chained as they laid.   790
Again she knew not how to frame her look,
Or speak to him who in a moment took

768 *alarm*: call to action.
773 *wring*: press tightly.
775–6 *this strife . . . the world*: Empedocles taught that strife cre-
    ated the world by separating the four elements, once
    mingled in chaos.
781–2 *Theban . . . Hesperides*: One of the labours of Hercules was
    to fetch apples, guarded by a fierce dragon, from the
    garden of the Hesperides, daughters of Atlas.
789 *them*: 'then' (1598). *Erycine*: Venus.
789–90 See ll. 151–2 and n.

That which so long, so charily she kept;
And fain by stealth away she would have crept,
795 And to some corner secretly have gone,
Leaving Leander in the bed alone.
But as her naked feet were whipping out,
He on the sudden clinged her so about,
That mermaid-like unto the floor she slid,
800 One half appeared, the other half was hid.
Thus near the bed she blushing stood upright,
And from her countenance behold ye might
A kind of twilight break, which through the hair,
As from an orient cloud, glims here and there;
805 And round about the chamber this false morn
Brought forth the day before the day was born.
So Hero's ruddy cheek Hero betrayed,
And her all naked to his sight displayed;
Whence his admiring eyes more pleasure took
810 Than Dis on heaps of gold fixing his look.
By this, Apollo's golden harp began
To sound forth music to the ocean;
Which watchful Hesperus no sooner heard,
But he the day-bright-bearing car prepared,
815 And ran before, as harbinger of light,
And with his flaring beams mocked ugly night,
Till she, o'ercome with anguish, shame, and rage,
Danged down to hell her loathsome carriage.

    Desunt nonnulla.

        Hero and Leander, 1598

804 *glims*: gleams.
810 *Dis*: Pluto, god of wealth.
813 *Hesperus*: here, the morning star.
818 *Danged*: flung.
Desunt nonnulla: 'Some things are lacking'.

WILLIAM SHAKESPEARE

[*Venus begins to woo Adonis*]
from *Venus and Adonis*

Even as the sun with purple-coloured face
Had ta'en his last leave of the weeping morn,
Rose-cheeked Adonis hied him to the chase;
Hunting he loved, but love he laughed to scorn.
    Sick-thoughted Venus makes amain unto him,   5
    And like a bold-faced suitor gins to woo him.

'Thrice fairer than myself,' thus she began,
'The field's chief flower, sweet above compare,
Stain to all nymphs, more lovely than a man,
More white and red than doves or roses are: 10
    Nature that made thee, with herself at strife,
    Saith that the world hath ending with thy life.

'Vouchsafe, thou wonder, to alight thy steed,
And rein his proud head to the saddle-bow;
If thou wilt deign this favour, for thy meed   15
A thousand honey secrets shalt thou know.
    Here come and sit, where never serpent hisses,
    And being set, I'll smother thee with kisses;

'And yet not cloy thy lips with loathed satiety,
But rather famish them amid their plenty,   20
Making them red, and pale, with fresh variety—
Ten kisses short as one, one long as twenty.
    A summer's day will seem an hour but short,
    Being wasted in such time-beguiling sport.'

VENUS AND ADONIS:
1 *purple-coloured*: crimson.
5 *Sick-thoughted*: lovesick.
9 *Stain to*: one whose beauty overshadows.
14 I.e. tie the horse's head to prevent him from straying.
19 *satiety* (1599): 'saciety' (1593).
24 *wasted*: spent.

25 With this she seizeth on his sweating palm,
The precedent of pith and livelihood,
And trembling in her passion, calls it balm,
Earth's sovereign salve to do a goddess good.
    Being so enraged, desire doth lend her force
30   Courageously to pluck him from his horse.

Over one arm the lusty courser's rein,
Under her other was the tender boy,
Who blushed and pouted in a dull disdain,
With leaden appetite, unapt to toy;
35   She red and hot as coals of glowing fire,
    He red for shame, but frosty in desire.

The studded bridle on a ragged bough
Nimbly she fastens—Oh, how quick is love!—
The steed is stallèd up, and even now
40 To tie the rider she begins to prove;
    Backward she pushed him, as she would be thrust,
    And governed him in strength, though not in lust.

So soon was she along as he was down,
Each leaning on their elbows and their hips;
45 Now doth she stroke his cheek, now doth he frown,
And gins to chide, but soon she stops his lips,
    And kissing speaks, with lustful language broken,
    'If thou wilt chide, thy lips shall never open.'

25 *sweating palm*: considered an indication of amorousness
    (cf. l. 143).
26 The sign of strength and vigour.
30 *Courageously*: lustfully.
39 *stallèd up*: tethered.
40 *prove*: strive.
47 *with lustful language broken*: i.e. interrupted with kissing.

He burns with bashful shame, she with her tears
Doth quench the maiden burning of his cheeks;   50
Then with her windy sighs and golden hairs
To fan and blow them dry again she seeks.
    He saith she is immodest, blames her miss;
    What follows more, she murders with a kiss.

Even as an empty eagle, sharp by fast,   55
Tires with her beak on feathers, flesh, and bone,
Shaking her wings, devouring all in haste,
Till either gorge be stuffed, or prey be gone:
    Even so she kissed his brow, his cheek, his chin,
    And where she ends she doth anew begin.   60

Forced to content, but never to obey,
Panting he lies and breatheth in her face;
She feedeth on the steam as on a prey,
And calls it heavenly moisture, air of grace,
    Wishing her cheeks were gardens full of flowers,   65
    So they were dewed with such distilling showers.

Look how a bird lies tangled in a net,
So fastened in her arms Adonis lies;
Pure shame and awed resistance made him fret,
Which bred more beauty in his angry eyes.   70
    Rain added to a river that is rank
    Perforce will force it overflow the bank.

Still she entreats, and prettily entreats,
For to a pretty ear she tunes her tale;
Still is he sullen, still he lours and frets,   75

    53   *miss*: improper behaviour.
    55   *sharp*: made ravenous.
    56   *Tires*: tears.
    61   *content*: accept.
    71   *rank*: brimming.

'Twixt crimson shame and anger ashy-pale;
　　Being red, she loves him best; and being white,
　　Her best is bettered with a more delight.

Look how he can, she cannot choose but love;
80　And by her fair immortal hand she swears
From his soft bosom never to remove
Till he take truce with her contending tears,
　　Which long have rained, making her cheeks all wet:
　　And one sweet kiss shall pay this countless debt.

85　Upon this promise did he raise his chin,
Like a dive-dapper peering through a wave,
Who, being looked on, ducks as quickly in;
So offers he to give what she did crave,
　　But when her lips were ready for his pay,
90　　He winks, and turns his lips another way.

Never did passenger in summer's heat
More thirst for drink than she for this good turn;
Her help she sees, but help she cannot get;
She bathes in water, yet her fire must burn.
95　　'Oh, pity,' gan she cry, 'flint-hearted boy,
　　'Tis but a kiss I beg; why art thou coy?

'I have been wooed as I entreat thee now,
Even by the stern and direful god of war,
Whose sinewy neck in battle ne'er did bow,
100　Who conquers where he comes in every jar;
　　Yet hath he been my captive and my slave,
　　And begged for that which thou unasked shalt have.

84　*countless*: measureless.
86　*dive-dapper*: dabchick.
90　*winks*: shuts his eyes.
91　*passenger*: traveller.
100　*jar*: fight.

300

'Over my altars hath he hung his lance,
His battered shield, his uncontrollèd crest,
And for my sake hath learned to sport and dance,   105
To toy, to wanton, dally, smile, and jest;
   Scorning his churlish drum and ensign red,
   Making my arms his field, his tent my bed.

'Thus he that overruled I overswayed,
Leading him prisoner in a red rose chain;   110
Strong-tempered steel his stronger strength obeyed,
Yet was he servile to my coy disdain.
   Oh, be not proud, nor brag not of thy might,
   For mast'ring her that foiled the god of fight!

'Touch but my lips with those fair lips of thine—   115
Though mine be not so fair, yet are they red—
The kiss shall be thine own as well as mine.
What seest thou in the ground? hold up thy head;
   Look in mine eye-balls, there thy beauty lies;
   Then why not lips on lips, since eyes in eyes?   120

'Art thou ashamed to kiss? then wink again,
And I will wink; so shall the day seem night.
Love keeps his revels where there are but twain;
Be bold to play, our sport is not in sight.
   These blue-veined violets whereon we lean   125
   Never can blab, nor know not what we mean.

'The tender spring upon thy tempting lip
Shows thee unripe; yet mayst thou well be tasted;
Make use of time, let not advantage slip;

---

104 *uncontrollèd crest*: unconquered helmet.
107 *churlish*: rough, vulgar.
127 *tender spring*: young growth.

130 Beauty within itself should not be wasted.
    Fair flowers that are not gathered in their prime
    Rot, and consume themselves in little time.

'Were I hard-favoured, foul, or wrinkled-old,
Ill-nurtured, crooked, churlish, harsh in voice,
135 O'erworn, despisèd, rheumatic, and cold,
    Thick-sighted, barren, lean, and lacking juice,
      Then mightst thou pause, for then I were not for thee;
      But having no defects, why dost abhor me?

'Thou canst not see one wrinkle in my brow;
140 Mine eyes are grey, and bright, and quick in turning;
    My beauty as the spring doth yearly grow;
    My flesh is soft and plump, my marrow burning;
      My smooth moist hand, were it with thy hand felt,
      Would in thy palm dissolve, or seem to melt.

145 'Bid me discourse, I will enchant thine ear,
    Or like a fairy trip upon the green,
    Or like a nymph with long dishevelled hair,
    Dance on the sands, and yet no footing seen.
      Love is a spirit all compact of fire,
150   Not gross to sink, but light, and will aspire.

'Witness this primrose bank whereon I lie:
These forceless flowers like sturdy trees support me.
Two strengthless doves will draw me through the sky
From morn till night, even where I list to sport me.
155   Is love so light, sweet boy, and may it be
      That thou should think it heavy unto thee?

133 *hard-favoured*: harsh-featured.
143 *with*: by.
149 *compact*: composed.
150 *aspire*: rise up.
152 *forceless*: weak.

'Is thine own heart to thine own face affected?
Can thy right hand seize love upon thy left?
Then woo thyself, be of thyself rejected;
Steal thine own freedom, and complain on theft.   160
  Narcissus so himself himself forsook,
  And died to kiss his shadow in the brook.

'Torches are made to light, jewels to wear,
Dainties to taste, fresh beauty for the use,
Herbs for their smell, and sappy plants to bear;   165
Things growing to themselves are growth's abuse.
  Seeds spring from seeds, and beauty breedeth beauty;
  Thou wast begot: to get it is thy duty.

'Upon the earth's increase why shouldst thou feed,
Unless the earth with thy increase be fed?   170
By law of nature thou art bound to breed,
That thine may live when thou thyself art dead;
  And so in spite of death thou dost survive,
  In that thy likeness still is left alive.'

By this the love-sick queen began to sweat,   175
For where they lay, the shadow had forsook them;
And Titan, tirèd in the mid-day heat,
With burning eye did hotly overlook them,
  Wishing Adonis had his team to guide,
  So he were like him, and by Venus' side.   180

And now Adonis, with a lazy sprite,
And with a heavy, dark, disliking eye,
His louring brows o'erwhelming his fair sight,

157 *to . . . affected*: enamoured with.
166 *to*: for.

303

Like misty vapours when they blot the sky,
185   Souring his cheeks, cries, 'Fie, no more of love!
The sun doth burn my face; I must remove.'

'Ay me,' quoth Venus, 'young, and so unkind!
What bare excuses mak'st thou to be gone!
I'll sigh celestial breath, whose gentle wind
190   Shall cool the heat of this descending sun.
I'll make a shadow for thee of my hairs;
If they burn too, I'll quench them with my tears.

'The sun that shines from heaven shines but warm,
And lo, I lie between that sun and thee;
195   The heat I have from thence doth little harm;
Thine eye darts forth the fire that burneth me;
And were I not immortal, life were done,
Between this heavenly and earthly sun.'

Venus and Adonis (1593) [1–198]

MICHAEL DRAYTON

[*Phoebe descends to earth to woo Endymion*]
from *Endymion and Phoebe*

The extract follows the opening description of Mount
Latmos, on the slopes of which the shepherd Endymion
tends his sheep.

Upon the top, a paradise was found
With which nature this miracle had crowned,
Impaled with rocks of rarest precious stone,
Which like the flames of Aetna brightly shone,

185 *Souring*: giving a sour expression to.
188 *bare*: paltry.
ENDYMION AND PHOEBE:
2   *miracle*: wonder, i.e. Mount Latmos.
3   *Impaled*: enclosed.

And served as lanthorns furnishèd with light 5
To guide the wand'ring passengers by night;
For which fair Phoebe, sliding from her sphere,
Used ofttimes to come and sport her there,
And from the azure starry-painted sky
Embalmed the banks with precious lunary; 10
That now her Maenalus she quite forsook,
And unto Latmos wholly her betook,
And in this place her pleasure used to take;
And all was for her sweet Endymion's sake—
Endymion, the lovely shepherd's boy, 15
Endymion, great Phoebe's only joy,
Endymion, in whose pure-shining eyes
The naked fairies danced the hay-de-guise.
The shag-haired satyrs, mountain-climbing race,
Have been made tame by gazing in his face; 20
For this boy's love the water-nymphs have wept,
Stealing ofttimes to kiss him whilst he slept,
And tasting once the nectar of his breath,
Surfeit with sweet, and languish unto death;
And Jove ofttimes, bent to lascivious sport, 25
And coming where Endymion did resort,
Hath courted him, inflamèd with desire,
Thinking some nymph was clothed in boy's attire;
And oftentimes the simple rural swains,
Beholding him in crossing o'er the plains, 30
Imaginèd Apollo from above
Put on this shape to win some maiden's love.
This shepherd Phoebe ever did behold,
Whose love already had her thoughts controlled;
From Latmos' top, her stately throne, she rose, 35
And to Endymion down beneath she goes.

7   *her sphere*: i.e. the lunar sphere of the Ptolemaic system.
10 *lunary*: the herb moonwort.
11 *Maenalus*: a mountain in Arcadia.
18 *hay-de-guise*: a country dance.

Her brother's beams now had she laid aside,
Her hornèd crescent, and her full-faced pride;
For had she come adornèd with her light,
40 No mortal eye could have endured the sight;
But like a nymph, crowned with a flow'ry twine,
And not like Phoebe, as herself divine.
An azured mantle purfled with a veil,
Which in the air puffed like a swelling sail;
45 Embosted rainbows did appear in silk,
With wavy streams, as white as morning's milk,
Which ever as the gentle air did blow,
Still with the motion seemed to ebb and flow;
About her neck a chain twice-twenty-fold,
50 Of rubies, set in lozenges of gold;
Trussed up in trammels and in curious pleats,
With sphery circles falling on her teats.
A dainty smock of cypress, fine and thin,
O'ercast with curls next to her lily skin,
55 Through which the pureness of the same did show
Like damask roses strewed with flakes of snow,
Discovering all her stomach to the waist,
With branches of sweet circling veins enchased.
A coronet she ware of myrtle boughs,
60 Which gave a shadow to her ivory brows.
No smother-beauty mask did beauty smother;
Great lights dim less, yet burn not one another;
Nature abhors to borrow from the mart;
Simples fit beauty, fie on drugs and art!

37 *Her brother*: i.e. Phoebus, the sun.
43 *purfled*: trimmed at the edges.
45 *Embosted*: embossed.
51 Fastened in tresses and in intricate braids (ll. 51–2 seem to refer to Phoebe's hair).
53 *cypress*: light transparent fabric.
58 *enchased*: adorned as if by engraving.
61 *mask*: i.e. of cosmetics.
62 *less*: i.e. lesser lights. *burn*: consume.
64 *Simples*: medicinal herbs.

Thus came she where her love Endymion lay,   65
Who with sweet carols sang the night away;
And as it is the shepherd's usual trade,
Oft on his pipe a roundelay he played.
As meek he was as any lamb might be,
Nor never lived a fairer youth than he.   70
His dainty hand the snow itself did stain,
Or her to whom Jove showered in golden rain;
From whose sweet palm the liquid pearl did swell,
Pure as the drops of Aganippa's well,
Clear as the liquor which fair Hebe spilt;   75
His sheephook silver, damasked all with gilt;
The staff itself of snowy ivory,
Studded with coral, tipped with ebony;
His tresses of the raven's shining black,
Straggling in curls along his manly back;   80
The balls which nature in his eyes had set,
Like diamonds enclosing globes of jet,
Which sparkled from their milky lids outright,
Like fair Orion's heaven-adorning light,
The stars on which her heavenly eyes were bent,   85
And fixèd still with lovely blandishment;
For whom so oft disguisèd she was seen,
As she celestial Phoebe had not been;
Her dainty buskins, laced unto the knee,
Her pleated frock, tucked up accordingly.   90
A nymph-like huntress, armed with bow and dart,
About the woods she scours the long-lived hart.

71   *stain*: blemish by comparison.
72   *her*: i.e. Danae, whose tower Jove entered in a shower of
     gold.
73   Cf. *Venus and Adonis* 25 and n.
74   *Aganippa's well*: the fountain of Aganippe, sacred to the
     Muses.
75   *Hebe*: cupbearer of the gods. *spilt*: poured.
76   *damasked*: richly patterned.
86   *blandishment*: allurement.
90   *accordingly*: suitably.

She climbs the mountains with the light-foot fauns,
And with the satyrs scuds it o'er the lawns.
95 In music's sweet delight she shows her skill,
Quavering the cithern nimbly with her quill.
Upon each tree she carves Endymion's name
In Gordian knots, with Phoebe to the same.
To kill him ven'son now she pitched her toils,
100 And to this lovely ranger brings the spoils.
And thus whilst she by chaste desire is led
Unto the downs where he his fair flocks fed,
Near to a grove she had Endymion spied,
Where he was fishing by a river side
105 Under a poplar, shadowed from the sun;
Where merrily to court him she begun:
    'Sweet boy,' quoth she, 'take what thy heart can
      wish;
When thou dost angle, would I were a fish!
When thou art sporting by the silver brooks,
110 Put in thy hand—thou need'st no other hooks.
Hard-hearted boy, Endymion, look on me!
Nothing on earth I hold too dear for thee.
I am a nymph and not of human blood,
Begot by Pan on Isis' sacred flood;
115 When I was born, upon that very day
Phoebus was seen the reveller to play;
In Jove's high house the gods assembled all,
And Juno held her sumptuous festival;
Oceanus that hour was dancing spied,
120 And Tithon seen to frolic with his bride;

---

98 *Gordian knots*: i.e. loveknots symbolizing indivisible love
    (Gordius's knot could not be untied).
99 *pitched her toils*: set her snares.
114 *Isis*: the river Thames. Phoebe's parentage is Drayton's
    invention.
120 *Tithon*: Tithonus lived in perpetual old age after Aurora
    (his 'bride') gave him immortality but not eternal youth.

The halcyons that season sweetly sang,
And all the shores with shouting sea-nymphs rang;
And on that day, my birth to memorize,
The shepherds hold a solemn sacrifice.
The chaste Diana nursed me in her lap,   125
And I sucked nectar from her down-soft pap.
The well wherein this body bathèd first,
Who drinks thereof shall never after thirst;
The water hath the lunacy appeased,
And by the virtue, cureth all diseased.   130
The place wherein my bare feet touch the mould,
Made up in balls, for pomander is sold.
See, see, these hands have robbed the snow of white,
These dainty fingers, organs of delight;
Behold these lips, the lodestones of desire,   135
Whose words enchant like Amphion's well-tuned lyre;
This foot art's just proportion doth reveal,
Signing the earth with heaven's own manual seal.
Go, play the wanton, I will tend thy flock,
And wait the hours as duly as a clock;   140
I'll deck thy ram with bells and wreaths of bay,
And gild his horns upon the shearing day;
And with a garland crown thee shepherds' king,
And thou shalt lead the gay girls in a ring;
Birds with their wings shall fan thee in the sun,   145
And all the fountains with pure wine shall run.
I have a choir of dainty turtledoves,
And they shall sit and sweetly sing our loves;
I'll lay thee on the swan's soft downy plume,
And all the wind shall gently breathe perfume;   150

121 *halcyons*: kingfishers.
131 *mould*: earth.
132 *pomander*: perfume.
136 *Amphion*: legendary lyrist, whose musical skill made stones form into a wall.
138 *manual seal*: personal imprint.

I'll plait thy locks with many a curious pleat,
And chafe thy temples with a sacred heat;
The muses still shall keep thee company,
And lull thee with enchanting harmony.
155   If not all these, yet let my virtues move thee:
A chaster nymph, Endymion, cannot love thee.'
   But he imagined she some nymph had been,
Because she was apparellèd in green;
Or happily some of fair Flora's train,
160   Which oft did use to sport upon the plain.
He tells her he was Phoebe's servant sworn,
And oft in hunting had her quiver borne,
And that to her virginity he vowed,
Which in no hand by Venus was allowed.
165   Then unto her a catalogue recites
Of Phoebe's statutes, and her hallowed rites,
And of the grievous penalty inflicted
On such as her chaste laws had interdicted.
Now he requests that she would stand aside,
170   Because the fish her shadow had espied;
Then he entreats her that she would be gone,
And at this time to let him be alone;
Then turns him from her in an angry sort,
And frowns and chafes that she had spoiled his sport.
175   And then he threatens her, if she did stay,
And told her great Diana came this way.
But for all this, this nymph would not forbear, . . .

Endymion and Phoebe (1595) [69–245]

159   *happily*: perchance.
164   *no hand*: no case.

Select Bibliography
and Biographical Notes

The bibliography contains (i) modern editions of sixteenth-
century anthologies and some useful modern anthologies of
Elizabethan poetry; (ii) general works on the period and on
the literary genres; (iii) under each poet's name, the modern
edition or editions which will be found most useful for wider
reading and for the textual commentary and detailed ex-
planatory annotation which is beyond the scope of this
anthology; and also the most helpful critical and biographical
studies of each poet. In all references London is the place of
publication unless otherwise stated.

ANTHOLOGIES

A Poetical Rhapsody [1602–21], ed. H. E. Rollins, 2 vols, Cambridge,
    Mass., 1931.
England's Helicon [1600, 1614], ed. Hugh Macdonald, 1949.
The Phoenix Nest [1593], ed. H. E. Rollins, Cambridge, Mass., 1931.
Tottel's Miscellany [1557–87], ed. H. E. Rollins, 2 vols, Cambridge,
    Mass., 1928–9.

Elizabethan Critical Essays, ed. G. Gregory Smith, 2 vols, Oxford, 1904.

Elizabethan Lyrics, ed. N. Ault, 4th edn, 1966.

Elizabethan Minor Epics, ed. Elizabeth S. Donno, 1963.

Elizabethan Sonnets, ed. Sidney Lee, 2 vols, 1904.

English Madrigal Verse, ed. E. H. Fellowes, 3rd edn, Oxford, 1967.

Lyrics from English Airs, ed. E. Doughtie, Cambridge, Mass., 1970.

Poetry of the English Renaissance, ed. J. W. Hebel and H. H. Hudson, New York, 1929.

Silver Poets of the Sixteenth Century, ed. G. Bullett, 1947.

The Oxford Book of Sixteenth Century Verse, ed. E. K. Chambers, Oxford, 1932.

GENERAL WORKS

Alpers, P. J., ed., *Elizabethan Poetry*, Oxford, 1967.

Berdan, J. M., *Early Tudor Poetry*, New York, 1920.

Brown, J. R., and Harris, B., eds, *Elizabethan Poetry*, Stratford-upon-Avon Studies No. 2, 1960.

Bush, Douglas, *Mythology and the Renaissance Tradition in English Poetry*, rev. edn, New York, 1963.

Buxton, John, *Elizabethan Taste*, 1963.

Craig, H., *The Enchanted Glass: The Elizabethan Mind in Literature*, New York, 1936.

Greg, W. W., *Pastoral Poetry and Pastoral Drama*, 1906.

Ing, Catherine, *Elizabethan Lyrics*, 1951.

John, Lisle C., *The Elizabethan Sonnet Sequences*, New York, 1938.

Johnson, Paula, *Form and Transformation in Music and Poetry of the English Renaissance*, New Haven, 1972.

Kernan, A., *The Cankered Muse: Satire of the English Renaissance*, New Haven, 1959.

Lever, J. W., *The Elizabethan Love Sonnet*, 1956.

Lewis, C. S., *English Literature in the Sixteenth Century*, Oxford, 1954.

Lievsay, J. L., *The Sixteenth Century: Skelton Through Hooker*, Golden-tree Bibliographies, New York, 1968.

Mason, H. A., *Humanism and Poetry in the Early Tudor Period*, 1959.

Pattison, Bruce, *Music and Poetry of the English Renaissance*, 2nd edn, 1970.

Peter, John, *Complaint and Satire in Early English Literature*, Oxford, 1956.

Peterson, D. L., *The English Lyric from Wyatt to Donne*, Princeton, 1967.

Powers, Doris C., *English Formal Satire: Elizabethan to Augustan*, The Hague, 1971.

Smith, Hallett, *Elizabethan Poetry*, Cambridge, Mass., 1952.

Stevens, J. E., *Music and Poetry in the Early Tudor Court*, 1961.

Tayler, E. W., *Nature and Art in Renaissance Literature*, New York, 1964.

Thompson, John, *The Founding of English Metre*, 1961.

Tillyard, E. M. W., *The Elizabethan World Picture*, 1943.

Tuve, Rosemond, *Elizabethan and Metaphysical Imagery*, Chicago, 1947.

Zocca, L. R., *Elizabethan Narrative Poetry*, New Brunswick, New Jersey, 1950.

INDIVIDUAL POETS

BARNES, BARNABE (1569?–1609), was born in Yorkshire, a son of the Bishop of Durham, and educated at Oxford. He was a prolific writer, chiefly of religious and love poetry.

Edition: Parthenophil and Parthenophe, ed. V. A. Doyno, Carbondale and Edwardsville, 1971.

BRETON, NICHOLAS (1545?–1626), was born in London of a wealthy family and educated at Oxford. He was stepson to George Gascoigne. With Mary Countess of Pembroke as his patroness, he wrote numerous lyrics, pastorals, satires and religious poems as well as prose.

Edition: Works in Verse and Prose, ed. A. B. Grosart, 2 vols, Edinburgh, 1879.

CAMPION, THOMAS (1567–1620), educated at Cambridge, Gray's Inn and abroad, was a physician and composer as well as poet. He published four books of airs between 1601 and 1617, and wrote several masques for James's court. In 1602 he wrote *Observations in the Art of English Poesy*, a treatise exhorting the use of classical quantitative measure, to which Daniel wrote a reply.

Edition: Works, ed. W. R. Davis, 1969.

Studies: Kastendieck, M. M., *England's Musical Poet, Thomas Campion*, New York, 1938.

Lowbury, E. *et al., Thomas Campion: Poet, Composer, Physician*, 1970.

DANIEL, SAMUEL (1562–1619), was born in Somerset, the son of a music-master. He was educated at Oxford and later toured the Continent. He became tutor to William Herbert and was introduced into the circle of the Countess of Pembroke. He was a conscientious verse craftsman and a prolific writer of sonnets, histories, verse plays and masques. He enjoyed court patronage under Queen Anne, but preferred the secluded life and spent his last years on his Somerset farm.

Edition: Poems and A Defence of Ryme, ed. A. C. Sprague, Cambridge, Mass., 1930.

Study: Rees, Joan, *Samuel Daniel: A Critical and Biographical Study*, Liverpool, 1964.

DAVIES, SIR JOHN (1569–1626), was educated at Oxford and at the Middle Temple, where his violent physical attack on a fellow student resulted in disbarment. He was allowed to return in 1601 and began an eminent legal and political career. He was knighted in 1606 and a month before his death was appointed Lord Chief Justice. His best known works are *Orchestra, or a Poem of Dancing* (1596) and a philosophical verse treatise, *Nosce Teipsum* (1599).

Edition: Poems, ed. R. Krueger, Oxford, 1975.

DEKKER, THOMAS (1570?–1632?), was born in London, where he lived for much of his life in poverty and debt. He wrote many plays, alone and in collaboration, and numerous popular pamphlets.

Edition: Dramatic Works, ed. F. Bowers, 4 vols, Cambridge, 1953–61.
Study: Hunt, Mary L., *Thomas Dekker: A Study*, New York, 1911.

DONNE, JOHN (1572–1631), son of a well-to-do London iron-
monger, was brought up a Roman Catholic, and educated
at Oxford, Cambridge and Lincoln's Inn. In 1596 he accom-
panied Essex on his expedition to Cadiz. He became secre-
tary to Sir Thomas Egerton, but his secret marriage to
Egerton's niece Anne More in 1601 resulted in imprisonment
and an end to his political career. He renounced Roman
Catholicism and in 1615 was ordained in the Anglican
Church. He gained fame as a preacher, and became Dean
of St Paul's in 1621. Almost all his poetry was written before
his ordination. Very little of it, and none of the *Satires*,
Songs and Sonnets, and *Holy Sonnets*, was published in his life-
time.

Editions: Divine Poems, ed. Helen Gardner, Oxford, 1952.
Elegies, and The Songs and Sonnets, ed. Helen Gardner, Oxford,
1965.
Satires, Epigrams and Verse Letters, ed. W. Milgate, Oxford, 1967.
Studies: Bald, R. C., *John Donne: A Life*, Oxford, 1970.
Legouis, P., *Donne the Craftsman*, Paris, 1928.
Leishman, J. B., *The Monarch of Wit*, 7th edn, 1965.
Sanders, W., *John Donne's Poetry*, Cambridge, 1971.
Smith, A. J., ed., *John Donne: Essays in Celebration*, 1972.
Stein, A., *John Donne's Lyrics*, Minneapolis, 1962.

DRAYTON, MICHAEL (1563–1631), born in Warwickshire of
yeoman stock, became page in the household of Sir Henry
Goodere, where he received his only formal education. He
was a professional poet and benefited from a number of
patrons, but was never financially secure for long; he was
a hack playwright for Henslowe at the turn of the century
and his ambition to be a court poet was never fulfilled. He
wrote with competence, and occasionally with brilliance,
in almost all of the contemporary genres. His longest work,
the historical-topographical *Poly-Olbion* (1612–22), was less

popular than were his sonnets, pastorals, and his *Heroical Epistles* (1597–9), written in the style of Ovid's *Heroides*.

Edition: Works, ed. J. W. Hebel, 5 vols, Oxford, 1931–41.

Studies: Elton, O., *Michael Drayton: A Critical Study*, 1905.

Hardin, R. F., *Michael Drayton and the Passing of Elizabethan England*, Lawrence, Kan., 1973.

Newdigate, B. H., *Michael Drayton and His Circle*, Oxford, 1941.

FLETCHER, GILES (THE ELDER) (1549–1611), was educated at Eton and Cambridge. He pursued a career as a lawyer and was sent as ambassador to Russia in 1588. His sonnet sequence *Licia* (1593) was his chief work of poetry.

Edition: English Works, ed. L. E. Berry, Madison, 1964.

GASCOIGNE, GEORGE (1539?–1577), studied at Cambridge and the Inns of Court. He was unsuccessful in gaining preferment at court and was imprisoned for debt in 1570. He served for a time as a soldier in the Low Countries. His largest collection, *Posies* (1575), was a miscellany which included lyrics, dramas, a novel, and a treatise on the writing of verse. His literary innovations were many and included the use of blank verse for satire, in his *Steel Glass* (1576).

Edition: Complete Works, ed. J. W. Cunliffe, 2 vols, Cambridge, 1907–10.

Study: Prouty, C. T., *George Gascoigne: Elizabethan Courtier, Soldier, and Poet*, New York, 1942.

GREENE, ROBERT (1558?–1592), born in Norwich and educated at Cambridge, was a prolific writer of plays, pamphlets and romances. He lived a dissolute and poverty-stricken life in London, some details of which are recounted in his writings.

Edition: Plays and Poems, ed. J. C. Collins, 2 vols, Oxford, 1905.

Study: Jordan, J. C., *Robert Greene*, New York, 1915.

GREVILLE, FULKE, LORD BROOKE (1554–1628), was educated at Shrewsbury, where he became a great friend of Sidney, a privilege he recorded in his own epitaph. After studying at

Cambridge he began a highly successful political career under Elizabeth and James, becoming Chancellor of the Exchequer in 1614. He was a generous patron as well as a poet and playwright. He was murdered by a servant who took issue over his will.

Editions: Poems and Dramas, ed. G. Bullough, 2 vols, Edinburgh, 1939.

Selected Writings, ed. Joan Rees, 1973.

Studies: Rees, Joan, *Fulke Greville, Lord Brooke, 1554–1628: A Critical Biography*, 1971.

Waswo, R., *The Fatal Mirror: Themes and Techniques in the Poetry of Fulke Greville*, Charlottesville, Va., 1972.

GUILPIN, EVERARD (b. 1572?), was born in London of a well-to-do family, educated at Cambridge and Gray's Inn. He lived much of his life in London. He was a friend of Donne and also of Marston, to whom he was distantly related and with whom he sided in literary quarrels against Hall and Weever.

Edition: Skialetheia, ed. D. Allen Carroll, Chapel Hill, 1974.

HALL, JOSEPH (1574–1656), was educated at Cambridge where, as a Fellow of Emmanuel College, he wrote his satires. He was ordained in 1600 and became Bishop of Exeter in 1627, Bishop of Norwich in 1641. He earned the distrust of Archbishop Laud and of Parliament and was imprisoned for some months in 1641. In 1643 his revenues were sequestrated and he was expelled from his palace in Norwich. He died in retirement in Norfolk.

Edition: Collected Poems, ed. A. Davenport, Liverpool, 1949.

Study: Kinloch, T. F., *The Life and Works of Joseph Hall*, 1951.

JONSON, BEN (1572–1637), was brought up in London, the stepson of a bricklayer, and educated at Westminster School. Although he never attended university, his learning, especially in the classics, was profound. After serving as a soldier in Flanders, he became an actor before beginning his long career as a playwright. On James's accession he wrote numerous masques and court entertainments. In 1616, when he published the first collection of his works, he was made Poet Laureate, although the post was not then an official one. He was an irascible man and was involved in many battles both of the pen and of the sword (he was imprisoned in 1598 for killing a man in a duel). However, he had as many firm friends as enemies, and was enormously popular and influential among his fellow-poets and disciples, the Tribe of Ben.

Edition: Ben Jonson, ed. C. H. Herford, P. and E. Simpson, 11 vols, Oxford, 1925–52.

Studies: Bamborough, J. B., *Ben Jonson*, 1970.

Gardiner, Judith K., *Craftsmanship in Context: The Development of Ben Jonson's Poetry*, The Hague, 1975.

Johnston, G. B., *Ben Jonson: Poet*, New York, 1945.

Nichols, J. G., *The Poetry of Ben Jonson*, 1969.

Trimpi, W., *Ben Jonson's Poems*, Stanford, 1962.

LODGE, THOMAS (1558?–1625), was educated at Oxford and Lincoln's Inn, but did not continue in a legal career. Like Greene, Peele, Nashe and other University Wits, he led an irregular and wild life in London. He wrote plays, romances and other prose writings as well as poetry. In 1600 he took a medical degree in Avignon, and settled down as a physician in London.

Edition: Complete Works, ed. E. W. Gosse, 4 vols, Glasgow, 1883.

Studies: Paradise, N. B., *Thomas Lodge: The History of an Elizabethan*, New Haven, 1931.

Tenney, E. A., *Thomas Lodge*, Ithaca, 1935.

LYLY, JOHN (1554?–1606), studied at Oxford and lived most of his life in London. He wrote several court comedies, and was particularly well-known for his prose romances of Euphues (1578, 1580), written in an elaborate rhetorical style which for a time became very fashionable.

Edition: Complete Works, ed. R. W. Bond, 3 vols, Oxford, 1902.

Studies: Hunter, G. K., *John Lyly: The Humanist as Courtier*, 1962.
Wilson, J. Dover, *John Lyly*, Cambridge, 1905.

MARLOWE, CHRISTOPHER (1564–1593), was born in Canterbury,
the son of a shoemaker, and educated at Cambridge. For a
time he was probably employed by the Government on a
secret mission abroad. During his brief career as a London
playwright he led a dissolute life, earning notoriety for his
atheism and unorthodox views. In 1593 he was summoned
by the Privy Council to answer charges, but in the mean-
time was killed in a quarrel in a Deptford tavern. His *Hero
and Leander* was his only long poem. His plays, particularly
Tamburlaine (written *c.* 1587), brought important develop-
ments to tragedy and to the use of blank verse.

Edition: Complete Works, ed. F. Bowers, 2 vols, Cambridge, 1973.

Studies: Boas, F. S., *Christopher Marlowe: A Biographical and Critical
Study*, Oxford, 1940.

Ellis-Fermor, Una M., *Christopher Marlowe*, 1927.

Levin, Harry T., *The Overreacher: A Study of Christopher Marlowe*,
Cambridge, Mass., 1952.

Steane, J. B., *Marlowe: A Critical Study*, Cambridge, 1964.

MARSTON, JOHN (1575?–1634), was educated at Oxford. His
satires all appeared in the 1590s before he turned to drama.
During his career as a writer he made many enemies and
indulged in several literary quarrels, notably with Joseph
Hall, and with Jonson in the War of the Theatres. In 1609
he was ordained, and from 1616 to 1631 was incumbent of
Christchurch, Hampshire.

Edition: Poems, ed. A. Davenport, Liverpool, 1961.

Studies: Allen, Morse S., *The Satire of John Marston*, Columbus,
Ohio, 1920.

Caputi, A., *John Marston, Satirist*, Ithaca, 1961.

NASHE, THOMAS (1567–1601), was educated at Cambridge, and
travelled through Europe. Thereafter he lived in London,
for much of the time in poverty. He was one of the Univer-
sity Wits, and wrote plays, satirical pamphlets and other

prose pieces, including a novel, *The Unfortunate Traveller* (1594).

Edition: Works, ed. R. B. McKerrow, 5 vols, Oxford, 1904–10; corr. and augm. F. P. Wilson, Oxford, 1958.

Study: Hibbard, G. R., *Thomas Nashe: A Critical Introduction*, 1962.

OXFORD, EDWARD DE VERE, EARL OF (1550–1604), inherited his title at the age of twelve. Arthur Golding, the translator, was his uncle and tutor; his guardian was Lord Burghley. As a courtier under Elizabeth he was known for his quarrel-someness, extravagance and eccentricity. He was a generous patron of the arts.

PEELE, GEORGE (1558?–1597?), was born of a humble family and educated at Oxford. He led a bohemian life in London as one of the University Wits. He wrote plays and court entertainments as well as lyrical and occasional poetry.

Edition: Life and Works, ed. C. T. Prouty, 3 vols, New Haven, 1952–70.

RALEGH, SIR WALTER (1552?–1618), after serving on several military expeditions to the Continent and to Ireland, became a leading courtier and favourite of the Queen, until, in 1592, he fell into disfavour after his relationship with Elizabeth Throckmorton was discovered. He took part in several voyages of discovery and colonization (notably of Virginia and Guiana), and in exploits against Spain. He was imprisoned for treason by James and narrowly escaped the block in 1603. While he was in prison (1603–16), he wrote his *History of the World* (1614). The failure of his final expedition to Guiana (1617–18) resulted in his execution.

Edition: Poems, ed. Agnes M. C. Latham, 1951.

Studies: Bradbrook, Muriel C., *The School of Night*, Cambridge, 1936.

Greenblatt, S. J., *Sir Walter Ralegh: The Renaissance Man and his Roles,* 1973.

Strathmann, E. A., *Sir Walter Ralegh: A Study in Elizabethan Skepticism*, New York, 1951.

SHAKESPEARE, WILLIAM (1564–1616), the son of a Stratford-upon-Avon merchant, was educated at the local free school. He married Anne Hathaway in 1582. By 1592 he had embarked on his career in London as actor and playwright. He wrote his narrative poems, *Venus and Adonis* and *The Rape of Lucrece*, in 1592–4, when the plague had closed the London theatres. On their reopening, he joined the Lord Chamberlain's Men, who took the title of the King's Men on James's accession. He was a busy theatre businessman and held shares in the Globe Theatre, where his company acted after 1599, and also in the Blackfriar's Theatre. He worked with the King's Men until he retired to Stratford (about 1610), where probably his last plays were written.

Editions: *Complete Works,* ed. P. Alexander, 1951.

Songs and Poems, ed. E. Hubler, New York, 1959.

Sonnets, ed. W. G. Ingram and T. Redpath, 1964.

Poems, ed. F. T. Prince, rev. edn, 1960.

Studies: Booth, S., *An Essay on Shakespeare's Sonnets*, New Haven, 1969.

Bradbrook, Muriel C., *Shakespeare and Elizabethan Poetry*, 1951.

Hubler, E., *The Sense of Shakespeare's Sonnets*, Princeton, 1952.

Knight, G. Wilson, *The Mutual Flame*, 1955.

Leishman, J. B., *Themes and Variations in Shakespeare's Sonnets*, 2nd edn, 1963.

Mahood, M. M., *Shakespeare's Wordplay*, 1957.

Martin, P. J., *Shakespeare's Sonnets*, Cambridge, 1972.

Seng, P., *The Vocal Songs in the Plays of Shakespeare*, Cambridge, Mass., 1967.

SIDNEY, SIR PHILIP (1554–1586), born at Penshurst in Kent, was educated at Shrewsbury and Oxford. He travelled widely on the Continent 1572–5, and as a favourite of the Queen was employed on several diplomatic missions abroad. He fell from favour in 1580, and retired for a time to Wilton, the home of his sister, Mary Countess of Pembroke. He produced all his major literary works in the period 1577–83:

the *Arcadia* (a prose romance with lyrics and eclogues), his sonnet sequence *Astrophil and Stella*, and his *Apology for Poetry*, a treatise written in reply to an attack on poetry and drama by Stephen Gosson. None of his works was published in his lifetime. In 1583 he was knighted, and married Frances Walsingham. He was sent to the Netherlands as Governor of Flushing in 1585, where he was fatally wounded in battle at Zutphen. Sidney was the friend of many men of letters including Spenser, Fulke Greville and Dyer. In his brief lifetime he excelled in every pursuit of the cultivated man; as the ideal Elizabethan noble, courtier and gentleman he combined education and culture with wit, charm and brilliance of personality.

Edition: Poems, ed. W. A. Ringler, Jr., Oxford, 1962.

Studies: Buxton, John, *Sir Philip Sidney and the English Renaissance*, 2nd edn, 1964.

Greville, Fulke, *Life of Sir Philip Sidney*, ed. Nowell Smith, 1907.

Kalstone, D., *Sidney's Poetry: Contexts and Interpretations*, Cambridge, Mass., 1965.

Montgomery, R. L., Jr., *Symmetry and Sense: The Poetry of Sir Philip Sidney*, Austin, Texas, 1961.

Myrick, K., *Sir Philip Sidney as a Literary Craftsman*, 2nd edn, Lincoln, Neb., 1965.

Nichols, J. G., *The Poetry of Sir Philip Sidney*, Liverpool, 1974.

Rudenstine, N. L., *Sidney's Poetic Development*, Cambridge, Mass., 1967.

SOUTHWELL, ROBERT (1561?–1595), born in Norfolk of a Roman Catholic family, was educated as a Jesuit in Paris, Douay and Rome. In 1586 he returned to England as a priest. He was arrested in 1592 and spent his last years in prison before he was finally executed.

Edition: Poems, ed. J. H. McDonald and Nancy P. Brown, Oxford, 1967.

Study: Devlin, C., *The Life of Robert Southwell*, 1956.

SPENSER, EDMUND (1552?–1599), born in London, was educated
at Merchant Taylors' School and at Cambridge. In 1579 he
was employed in the household of the Earl of Leicester. His
Shepheardes Calender (1579) was dedicated to Leicester's nephew,
Sidney. In the same year he married his first wife Macha-
byas Chylde (she died in 1591), and in 1580 was appointed
secretary to Lord Grey in Ireland. After Grey's return to
England in 1582, he lived in Dublin and later at Kilcolman
in County Cork, which became his home for the rest of his
life. In 1589 his friend Ralegh persuaded Spenser to accom-
pany him to England to publish the first Part of his *Faerie
Queene* (1590). He was introduced to the Court and was
granted a pension of £50 by Elizabeth. He returned to
Ireland, where he married Elizabeth Boyle in 1594. The
Amoretti and *Epithalamion*, which were based on his courtship
and marriage, were published in 1595. He was in London
again when the second Part of the *Faerie Queene* appeared in
1596. He was appointed Sheriff of Cork in 1598, but during
Tyrone's rebellion, Kilcolman Castle was destroyed and he
fled to England, where he died soon afterwards.

Edition: Poetical Works, ed. J. C. Smith and E. de Sélincourt,
Oxford, 1909–10.

Studies: Davis, B. E. C., *Edmund Spenser: A Critical Study*, Cam-
bridge, 1933.

Hieatt, A. K., *Short Time's Endless Monument*, New York, 1960.

Hough, G., *A Preface to The Faerie Queene*, 1962.

Jones, H. S. V., *A Spenser Handbook*, New York, 1930.

Nelson, W., *The Poetry of Edmund Spenser*, New York, 1963.

Renwick, W. L., *Edmund Spenser: An Essay on Renaissance Poetry*,
1925.

Tonkin, H., *Spenser's Courteous Pastoral: Book Six of the Faerie
Queene*, Oxford, 1972.

Welsford, Enid, *Spenser: Fowre Hymnes, Epithalamion: A Study of
Edmund Spenser's Doctrine of Love*, Oxford, 1967.

Williams, A., *Flower on a Lowly Stalk: The Sixth Book of the Faerie
Queene*, Michigan, 1967.

SURREY, HENRY HOWARD, EARL OF (1517?–1547), was a courtier of Henry VIII, and served on several military campaigns in France. He was hot-tempered and quarrelsome, and was several times imprisoned for various offences. In 1546 he was arrested for treason and soon afterwards was beheaded. None of his poems was published during his lifetime; a great many appeared in *Tottel's Miscellany* (1557).

Edition: Poems, ed. F. M. Padelford, rev. edn, Seattle, 1928.

Study: Casady, E. R., *Henry Howard, Earl of Surrey*, New York, 1938.

TICHBORNE, CHIDIOCK (1558?–1586), born of Roman Catholic stock, was a conspirator in the Babington Plot against the Queen in 1586. He was arrested, and hanged for treason.

TURBERVILE, GEORGE (1540?–1610?), born in Dorset, was educated at Oxford and at one of the Inns of Court. He was secretary to Sir Thomas Randolph on a political mission to Russia in 1568. His collection of poems, *Epitaphs, Epigrams, Songs, and Sonnets*, appeared in 1567. He also translated works of Ovid, Boccaccio, Tasso and Mantuan, and wrote treatises on falconry and venery.

Edition: The Eclogues of Mantuan, Translated by George Turbervile, ed D. Bush, Scholars' Facsimiles & Reprints, New York, 1937.

Study: Hankins, J. E., *The Life and Works of George Turbervile*, Lawrence, Kans., 1940.

WYATT, SIR THOMAS (1503–1542), was born in Kent and educated at Cambridge. He became a courtier, and was sent on a number of European embassies. In France and Italy he became familiar with the poetry of the Continental Renaissance. He was probably a lover of Anne Boleyn before she became Queen in 1533. He was in and out of court favour and was several times in prison. He was knighted in 1536. In 1541 he was charged with treason but was acquitted. His poems survive in manuscript; many were published posthumously in *Tottel's Miscellany* (1557).

SELECT BIBLIOGRAPHY

Edition: *Collected Poems*, ed. K. Muir and Patricia Thomson, Liverpool, 1969.

Studies: Chambers, E. K., *Sir Thomas Wyatt, and Some Collected Studies*, 1933.

Muir, K., *Life and Letters of Sir Thomas Wyatt*, Liverpool, 1963.

Southall, R., *The Courtly Maker: An Essay on the Poetry of Wyatt and his Contemporaries*, Oxford, 1964.

Thomson, Patricia, *Sir Thomas Wyatt and his Background*, Stanford, 1964.

Index of First Lines

if I didn't
need this as
a requirement, I
would write an
obnoxious letter
to the Eng. chairperson
& switch classes.